ILLINOIS CENTRAL COLLEGE
PR778.P55H3 1981
STACKS
The omnipresent debate :
A12900 728444

W9-AOD-299

THE

OMNIPRESENT DEBATE

THE OMNIPRESENT DEBATE

Empiricism and Transcendentalism in Nineteenth-Century English Prose

WENDELL V. HARRIS

Northern Illinois University Press

DEKALB

Library of Congress Cataloging in Publication Data

Harris, Wendell V.
The omnipresent debate.

Bibliography: p.
Includes index.
1. English prose literature—19th century—History and criticism. 2. Philosophy, English—19th century. 3. Empiricism. 4. Transcendentalism.
I. Title.
PR778.P55H3 828′.8′08 80–8663
ISBN 0–87580–076–9 AACR2

Published by the Northern Illinois University Press,
DeKalb, Illinois 60115
Manufactured in the United States of America

Design by Guy Fleming

CONTENTS

PREFACE

THIS STUDY is an attempt to exemplify an approach to the essayists, "sages," and cultural critics who participated in the ongoing intellectual debates of nineteenth-century England which grants their basic metaphysical assumptions more significance than is currently the fashion. By "metaphysics" I intend the older, larger scope of the word that includes both ontology (the question of being, of what exists) and epistemology (the question of what can be known and how it can be known). The nineteenth century boasts an unusually large number of influential cultural, social, and aesthetic critics, most of them both prolific and many-faceted in their interests. A century that saw three major electoral reform bills, the hectic growth of cities, the transition from what we vaguely call the industrial revolution to an undoubted age of mechanization, the growth of dissenting sects alongside the Oxford movement, and aestheticisms as different as those of Keats, Ruskin, Whistler, Arnold, and Wilde is obviously enormously complex.

There can be no royal route to the understanding of this complexity, no single thread leading through the labyrinth. A multiplicity of perspectives on nineteenth-century thought, literature, and art, and on the social, economic, and political changes over the century is essential. Among classic treatments are *The English Utilitarians* by Leslie Stephen, Basil Willey's two studies of the moral and religious ideas of important nineteenth-century figures, Raymond Williams's analysis of "the discovery of the idea of culture" in *Culture and Society, 1780–1850*, D. C. Somervell's *English Thought in the Nineteenth Century*, Crane Brinton's *English Political Thought in the Nineteenth Century*, and Walter Houghton's *The Victorian Frame of Mind, 1830–1870*. More recent examples are John Holloway's *The Victorian Sage*, Gaylord Leroy's analysis of the personal responses of six Victorian writers to major societal problems in *Perplexed Prophets*, Peter Allan Dale's *The Victorian Critic and the Idea of History*, and David DeLaura's examination of one of the major intellectual currents in *Hebrew and Hellene in Victorian England*.

More narrowly focused studies that nevertheless cast light well beyond their titular topics are Emory Neff's *Carlyle and Mill* and Edward Alexander's two volumes, *Matthew Arnold and John Stuart Mill* and *Matthew Arnold, John Ruskin, and the Modern Temper*. And then there are the many excellent studies of individual writers, for instance John Rosenberg on Ruskin and John Robson on J. S. Mill. It is among the studies of individuals that most of the strongly psychological studies are to be found: J. L. Halliday on Carlyle, R. H. Wilenski on Ruskin, Bruce Mazlish on the Mills. Surveying a set of later Victorian psychological perturbations is Barbara Charlesworth's *Dark Passages: The Decadent Consciousness in Victorian Literature*.

More philosophically technical surveys also exist, of course, from the histories of English philosophy by James Seth and W. R. Sorley to ever more detailed analyses of movements like J. H. Muirhead's *The Platonic Tradition in Anglo-Saxon Philosophy*, Elie Halévy's *The Growth of Philosophical Radicalism*, René Wellek's *Immanuel Kant in England, 1793–1838*, and G. N. G. Orsini's *Coleridge and German Idealism*.

This brief sampling can be greatly extended, but whatever the list one compiles, the background of warring metaphysical assumptions will be found to be more often simply acknowledged than pursued in the major works of the nineteenth-century prose writers—prophets, sages, men of letters, essayists. However, to the extent that correlations can be established between social, moral, and aesthetic doctrines and the deepest assumptions about the nature of existence and knowledge, we acquire an additional powerful means of grasping and assimilating the rich variety of the century.

ACKNOWLEDGMENTS

Portions of chapters II, IV, and VII have been revised from articles originally appearing in *Modern Philology*, *Studies in English Literature*, *The Victorian Newsletter*, and the *University of Toronto Quarterly*. I am appreciative of permission to reprint these materials as granted by the University of Chicago Press, the editors of *SEL* and *VNL*, and the University of Toronto Press.

I wish also to express my especial appreciation to Richard T. Congdon for his faith in the present endeavor.

THE
OMNIPRESENT
DEBATE

Introduction:

The Philosophical Antagonists

A

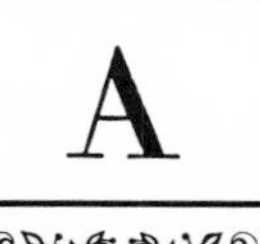

T THE BEGINNING of his essay on Bentham, John Stuart Mill remarks that Bentham and Coleridge "were destined to renew a lesson given to mankind by every age, and always disregarded—to show that speculative philosophy, which to the superficial appears so remote from the business of life and the outward interests of men, is in reality the thing on earth which most influences them, and in the long run overbears every other influence save those which it must itself obey."[1] The lesson is a singularly hard one to learn; in that essay, Mill himself scarcely touches on Bentham's deeper philosophical assumptions, and when he came to write his companion piece on Coleridge, he dismissed Coleridge's metaphysical

[1]J. S. Mill, *Collected Works*, X, 77. Coleridge acknowledged the importance of philosophy in a strikingly similar statement: "To the immense majority of men, even in civilized countries, speculative philosophy has ever been, and must ever remain, a terra incognita. Yet it is not the less true, that all the epoch-forming revolutions of the Christian world, the revolutions of religion and with them the civil, social, and domestic habits of the nations concerned, have coincided with the rise and fall of metaphysical systems" (*The Statesman's Manual*, in *Complete Works*, I, 428).

beliefs as wholly erroneous and virtually ignored the way his doctrines grew out of those beliefs.

Twentieth-century scholarship, especially, has tended to follow Mill's practice rather than his precept in undervaluing the role of "speculative philosophy," or metaphysics, in shaping many of the great Victorian cultural debates. Every student of course recognizes the antagonism between the kind of thought represented by Coleridge and that represented by Bentham, especially since the importance of the opposition was underlined both in the nineteenth century by Mill and in our own by F. R. Leavis's republication of Mill's essays on Bentham and Coleridge. However, the literary and cultural historian more naturally turns to the elucidation of the particular questions that interest him at the moment—literary, economic, political, or psychological questions—than to the basic metaphysical beliefs that link together the views held by an individual, a group, or an age.

The view that metaphysics was irrelevant to nineteenth-century interests appears to have the endorsement of the Victorians themselves. Its influence is almost universally discounted: Carlyle tells us in 1829 that "it is admitted, on all sides, that the Metaphysical and Moral Sciences are falling into decay," and speaks of the "Disease of Metaphysics" which at best serves to destroy outworn systems;[2] Bentham and the utilitarians frequently use the word as a term of opprobrium; Lewes as well as Comte use it to describe beliefs that the thoughtful portion of mankind have long abandoned; Henry Sidgwick and Mark Pattison discuss the decline of interest in all formal philosophical speculation in their 1876 articles on philosophy at Cambridge and Oxford;[3] David Masson finds it better to

[2] Carlyle, *Complete Works*, XIII, 468; XIV, 367–69.

[3] Sidgwick, "Philosophy at Cambridge," *Mind*, I (1876), 235–45; Pattison, "Philosophy at Oxford," *Mind*, I (1876), 82–97.

avoid the very word when he comes to write his history of philosophy in 1865.

But as a result of this tendency to shun metaphysics, references to the "philosophy" of one of the participants in the nineteenth-century intellectual controversies can easily become a random catalogue of that person's opinions rather than an attempt to trace particular pronouncements back to their metaphysical bases, or even to establish which are the basic assumptions, which the derivative or subsidiary positions. Explanations of the grounds of an essayist's beliefs, attitudes, and opinions tend to be largely biographical, sometimes sought in an almost random sequence of external influences, more often through the heavily psychoanalytical interpretation of biographical facts. But the attempt to analyze either the author or the work in terms of psychoanalytical categories has a tendency to slide into an explanation of an author's limitations (the psychological problems *not* surmounted) rather than the reasons his work is valued. However, our ultimate estimate of the value of a writer is, I believe, much more likely to depend on the degree to which he has been able to reduce his thoughts, feelings, and reactions to order and convey this achieved order through appropriate form than on the picturesqueness of his aberrations. In any case, the psychological and social contexts of nineteenth-century literature have been enough explored that placing the emphasis elsewhere for the nonce may restore a balance.

We have become so accustomed to regarding mankind as fundamentally irrational and inconsistent that we forget that everyone, to some extent, reasons deductively from basic assumptions which are ultimately metaphysical postulates, and that when individuals engage strenuously in more or less abstract thought, it is generally with the intention of making their thoughts as consistent as possible with their basic beliefs. It is, of course, very likely that a thinker's metaphysical orientation is grounded in something more primordial than logical ratiocination. Writes Basil Willey, "The original impulse, towards, say, 'materialism,' or 'idealism,' is usually something sublogical; not, that is, a 'conviction' resulting from an intellectual process, but a quite simple set of the whole being towards a particular way of life."[4] But the result of this 'set' will be a cluster of more or less consciously articulated basic assumptions about what exists, what is true, and what we know.

Assumptions about the nature of what we know and how we know it, the root problems of metaphysics, are like the soil and climate out of which all the rest of a person's thought grows: they determine what can and what cannot grow in a particular place. To establish a man's premises is to establish his intellectual ecology; one cannot predict the exact variety and extent of the vegetation of a region on the basis of ecological information alone, but one can state what can and what cannot flourish there. As David Masson put it one hundred years ago in *Recent British Philosophy*, "Let there be a difference between two thinkers as to their root-principles, and the difference will shoot its correspondences into all the subjects about which they speculate."[5]

Certain areas of philosophical debate tend to fall out of concern in the essays of the great nineteenth-century prose writers or "sages," to use John Holloway's happy term. Whether there are truly both primary and secondary qualities, whether God's will or reason or love determines the nature of reality, the validity of the ontological argument for Deity, whether the concept of cause is the result of real relations between external objects, God's will, or association—these remained intriguing questions, but they were not in the forefront. However, whether there were ideas somehow innate in the mind determinate of good or whether the criteria for good have to be constructed by the analysis of human experience was a question of major por-

[4] Willey, *The Seventeenth Century Background*, p. 94.

[5] Masson, *Recent British Philosophy*, p. 20.

tent for it determined the ground of ethical principles and the strategies for inculcating ethical action. The more comprehensive form of the same dispute between believers in innate ideas and thorough-going associationists determined the questions of how not only children but society should be educated to pursue proper goals. The major interest of the Victorian sages and lesser essayists was on what may be called, in the broadest sense, the conduct of life. (It is a nice question whether a concern for human conduct is not, alongside stylistic felicity and imaginative power, one of the central criteria by which we distinguish "literature" from writing in general.)

How inadequate has been the perception of the significance and basis of the fundamental metaphysical opposition of the nineteenth century is indicated by the difficulty of finding adequate terms to designate the two primary positions. Those who belong in each grouping are clear enough: Bentham, the Mills, Morley, Huxley, and Harrison are outstanding examples on one side, Coleridge, Carlyle, Ruskin, and Newman on the other. The essential question that divides the group is, as I should like to emphasize, the very old one of whether all understanding of the world as it is and all formulation of the goals that would make the world what it should be depend on the application of logic to careful observations, or on faculties superior to logic and observation. It thus includes, but is ultimately of much wider significance than, the much-analyzed conflict between science and religion.

According to one view, the discovery of truth depends on the analysis of relations between those things which make up our experience, relations not always directly observable but deducible by logic; according to the other it depends on insight into a structure which is not only invisible but which cannot be deduced from the phenomena of experience. To those who hold the latter view, the world often seems more purposive, more mysteriously wonderful than to the others and is more likely to be seen as a structure of "vital" or "spiritual" forces (such adjectives of course are susceptible of wide interpretation). But the essential difference is that those who hold the latter view regard human experience as necessarily misleading as long as it is uninformed by a higher kind of knowledge which sees beyond all observable phenomena and is governed by something beyond logic. The one kind of thought is designated variously (and confusingly) as "utilitarian," "materialist," "rationalist," or "empiricist," and the other "intuitionist," "idealist," "mystic," or "transcendentalist."

There are objections to each of these terms—formal philosophical designations rarely fit neatly an actual system of thought and are not seldom ambiguous in themselves. "Utilitarianism" most often suggests the system of ethics and legislation somehow allied with the Ricardian economics that came to be adopted by the leaders of the utilitarian or Benthamite movement. It almost never is used to denominate the metaphysical presuppositions which lie behind the arguments of the utilitarian school. "Rationalist" is in general use to refer both to that system of thought which optimistically looks upon human reason as sufficient to understand the world and lay out the lines upon which almost unlimited progress and improvement would be possible—and in this sense is applicable enough to the Benthamite group—and to the belief in innate ideas, a doctrine vigorously attacked by that group. It is also frequently employed in the limited sense A. W. Benn gives to it in *The History of English Rationalism in the Nineteenth Century*: "the mental habit of using reason for the destruction of religious belief."[6] "Materialist" is perhaps the least helpful, invoking as it does the controversies over whether "mind" and "spirit" are reducible to "matter," or the status of primary and secondary qualities. On the other side, "idealist" suggests to many simply one pole of the controversy over the "real" existence of objects, while "mystic" and "in-

[6] Benn, *The History of English Rationalism*, p. 4.

tuitionist" suggest wholly anti-intellectual positions.[7] "Aristotelian" and "Platonic" are even less helpful, both because there exist conflicting interpretations of each system of thought and because to call a writer "Aristotelian," for instance, leaves undetermined the extent and nature of the inevitable disagreements between that particular "Aristotelian" and the whole of Aristotle's major positions.

"Empiricist" seems the best designation for the former position, if we interpret it in accordance with definition 2.b of the *OED*: "The doctrine which regards experience as the only source of knowledge." Empiricism so defined does not necessarily rely upon traditional logic nor Lockian doctrines of association for the organization and interpretation of experience which transforms it into knowledge, although it is difficult to find a nineteenth-century empiricist who does not depend on logic and some form of associational psychology. The term "empiricism" then will be employed here to mean what J. S. Mill referred to as the doctrine of his *System of Logic*: "that which derives all knowledge from experience, and all moral and intellectual qualities principally from the direction given to the associations." "The notion that truths external to the mind may be known by intuition or consciousness, independently of observation and experience, is, I am persuaded, in these times, the great intellectual support of false doctrines and bad institutions."[8]

The word "transcendentalist" seems the most accurate with which to refer to the opposing position, though it is not without its liabilities, the major one of which is the confusion engendered by Kant's use of the terms "tran-

[7] In an excellent study of the moral philosophies of Victorian novelists, Jerome B. Schneewind uses the terms "Utilitarian" and "Intuitionist" ("Moral Problems and Moral Philosophy in the Victorian Period," *Victorian Studies*, IX, Supplement, Sept. 1965, 29–46), but these are rather too narrow to apply to the total range of oppositions I am here considering.

[8] J. S. Mill, *Autobiography*, pp. 144–45. Mill went so far as to make mathematical propositions generalizations from experience.

scendental" to refer to the universal and necessary conditions of experience and "transcendent" to refer to that which is not a possible object of experience and which, therefore, though thinkable, is not a possible object of knowledge. Kant is not a "transcendentalist" in the sense in which the term was most commonly employed in England in the nineteenth century, where it signified one who affirmed the existence of a realm beyond ordinary experience which was somehow *knowable*.[9] Nevertheless, for our purposes, the term has the advantage of having been the one that those who denied the source of knowledge beyond experience most often used in referring to their opponents and is much broader than such special designations as the "Germano-Coleridgean," which J. S. Mill coined in his essay on Coleridge. It can include both those whose belief in a transcendent realm is the result of orthodox religious faith and those whose belief is philosophical or even mystical. It can include those who believe in universal innate ideas. (Believers in innate or intuitive ideas almost inevitably look toward a transcendental system; though they may not explicitly develop this aspect of their thought, most seem to assume that the innate ideas whose existence they assume do not mislead, that they are in harmony with some eternal plan, and that their presence is to be explained by divine sanction.) It can include those who believe in special revelation or vision as well as those who hold to the main tradition of Natural Law.[10] It

[9] Neither Coleridge nor Carlyle, for instance, followed Kant in his limitation of man's knowledge to phenomena, although they were both happy enough to use as much of Kant as they could as a buttress for transcendentalism in its more unusual sense. See Coleridge, *Biographia Literaria*, ed. John Shawcross, I, 100; René Wellek's *Immanual Kant in England, 1793–1838*, pp. 82–135, 182–202; C. F. Harrold's *Carlyle and German Thought: 1819–1834*, pp. 13, 87–95. On the other hand, there is of course a close relationship between Kant's view of the regulative function of the Ideas of the Reason and the transcendentalist's belief in implanted mental principles.

[10] I refer to Natural Law as summed up by Peter Stanlis in *Edmund Burke and the Natural Law*, p. 7: "Until the time of Hobbes, the classical and Scho-

embraces, in other words, all those who in some way look to what Ernest Tuveson calls "the supranatural mooring of the mind."[11]

I am mindful of the ease with which terms such as "empiricist" and "transcendentalist" mask the vital differences between the modes of thought of the multitudes of thinkers who can be ranged under one or the other rubric. In the rich review of the problems and potentials of the pursuit of intellectual history which makes up the first chapter of *The Great Chain of Being*, A. O. Lovejoy is at pains to describe broad philosophical "isms" as "trouble-breeding and usually thought-obscuring" because they are "names of complexes, not of simples."[12] Yet in the present case, where it is broad affinities between writers tending strongly to one of two radically divergent modes of thought that is of interest, the very inclusiveness of each of these two terms is useful. So long as one thinks of "empiricism" and "transcendentalism" as designating the polar halves of a mental compass rather than as names of specific philosophical doctrines, they provide a kind of intellectual orientation that is otherwise difficult to achieve among the strong currents and countercurrents of nineteenth-century English thought.

The most likely differences in the conclusions toward which each set of metaphysical assumptions leads can be briefly outlined. David Masson well stated the peculiarity

lastic conceptions of Natural Law were in agreement upon the following basic principles: Natural Law was an emanation of God's reason and will, revealed to all mankind. Since fundamental moral laws were self-evident, all normal men were capable through unaided 'right reason' of perceiving the difference between moral right and wrong. The Natural Law was an eternal, unchangeable, and universal ethical norm or standard, whose validity was independent of man's will; therefore, at all times, in all circumstances and everywhere, it bound all individuals, races, nations, and governments. True happiness for man consisted in living according to the Natural Law."

[11] Tuveson, *The Imagination as a Means of Grace*, p. 14.

[12] Lovejoy, *The Great Chain of Being*, p. 6.

of the question of the existence of an at least partially knowable supernatural, absolute, or noumenal world: "The history of the question, we may say confidently, has consisted in a negative answer to the question, accompanied all the while by modes of thought, speech, and conduct, in which a positive answer to it, and very definite forms of a positive answer, have been practically assumed."[13] The positive answer, which maintained itself in various forms in the nineteenth century, has important consequences. If there is a knowable unchanging ideal pattern or set of innate principles, "beauty," "truth," and the "good" mean simply conformity with the ideal, and the three must ultimately be identical and unchanging. Man will necessarily find appearance misleading; truth is not found by collecting appearances; the good is not found by asking simply what men appear to desire; beauty is not created by the imitation of appearances. Therefore, seers of special insight are required; they are to lead, others to follow. Thus, there are times at which dissent ought not to be tolerated. They who can see the ideal begin the movement toward it by reforming the individual; those whose taste and judgment have been reformed or purified will perhaps see the ideal, but if they do not, they still have been led closer to it. Finally, authors who view the world in this way must find a way of leading readers to disregard habitual dependence on ordinary experience; in order to do this effectively they are likely to break through literary traditions and create unique styles and forms.

On the other view, all truth is found, all good recognized, and all beauty created by the observation of the only world there is, that which presents itself to the senses. Where the transcendentalist is, or aspires to be, a traveler securely tracing the correspondence between a model or map in his possession and the land through which he is born to travel, the empiricist is like an explorer in a largely

[13] Masson, *Recent British Philosophy*, p. 57.

unknown, partially hostile environment, carrying what amounts more to a set of "principles of exploration" than a map. Or, to put it another way, to the extent he feels possessed of a map, it is a sketchy one which must constantly be corrected. There is no necessary identity between the good, true, and beautiful, nor is there any reason that our judgments of them cannot change as conditions change. "Truth" becomes the approximation of fact and is arrived at by analyzing objects; the "good" is the goal toward which men elect, or are forced by circumstance, to strive. Though few are able to detect subtle connections and make new discoveries, most can be made to understand these once found. Education, discussion, and even controversy help make facts or truths clear, or at least create the right associations. The ideal is not a pre-existent model to which one constantly tries to approximate; it is the best next step which the operation of logic or experience can suggest. Reforms are to be initiated by changing laws and procedures, not by appealing to the individual to recognize inherent moral laws. Finally, again, empiricists are likely to feel themselves to be simply contributors to a tradition of thought, speaking as clarifiers and interpreters, not as prophets. As a result, they are often content to retrace the arguments they have found convincing without feeling the need to impress an individual stamp on them.

Whereas pure empiricism and pure transcendentalism are both incompatible with revealed, dogmatic religion, orthodoxy to some extent modifies both empiricist and transcendental allegiances. However, the accommodations Christian belief elicits from the empiricist or the transcendentalist exhibit characteristic patterns. The empiricist believer in the Thirty-Nine Articles must believe in a final cause, however much he denies that it can serve to explain phenomena; the transcendentalist who believes in those same articles need not depend wholly on his own transcendental vision for guidance. Although the chronological order differs in the two cases, one could say for instance that

Paley's system of thought is to Bentham's as Coleridge's is to Kant. Both Coleridge and Paley short-circuit the more elaborate systems by the introduction of a revealed Deity. (Paley's impulses were of course strongly empiricist—thus the importance he gives to arguments from design on the one hand and miracles on the other—both of which the transcendentalist Coleridge, whose allegiance was to the same Anglican dogmas, found contemptible.)

No one will be surprised that these paradigmatic systems of thought conform in general to the two great streams actually found in nineteenth-century England. However, failure to keep the whole thrust of each system in mind when discussing specific differences and similarities between two or more figures can obscure more basic issues. In other words, it is so easy to point out that Carlyle thought *x* while Mill thought *y*, or that Ruskin and Carlyle both thought *z*, that we sometimes fail to penetrate to the more basic oppositions and similarities. It is particularly easy to oversimplify the nineteenth century by directing one's attention primarily to points of agreement while ignoring more significant differences.[14] Thus Coleridge's theory of the syllogism[15] is very close to Mill's explanation of the sources of novelty in syllogistic reasoning and Coleridge's "to whom do we owe our meliorated condition?—To the successive few in every age. . . ."[16] could have been incorporated directly into *On Liberty*. But despite both such similarities and Mill's tribute to Coleridge's importance, the barriers between their modes of thought are impassable. Similarly, education was supported from almost all philosophical positions, but to understand the grounds of the

[14]Edward Alexander has made this point very well in "Mill's Marginal Notes on Carlyle's 'Hudson's Statue,'" *English Language Notes*, VII (1969), 120–21.

[15]As set forth by Alice D. Snyder in *Coleridge on Logic and Learning*, pp. 53–54.

[16]Coleridge, *The Friend*, in *Complete Works*, II, 63.

bitter controversy over forms of education we must realize that the empiricists tended to regard education as the instilling of certain associations (and cancelling of others) while the transcendentalists regarded education as the instilling of disciplined obedience to a seer, or the creation of a sense of phenomena-dissolving wonder, or the brushing away of the corruption of the mind that overlaid and obscured the moral sense.

So long as the position a writer takes on issues is viewed without reference to his metaphysical orientation, paradoxes abound. Bentham's attitude toward the punishment and reform of criminals is, despite the horror with which certain commentators regard his proposed "panopticon," instinct with mild beneficence beside Carlyle's desire to wreak the Lord's vengeance on the miscreant in the Latter-Day Pamphlet "Model Prisons." Yet Carlyle's denunciation of the Benthamite Poor-Law Amendment Act in "Chartism"—"To believe practically that the poor and luckless are here only as a nuisance to be abraded and abated, and in some permissible manner made away with, and swept out of sight, is not an amiable faith"[17]—makes him seem a very champion against the heartless cruelty of the utilitarians. And, yet again, Carlyle's impatience with the religious opposition to a universal and effective education in the same essay[18] is almost indistinguishable from James Mill's, while one can find passages in James Mill which anticipate Ruskin's protest against chaining men to dull and tedious work.[19] But both the reasoning which leads to these outwardly similar positions and the responses which they suggest will be found to be in distinct opposition.

Even the meaning of such an apparently unquestionable assertion as that man's happiness and success depend

[17] Carlyle, *Complete Works*, XVI, 48.

[18] *Ibid.*, XVI, 110–11.

[19] See, for instance, *James Mill on Education*, p. 89.

on his adaptation to certain unchangeable laws of nature depends upon metaphysical assumptions. As we shall see, for Bentham and James Mill such laws reduce to the laws governing matter, which it is the task of physical science to discover, and the laws governing the human mind. For Carlyle they include a supranatural moral accounting system: "Nature keeps silently a most exact Savings-bank, and official register correct to the evanescent item, Debtor and Creditor, in respect of one and all of us; silently marks down, Creditor by such and such an unseen act of veracity and heroism; Debtor to such a loud blustery blunder . . . rigorously as Fate (for this *is* Fate that is writing); and at the end of the account you will have it all to pay my friend."[20] The celestial account book has been transferred from the angels to a Fate conceived of somewhat after the classical manner, though with Lachesis doubling as a knitter of coded records as well as spinner of the thread of life. (One finds the same sort of thing in Ruskin.) To say that an action cannot finally achieve its end because it fails to take into account the laws by which the mind works, and to say that an action is damnable because it violates an eternal law, may seem much the same, but the attitude toward the action held by the person who thinks in the second set of terms, and the means proposed for discouraging such action, are very likely to be quite different. Carlyle, who urges that the Laws of England be made an "exact transcript" of "The Laws of this Universe,"[21] will naturally find it impossible to conceive the use of a utilitarian analysis of government based on assumed psychological principles such as Bentham offers in *Principles of Morals and Legislation*.

Isolated passages will mislead us about the metaphysical views of an author only if we do not look to the body of his or her writing as a whole. The famous passage from "A

[20] Carlyle, *Complete Works*, II, 448.

[21] Carlyle, "Parliaments," in *Complete Works*, XII, 306.

Liberal Education" in which Huxley compares life to a chess game played against a hidden player who "is always fair, just, and patient" but who "never overlooks a mistake, or makes the smallest allowance for ignorance" sounds rather like Carlyle's sternly judging Sphinx-fate in *Past and Present*. But what we have here is a case illustrating the danger of introducing figurative language into an empiricist argument, which the utilitarians have been so often damned for insisting on. For Huxley goes on to equate that hidden player with "things and their forces" and "men and their ways," in other words, with the laws governing matter on the one hand and the human mind on the other. If there is any set of moral accounts being kept, it is useless for us to speculate on or point to them; they belong to the same realm as those questions of lunar politics about which Huxley elsewhere advises us not to speculate.

No less a thinker than J. S. Mill announced in the essay on Coleridge that "whoever could master the premises and combine the methods" of Bentham and Coleridge "would possess the entire English philosophy of his age."[22] But an attempt to combine the premises and modes of thought based on those premises could not in itself succeed; the premises are irreconcilable. Mill remarks in the *Autobiography*, "The acquaintance I had formed with the ideas of the Coleridgeans, of the German thinkers, and of Carlyle, all of them fiercely opposed to the mode of thought in which I had been brought up, had convinced me that along with much error they possessed much truth, which was veiled from minds otherwise capable of receiving it by the transcendental and mystical phraseology in which they were accustomed to shut it up, and from which they neither cared, nor knew how, to disengage it. . . ."[23] That what

[22] J. S. Mill, *Collected Works*, X, 121.

[23] J. S. Mill, *Autobiography*, pp. 157–58.

seemed to him transcendental and mystical were precisely the basic principles that sustained the conclusions he wished to disengage and that these had been presented through modes of expression especially calculated to prepare for their reception apparently never fully came home to Mill. His own venture into leavening the strictness of Bentham's philosophy with Coleridgean views led to the well-known inconsistencies in the first part of his essay "Utilitarianism."

John Stuart Mill was not at all alone in attempting to reconcile the two metaphysical modes. Coleridge himself felt that he had in some sense done so. Ruskin combined incredibly patient empirical observation with an unswerving devotion to certain transcendentally guaranteed principles. The struggle between the two modes of thought is evident in Arnold, and Pater's extraction of the last nuance from experience takes place against a transcendental backdrop of universal fugacity. We shall see that Vernon Lee devoted most of her life to the attempt to adjust her allegiance to empiricism with certain persistent transcendental inclinations.

This study is an attempt to indicate the value of keeping in mind the metaphysical assumptions of each side as significant though not invariable determinants of the positions its adherents adopt, the conclusions at which they arrive, the weaknesses they are most likely to exhibit, the conflicts that arise within their own thought, and even the formal characteristics of their work. My intention is not to offer novel insights into this material but rather to analyze selected instances of opposition in terms of the internal coherence of the opposing modes of thought. In order to maintain the emphasis on this presently unfashionable approach, very little space has been given to rehearsing the results of the many excellent existing biographical and literary-historical studies of the writers treated. The omission in no way questions the legitimacy of such approaches but rather reflects the attempt to insist that the necessity of

grounding speculation in one of two sets of opposed premises did indeed heavily influence the content of some of the most interesting cultural and aesthetic criticism in nineteenth-century England.

The first brief chapter is a quick gallop through the most influential and immediate of the philosophical arguments and systems which the nineteenth century inherited. The philosophical interplay of the previous 200 years both set the problems and suggested the approaches to their solution. The second and third chapters are devoted to the philosophical positions of Coleridge and James Mill, the two being the great contemporaneous representatives of the transcendental and empirical schools. (I cite Mill rather than Bentham not only because he is a more exact contemporary of Coleridge and more representative of nineteenth-century thought but because he draws the empiricist position together into a more precise focus than Bentham, just as Coleridge more comprehensively than anyone else draws together the various strains of transcendentalism in England at the beginning of the nineteenth century.) These chapters are more technical than those which follow, but they provide a necessary foundation as well as offer a useful general survey of the thought of Coleridge and of the Mills in briefer compass than I know to exist elsewhere. The succeeding chapters are intended to offer examples of the way a metaphysically informed approach to nineteenth-century literature and thought can provide a widely applicable guide to the prose of the period. They are illustrative essays, not links in a concatenated argument. At times the writers under consideration will be found speaking more or less directly to metaphysical questions; at other times implicit empiricist or transcendental assumptions are in the background. But questions about which these writers feel strongly always reach toward these assumptions.

In re-reading the final draft I find that I have dwelt particularly strongly on the weaknesses of the transcendentalist position. On no issue could empiricists or transcendentalists be expected to be unexceptionably in the right, wholly consistent, or indubitably convincing. Nevertheless, one of the phenomena that must be accounted for in the nineteenth century is the victory of empiricism in all areas, except, curiously enough, formal philosophy itself, where the idealism of T. H. Green and F. H. Bradley dominated the closing years of the century. But for three quarters of a century the gods of the Mills were slowly grinding out all effective opposition, except that which found ways of using their own weapons, that is, their own premises, against them.

I

Philosophical Background and Milieu

T

THE CONTEXT of any major philosophical issue extends almost indefinitely. Through the centuries, key terms acquire additional and complicating meanings; old assumptions are undermined; previously unimaginable questions are asked; interests and emphases shift. But despite all such twists and turns, certain central problems of ontology, epistemology, ethics, and aesthetics have been more or less continually under debate since man's earliest recorded thought. At the same time, because of such twists and turns, the form in which issues are debated at any one time is especially influenced by the preceding century or so of philosophical disputation. This chapter attempts to sketch the issues primarily intertwined in the opposed modes of thought upon which I focus from early in the seventeenth to the end of the nineteenth centuries.

Among metaphysical oppositions, that between the tendencies I subsume under the terms "empiricist" and "transcendentalist" is surely one of the most radical. It is because the essences of these mighty opposites seem to lie imbedded in the preserved fragments of Parmenides and

Heraclitus that these names stand out so prominently among the pre-Socratic Greek thinkers. "How could Being perish?" asks Parmenides. "How could it come into being? If it came into being, it Is Not; and so too if it is about-to-be at some future time. . . . Nor is Being divisible, since it is all alike . . . all is full of Being." In sum, "For nothing else either is or shall be except Being, since Fate has tied it down to be a whole and motionless; therefore all things that mortals have established, believing in their truth, are just a name: Becoming and Perishing, Being and Not-Being, and Change of position and alteration of bright colour."[1] Beyond the gate opened by Parmenides' vision of ultimate Being—a perfect, unchanging whole underlying illusory becoming, change, and decay—lies the way to eternal forms, transcendental permanences, immutable verities, and innate ideas.

Those of Heraclitus' sayings which announce evanescence and fugaciousness as the central truth of existence are those by which he is primarily remembered. Heraclitus is reported to have held not only that it is impossible to step twice "into the same river" but that "it is impossible to touch the same mortal substance twice, but through the rapidity of change they scatter and again combine, or rather, not even 'again' or 'later,' but the combination and separation are simultaneous and approach and separate."[2] In such a doctrine lies the gate to empiricism, associationism, and universal contingency.

We need not for our purposes follow these ever-branching and occasionally reuniting intellectual paths through the decline of Greece, the rise of Roman thought, the shift of the world's intellectual center to Byzantium, and the subsequent reign of scholasticism. It is sufficient to pick up the trail where the two modes of thought are

[1] Freeman, ed. and trans., *Ancilla to the Pre-Socratic Philosophers*, pp. 43–44.

[2] *Ibid.*, p. 31.

briefly and uneasily combined in the speculations of René Descartes, father of modern philosophy.

Descartes was of course consciously attempting to make a new beginning far back of what had become the sterile habit of explaining all things by final causes and the ceaseless churning of principles drawn from Plato, Aristotle, Plotinus, the Pseudo-Dionysius, and Augustine, principles which could never finally be harmonized. No philosophical utterance is better known than "I think, therefore I am," which lays the indubitable foundation on which Descartes will build. And nothing is perhaps more widely remembered by laymen with the scantest knowledge of philosophy than that the result of Descartes' maneuver was a philosophical dualism that opposed thought and extension, or more loosely stated, mind and matter. As Basil Willey phrases it, Descartes authorizes two kinds of certainty: one for the external world, one internal to the mind.[3] This set the problem of the possible relationship between the two apparently wholly opposed modes of existence. It further set the problem of how the consciousness could know anything outside itself, especially how it could know that which was extended. Traditional cosmological and ontological questions now give way to epistemological ones: What can we know and how do we know it?

English thought was especially aware of the importance of those questions. Francis Bacon, who is second only to Descartes in drawing speculative interest away from scholasticism, had already raised the claims of induction from experience above those of deduction from authority. Bacon challenged scholasticism to insist on the utilitarian ends of knowledge: practice was henceforth to be the end, not the splendors of an intellectually satisfying system. Again, Thomas Hobbes, who in offering a deductive argument for materialism took quite a different line from Bacon's, had an early chance to question Cartesian

[3] Willey, *The Seventeenth Century Background*, p. 76.

conclusions when he was asked to criticize the *Meditations* prior to their publication in 1641. But it is not with Bacon, who had been dead fifteen years when Descartes' *Meditations* appeared, nor yet with Hobbes who had many more foes than disciples, but with John Locke that the empiricist alternative to dualism—one of the two major philosophical currents against which nineteenth-century thought must be viewed—emerges.

Locke was not directly replying to Descartes, but the effect was the same. Yes, one had intuitive certainty of one's own existence, but no, there were no ideas innate in the mind as Descartes believed, and no, there was no need to invoke (as Descartes' Continental successors found necessary) the constant intervention of the Divine Being to explain how new ideas entered the mind. They entered as simple ideas through the senses and were elaborated by association. Once he had asked the question of what the limits of the understanding, or mind, might be, Locke found ample arguments for dismissing the belief in innate ideas and tracing everything found in the mind either to the senses or to the associations of ideas that had originated from the senses. Locke's famous conclusion that there indeed exist external objects but that we cannot know the true constitution of or relationship between the qualities of any object was of course the first step in a well-known progression. Bishop Berkeley was able to show that Locke's own arguments, if carried further, deny any reason for belief in material objects. He announced the idealist solution of Cartesian dualism; in James Seth's summary, Berkeley followed Locke's road to the position that "the primary reality is spiritual and the reality of the material world mind-dependent; that matter and extension are neither substantial nor attributes, coordinate with thought . . . but in their very nature subordinate to thought and the thinking mind."[4] But Berkeley could also be accused of stopping

[4]Seth, *English Philosophers and the Schools of Philosophy*, p. 127.

his analysis too soon: if material substance was nothing more than a sequence of perceptions and thus not given in experience, why would we not recognize that ideas such as existence, space, time, and causality are ideas never given in experience either. All such judgments for David Hume were the result of association; however, because reasoning is so dependent on establishing causal relationships, Hume's reduction of causal judgments to habitual associations of the perceptions we call experience had the greatest impact on philosophical thought.

Seen in another way, what seems an almost uniform progression from Locke to Berkeley to Hume is actually a fascinating zig-zag movement. While Locke's philosophy moved toward realism as well as empiricism, Berkeley's more radical analysis made a sharp turn into a wholly idealist philosophy, while Hume's even more radical conclusions were again squarely empiricist. A. O. Lovejoy's warning about the slipperiness of philosophical labels is here clearly exemplified.

For those primarily interested in human conduct, associationist theory had penetrating implications—and in early eighteenth-century England, associationist theory hung like a mist in the intellectual air. In approximately the same years that Hume was working out first his *Treatise* and then his *Inquiry*, John Gay and David Hartley were elaborating Lockian associationism. Indeed, succeeding empiricist writers were able to pay tribute to Hume's "metaphysical" genius while employing their own powers in working out the practical effects of the associative theory as developed not by Hume but by Hartley. Moreover, Hume's skeptical empiricism was much more thoroughgoing than that of succeeding empiricists who devoted themselves to translating theoretical systems into practical application.

It may as well be noticed here that Locke believed that man in a state of nature was an admirable enough creature. The need for a social contract protecting property rights was the result of the excess of human beings over the unassisted resources of nature, not of an intrinsically selfish or evil quality in mankind. The contrast of this view with Hobbes's description of man's short, nasty, brutish life in a state of nature is striking. The fact is that, while not required as a consequence of the empiricist's theory of knowledge, Locke's view harmonizes more easily with it than does that of Hobbes. If moral knowledge is not to be regarded as a reflection of laws beyond experience, it is most comfortably seen as something easily discovered by man's reasoning powers.

Hume was less sanguine about man's natural benevolence than Locke, but what is lacking in charity is provided by man's inventiveness. "Tis only from the selfishness and confined generosity of men, along with the scanty provision nature had made for his wants, that justice derives its origin." But, "Mankind is an inventive species; and where an invention is obvious and absolutely necessary, it may as properly be said to be natural as anything that proceeds immediately from original principles. . . . Tho' the rules of justice be *artificial*, they are not arbitrary. Nor is the expression improper to call them *Laws of Nature*; if by natural we understand what is common to any species. . . ."[5]

The empiricist line that begins with Locke enters the nineteenth century primarily under the sponsorship of Jeremy Bentham. However, many lines of thought were converging toward English utilitarianism at this time. The curious but long-influential theological utilitarianism of William Paley owed much to earlier English thinkers; his *Principles of Moral and Political Philosophy* (1785) was indebted primarily to Abraham Tucker, whose debts, in turn, are to Locke, Gay, and Hartley.[6] Paley argued, in essence, that revelation is an insufficient guide to human ac-

[5]D. Hume, *A Treatise of Human Nature*, Book III, Part II, section 1.

[6]On this set of relationships, see Seth, *English Philosophers*, p. 217, and Sorley, *A History of British Philosophy to 1900*, p. 200.

tion, but that since God was benevolent and therefore wished man's happiness, calculations of human happiness should serve as the basis for ethical rules. Moreover, the ethical rules arrived at by such calculation are given strong sanction by a further application of utilitarian calculation to theology. Since there is probability on the side of the existence of God and of the truth of Christian doctrines, argues Paley, the pains of hell are to be balanced against the pleasures of this life; the resulting calculation is much in favor of adhering to Christian beliefs.

In addition to Paley's religious utilitarianism, which was viewed with distaste both by Coleridge and Bentham, secular utilitarianism seems almost to have been in the air. Joseph Priestley in the 1760s and 1770s was not only restating Hartley's associationism in a more attractive form (freed of physiological speculations) but making the maximizing of happiness the end of government. Hume had long before made pursuit of pleasure and avoidance of pain the ultimate ends of human action, and Hume's influence on Bentham was not only through English thinkers but through the French writer Helvetius and his Italian disciple Beccaria.

By making all knowledge dependent on passively received sensations that could never be wholly accurate representations of the assumed external objects, Locke, who stands at the source of various streams of speculation which were coming together again in Bentham, not only provided the foundation for empiricism but opened the door to idealism. But in his scheme, those ideas entering through the senses were all the mind had to work with; hence the emphasis on experience as the source of all knowledge. Thinkers like Bentham simply took that empiricism (and the associationism which in England had become so closely identified with it) and let the idealism go. "Nature has placed mankind under the governance of two sovereign masters, pain and pleasure," writes Bentham as his first sentence in *Principles of Morals and Legislation*

(1789), and he is off and running. It is left to James Mill and other first generation disciples, and to John Stuart Mill and others of the second generation, to mend speculative fences as necessary once the Benthamic calculus has begun to make its way.

We may leave empiricism for the moment to turn to the immediate lineage of the other great intellectual stream on which the nineteenth-century debate drew. On the Continent, the problems posed by Cartesian dualism—specifically, that of how man's mind and will could act on the external world—led to the Occasionalism of Géraud De Cordemoy, Arnold Geulincx, and Nicolas Malebranche. The Deity already played an essential role in Descartes' system of thought; it was not, therefore, a long step to the nevertheless somewhat startling conclusion that all correspondence between the mind and matter occurs through God's action. Thus, God becomes not only the final but the efficient cause of all experience.

In England, the seventeenth-century group of religious philosophers known as the Cambridge Platonists, opposing the mechanism of Hobbes, found Descartes' dualism both a stimulation and a challenge. Henry More, one of the major figures in the Cambridge group, began with a strong admiration for the French philosopher but could not finally rest in a dualism that left the material world under the rule of a merely mechanical power. Seeking to reconcile Plato and Descartes, he not only reaffirmed the importance of innate ideas but found the material world pervaded by spirit. Nor had he any difficulty in finding evidence of a "boniform" faculty which is able to savor the sweetness of and thus certify the good recognized by right reason. Ralph Cudworth was equally sure that there are in the mind anticipations of experience which lie waiting to be excited by objects of the senses. While never reaching the extreme of Occasionalism, he nevertheless saw the human mind as participating in the Divine "system of mind-sustained truth." For him, God's essence included the equivalent of Platonic Ideas. Not only did he offer a model of the human mind as more than Locke's passive receptacle, he suggested that there is an underlying active organizing principle in nature, not merely a set of mechanistic structures.

The most Platonic of these Cambridge writers, John Smith, constructs something like the Platonic ladder:

> Those dismall apprehensions which pinion the Souls of men to mortality, churlishly check and starve that noble life thereof, which would alwaies be rising upwards, and spread itself in a free heaven: and when once the Soul hath shaken off these . . . it finds a vast Immensity of Being opening itself more and more before it, and the ineffable light and beauty thereof shining more and more into it; when it can rest and bear up itself upon an Immaterial centre of Immortality within, it will then find itself able to bear away by a self-reflexion into the contemplation of an Eternall Deity.[7]

More, Cudworth, Smith, and others of the Cambridge group wrote primarily to discredit the Hobbesian materialism which denied that God's activity could be discovered in the mind; their metaphysics are not developed to the degree nor presented with the strictness of a Locke, Hume, or Kant. Rather, as devout churchmen with strong Platonic affinities, they were concerned to rescue religion from doctrinal controversy, philosophy from hedonistic theorizing, and morality from sterile hairsplitting. J. H. Muirhead remarks on their fondness for the formula "the spirit of man is the candle of the Lord," a metaphor interpreted by means of doctrines drawn from the Platonic tradition.[8] Whether a strange or a natural alliance (A. O. Lovejoy thinks it the first, J. H. Muirhead the second), Platonism and Christi-

[7] *J. Smith, Selected Discourses*, p. 125.

[8] Muirhead, *The Platonic Tradition in Anglo-Saxon Philosophy*, p. 29.

anity had become closely intertwined by the seventeenth century.[9] In general, as summed up by James Seth, the Cambridge Platonists undertook to support "three main positions: (1) the unity of faith and reason, of religion and life; (2) the spiritual constitution of the universe; and (3) the reasonableness . . . of morality."[10] Reason, as they understood it—buttressed by innate ideas or anticipations of experience, having access to ideas, including moral ones, which are finally reflections of the very nature of God, and undivorced from the external world because both mind and matter partake of spirit—is very different from what a Locke or Hume would mean by man's reason. Except for the intuitive knowledge of one's own existence and the demonstrable existence of God, reason for the empiricists could only mean the association of ideas presented initially through the senses.

There was yet another philosophical current flowing into nineteenth-century thought, the reaction of what is known as the Scottish School of Common Sense, as exemplified particularly by Thomas Reid, to the line of argument culminating in Hume's skepticism. Returning to the views of the mind that Locke accepted from Descartes, Reid asked whether it is really true that we sense bare ideas of objects; his answer is no, whatever we apprehend is already accompanied by a judgment. These judgments are the result of the constitution of the mind and therefore may be called principles of common sense. This was the general line of argument further pursued by Dugald Stewart, Reid's pupil. However, while furnishing plentiful occasion for philosophical controversy, the Scottish Common Sense philosophy had little direct influence on the writers of the time who were not professional philosophers—ex-

[9] Lovejoy, *The Great Chain of Being*, chapter III, *passim*; Muirhead, *The Platonic Tradition*, p. 26: "It is difficult to exaggerate the essential unity of principle and spirit that pervades these two great systems."

[10] Seth, *English Philosophers*, p. 83.

cept in serving (as did the Cambridge Platonist, Cudworth) to help accustom thinkers to regard the mind as having certain fixed principles by which sensations are immediately judged and thereby transformed into perceptions. One who accepted such a view of the mind would have much less difficulty with the critical philosophy shortly to issue from Kant.

Immanuel Kant was the first major Continental influence on English thought after Descartes. My brief summaries of key philosophical themes since Descartes have been offered as no more than reminders of the immediate sources on which nineteenth-century English thought would draw and the questions it would inherit; the reader who is unfamiliar with the English philosophers of the seventeenth and eighteenth centuries will wish to consult standard histories of philosophy, if not key passages in the primary sources. To convey the richness of Kant's thought, not to mention that of the thinkers who pursued directions emanating from Kantian idealism (Fichte, Schelling, Hegel) is even less something to be attempted within the scope of the present study. Fortunately, the difficulty is somewhat mitigated by recognition that it was a very imperfectly understood and partial version of Kant that first began to influence English thought.

The native idealism of the Cambridge Platonists was a response to Hobbes. The version of idealism imported from Germany about the beginning of the nineteenth century was not wholly exotic to England since it had been excited by Hume, the philosopher generally regarded as England's greatest. Those who know little else of Kant are likely to be familiar with his statement that he was awakened from his dogmatic slumbers by Hume. Kant begins with much the same initial question as Locke: "To examine our own abilities, and see what objects our understandings were, or were not fitted to deal with" had been the task Locke set himself. In Harald Höffding's single-sentence summary, Kant's critical philosophy "is distinguished from the dogmatic by the fact that it examines the faculty of knowledge itself, and, by the light of this inquiry, decides which are the problems this faculty is able to solve, and which are those which lie beyond its reach."[11] Among other advantages, Kant had that of knowing that Locke's solution to the question had led by seemingly necessary logical deduction to Hume's skepticism. If all the contents of the mind are impressions, and if these are there ordered by association only, we can know nothing of necessary connections. And, in particular, if the connections we designate as cause and effect cannot be shown to be necessary, reasoning in both science and metaphysics lies open to doubt. The specific question is the grounds of necessary, that is, *a priori* (not dependent on experience) synthetic (not tautological) judgments.

Kant's answer is easier to follow in the *Prolegomena to Any Further Metaphysics* than in the *Critique of Pure Reason*. In the *Prolegomena*, the argument runs that the possibility of synthetic *a priori* judgments seems guaranteed by the success of mathematics. But such judgments can only be the result of an activity of the mind which imposes location in space and time on all sensations. Space and time thus become forms imposed by the mind, which transform sensations into perceptions. But the synthetic *a priori* judgments of science require that perceptions also be ordered by the concepts of causality, number, etc. These concepts, or categories of the Understanding, then, of which Kant deduces twelve, are imposed on perceptions to transform them into experience. Since we cannot go behind the activity of the mind in imposing the forms and categories, we cannot know the external objects that are the sources of our sensations as they are in themselves. This realm of things-in-themselves or *noumena* presumably does exist, but we can know it only as the *phenomena* in our minds, that is, as sensations upon which have first

[11] Höffding, *A History of Modern Philosophy*, II, 50.

been imposed the forms of space and time and then the twelve categories of the understanding. It is true that the mind's desire for completeness produces what Kant calls the Ideas of the Reason: of the soul, the world, and God. However, these three, which are produced by a separate faculty, the Reason, not the Understanding, can never be experienced nor can anything be known about them.

In his second great treatise, the *Critique of Practical Judgment*, Kant finds grounds for belief in the soul, free will, the universe, and God, but these guarantees are of a different order from the necessary judgments to be made about experience. Moreover, the Practical Reason, or the moral will, searching for an end not given in experience (only the Understanding can make judgments about experience), is able to generate the moral law: "Act as if the maxim from which you act were to become through your will a universal law." Thus emerges the famed "categorical imperative," "categorical" because it is unconditionally binding regardless of empirical circumstances. Since Kant's critique moves ethics away from calculation based on experience, it is, he recognizes, a reversal of the "moving springs" of man's action.

Clearly, Kant's system is "transcendental" with a difference: it denies that pure reason can know things-in-themselves or assert anything, even the existence of the objects of the Ideas. ("Transcendental" for Kant refers to the method of his critical philosophy, which "transcends" experience by analyzing how it comes about; it does not refer to discovering the *existence* of objects, or moral laws, or Platonic Ideas beyond experience.) However, by grounding the Ideas of the Soul, World, and God—and the moral law itself—outside experience, Kant was clearly opposing those systems of thought which had developed out of Lockian empiricism. Moreover, his argument that consciousness contained more than sensation encouraged many other thinkers to regard the mind as active, not passively dependent on sensation. And finally, the gulf between the worlds of *noumena* and *phenomena*, which Kant bridged in his own way in the *Critique of Practical Reason* and *Critique of Judgment*, challenged his German successors to find ways out of this new kind of dualism, while English thinkers influenced by Kant tended from the first to leap back and forth over the gulf as though it were not really there.

Johann Gottlieb Fichte took the first step toward collapsing Kant's hard-won distinctions by asserting the mind's power to know things-in-themselves: if all our speculations indeed start from thought, all experience must be deducible from thought without the necessity of assuming things-in-themselves as the source of the sensations the mind transforms into experience. (Things-in-themselves, or *noumena*, could not be regarded as the cause of our sensations, he argued, since cause was one of the categories of the Understanding and could therefore not be applicable to things-in-themselves.) The mind, the ego in Fichte's terms, must produce all that is found in consciousness through the opposition of the unbounded will or ego and the limits of the non-ego it constructs. But there must be a deep ground of identity between egos guaranteeing some agreement between consciousnesses. Behind the finite empirical ego then must lie an infinite, encompassing ego. As a result, for Fichte, *noumena* become knowable objects because they are the product of the universal ego.

F. W. J. Schelling took the next step, in which the infinite ego becomes the Absolute Ego or God. What happens at this point is nicely summed up in an otherwise largely superseded article by Thomas Case in the thirteenth edition of the *Encyclopaedia Britannica*: "Schelling attributes to man an intellectual intuition of the Absolute God; and as there is, according to him, but one universal reason, the common intelligence of God and man, this intellectual intuition at once gives man an immediate knowledge of God, and identifies man with God himself."[12] This Absolute is not simply thought but spirit, spirit found in consciousness and nature, the latter existing for Schelling more through its participation in spirit than through the activity of the ego. Thus Schelling's pantheism.

The systems of Fichte and Schelling are peculiarly intractable to summary, as readers of histories of philosophy well know; unfortunately, any attempt to encompass Hegel in brief formulations is even more certain to degenerate into elliptical travesty. To say that Hegel was able to employ the dialectical logic that Fichte had developed in which principles or postulates not deducible one from another and apparently contradictory are reconciled in a higher synthesis in order to demonstrate that everything is interconnected, everything is spirit, and everything can be thought is perhaps less helpful than inclusive. But again, until late in the century, these latter developments of German Idealism served British thinkers more nearly as inspiring incantations than as reasoned arguments. J. H. Muirhead's overview of the high road down which German Idealism traveled is perhaps the best way to summarize it:

> The stages of the post-Kantian development of thought in Germany are by this time familiar matter of history: first Fichte's Moralism with its emphasis on the Ego; next the reaction against it in the Natur-Philosophie of Schelling, with its emphasis on the Absolute as the neutral basis both of self and nature: the so-called Philosophy of Identity; lastly Hegel's Absolute Idealism, which sought to establish Mind or Spirit as the principle that has been manifesting itself under the forms of space and time in nature, of consciousness and the creations of science, art, morality, religion, that are the embodiments of its ideals in the life of man.[13]

[12] *Encyclopaedia Britannica*, 13th edition, s.v. "Metaphysics," XVIII, 231.

[13] Muirhead, *The Platonic Tradition*, p. 147.

For our purposes, at this point it is enough to bear in mind for how brief a moment Kant's inherently unstable system held together, paying its simultaneous respects to the existence of real external objects and to the active powers of the mind that guarantee an at least functional objectivity to our experience of space, time, and causality, and setting a limit to what could be known while at the same time finding a ground for religious belief and ethical principle beyond that limit.

This brief sketch brings us to the early years of the nineteenth-century intellectual drama, but it may be useful to glance on down the century and recognize how fully the central positions that dominate nineteenth-century English thought were laid out by 1800.

The rigor of Kant's Critical method, and the limits to the mind set by his "transcendental" idealism, were not part of the aspects of Kantian and post-Kantian thought conveyed to English readers by Coleridge or, a little later, by Carlyle. Unfortunately for the assimilation of Kant's philosophical system in England, the professional philosopher who first drew attention to the merely phenomenal nature of all knowledge was Sir William Hamilton. Prepared by Thomas Reid's recognition of the active judgments of the mind, Hamilton grafted onto the Scottish Common Sense philosophy the Kantian position that space and time are forms of experience and that the mind conditions all experience. Hamilton went on to emphasize so heavily the resulting phenomenal nature of all knowledge that man's ignorance, not his knowledge, appears to claim priority. This is the other side of Kant from that which Schelling or Coleridge developed, but it is equally partial. Hamilton is able, by the aid of Christian doctrine, to assert the necessity of faith all the more strongly where indubitable knowledge is necessarily beyond the reach of the human mind. But if one goes down the road he has marked out unattended by Christianity, one arrives, as James Seth reminds us, at the agnosticism of Spencer and Huxley.[14]

Not until the middle of the century was a true idealism asserted in England; this was the system set forth in the *Institutes of Metaphysics* (1854) by J. F. Ferrier, a system that he attributed to the influence of Berkeley rather than German thought. Historians of philosophy seem agreed that only with Hutchison Stirling's *The Secret of Hegel* (1865) and *Textbook to Kant* (1881), and Edward Caird's *Philosophy of Kant* (1878) did the German philosophers begin to be adequately interpreted in England. And only in the 1880s in the writing of Thomas Hill Green, and in the 1890s with the works of F. H. Bradley, did an English Idealist philosophy begin to appear which took a thorough understanding of Kant and Hegel as the starting point.

I have hurried through these nineteenth-century English idealists—about whose systems I am not competent to speak in any case—because before the end of the century they did not in the main much affect English thought beyond the regions in which professional philosophers dwell. The fact is that as the atmosphere in which philosophical discussion occurred became more rarified—increasingly technical, turning back more toward questions of innate versus wholly empirical knowledge and principles, and finally much less readily translatable into moral, political, and aesthetic theory—it became insulated from those whose primary interests were more immediately pragmatic. Moreover, metaphysical systems have generally required a generation to announce themselves to the world of letters. More than forty years after Locke's *Essay on Human Understanding* his doctrines of association were being developed by Hartley, and after another forty years Archibald Alison was building his *Essay on the Nature and Principles of Taste* on Hartley. Some thirty years after its publication Kant's *Critique of Pure Reason* begins

[14] Seth, *English Philosophers*, pp. 305*ff.*

to be championed by Coleridge; Bradley's *Appearance and Reality* finds a place in the essays of T. S. Eliot after a similar interval.

Nineteenth-century empiricism as developed under the utilitarian banner by the Mills extended and ramified Bentham's system, but with fewer essential changes than is often thought. (See the discussion of J. S. Mill in chapter IV.) Major modifications occur only as the influence of Comte, Huxley, and, more rarely, Spencer merge with the utilitarian tradition in the minds of some of the later Victorians.

Comte's *Cours de Philosophie Positive* was published in 1840–1842 and condensed and translated by Harriet Martineau in 1853. J. S. Mill, chief contemporary spokesman for utilitarianism, found much to admire in it. Since the primary meaning of "positive" for Comte is "scientific," where that means the methodical analysis of experience, there was naturally much in Comte's positivism that seems simply empiricism stated in mid-nineteenth-century terms. While Comte insists that his Positive Philosophy is not empiricism, his explanation of the differences is less clear than their similarity. Comte's three stages of history—theological, metaphysical, and positive—fitted well enough with the Saint-Simonianism that influenced Mill in those early essays emphasizing the changes in social structure and thought from one period to the next. Even the attempt to transform the positive philosophy into a religion had its appeal to Mill, who was less eager than Bentham to rely on law as the major weight thrown into the balance to help associate pain with acting *against* the greatest happiness for the greatest number. A Religion of Humanity would rather help encourage the association of pleasure with acting *for* the greatest happiness of the greatest number. One can argue that for all the vagueness of his epistemology, Comte's basically empiricist standpoint made it a much more natural source of influences to soften Mill's basic

Benthamism than the thoughts of Coleridge or Carlyle, to which Mill at times looked. Nevertheless, Mill found much to criticize in Comte, most of it instances of deviation from the canons of empiricism.

Though known by leaders of utilitarianism and eminent scientists like Huxley, and significant in helping to focus interest on possible larger ramifications of the Darwinian evolutionary theory, Herbert Spencer remained very much a thinker apart. While the intellectual climate more and more accommodated itself to thinking of all things as evolving, Spencer's attempt to bring all areas of knowledge under a single principle and trace the workings of the evolutionary principle in each proved not to amalgamate easily even with the empiricist or positivist systems with which one would expect it to be nearly allied.

Epistemologically, Spencer's views took an intriguing turn that put him somewhere between empiricist and transcendentalist positions, between Locke and Kant, between Hamilton and Mill. Yes, all knowledge came from experience, but that experience has in itself over the millenia created certain forms of thought now inherent in ("inherited by" to use a term closer to the evolutionary mode of thought) the mind. Moreover, his exposition of his system begins with an account of the unknowable—a something rather like Hamilton's Unconditioned. Though Locke's distinction between primary and secondary qualities stands at the head of the trail leading to those unplumbed depths referred to as things-in-themselves, the Unconditioned, or the unknowable, such assumptions make empiricists decidedly uncomfortable. On the other hand, the flickering lamp of transcendentalism being at this time primarily in the care of thinkers more inclined to theology than metaphysics, little fellowship was to be expected there. Moreover, as the unknowable could alternately be seen as the source of that "persistence of force" which Spencer regarded as the primary principle that even evolution obeyed, it was hardly available for a transcendental cornerstone. Although Spencer accepted the necessity of an empirical utilitarianism until such time as a rational one (deduced from evolution) could be adequately developed, how this was to occur was questionable. The transition from Spencer's three principal directions of evolution—homogeneity to heterogeneity, diffusion to integration, and incoherence to coherence—to political and ethical principles was much less direct than from Bentham's first principle.

Finally, though Spencer saw the movement of evolution as toward greater happiness for mankind, its progress would have to be slow indeed since it depended on the gradual modification of the human character. No Benthamic calculus would provide a short cut. For Spencer, nevertheless, the essence of ethics lay in cooperating with evolution. But to see the evolutionary process, at least as illustrated in nature, as an ethical guide was repugnant to many of different philosophical persuasions. Matthew Arnold had dismissed it in "In Harmony with Nature," Huxley repudiated "the gladiatorial theory of existence," and Mill argued against it in his late essay "Nature."

Not only as a result of his difficulties in distilling ethics from evolution but because of the general difficulties of drawing practical consequences from evolution, Spencer's system failed to effect the revolution he desired. By his death in 1903, it had already lost its attractiveness. But John Stuart Mill had by then been dead for thirty years, and the utilitarianism for which he had been so eloquent a spokesman had lost its potency. Those of a speculative turn of mind were intrigued now by the idealism of Green and Bradley; but at the turn-of-the-century moment, empiricism was triumphant in social and political theory, ethics, and aesthetics.

We may turn back to the early part of the nineteenth century, having briefly surveyed the cardinal issues and shifting emphases in the continual struggle between empiricism and transcendentalism to the opening of the present century. The contest between the great metaphysical world views at this time was open, straightforward, and between rivals of very nearly equal strength. Coleridge and Carlyle were formidable champions of the one metaphysical tradition, Bentham and the Mills, in quite a different way, of the other.

II

Samuel Taylor Coleridge

OLERIDGE was of a strongly eclecticizing mind, capable of drawing on Hartley, Kant, Bacon, Plato, Newton, Shakespeare, Leighton, and Schelling among many others. He worked hard to make his thought comprehensive—and there is indeed considerable breadth in the thought of a man who can be cited as an important influence in the founding of both the Broad Church and Oxford movements.[1] However, the bias of Coleridge's thought, certainly from the time he renounced Hartleian psychology, was transcendental. One might indeed say that his major eclectic effort was to bring the thought of Kant into harmony with the succeeding German Idealists and even more with the Neo-Platonic tradition, an effort which ultimately heavily Platonized Kant, largely dissolving the distinction he had labored to make between "transcendental" and "transcendent," returning both terms to their older senses. And, though Carlyle is perhaps more wholeheart-

[1]To some extent there is confusion as well as breadth. René Wellek went so far as to say, "It will sound paradoxical . . . but . . . Coleridge has little insight into the incompatibility of different trends of thought" (*Immanuel Kant in England, 1793–1838*, p. 67).

edly the transcendentalist than Coleridge, Coleridge's conscious effort to order his thought into a philosophical system makes him the best example of early nineteenth-century transcendental thought.[2] It also makes him a very good example of the way in which even an eclectic thinker filters out whatever clashes directly with the basis of his thought.[3]

What follows is an outline of Coleridge's philosophy, traced primarily in his formulation of the all-important relationship between the Reason and the Understanding in the area of politics, aesthetics, and religion, as they appear in his major pronouncements, either published or presented in public lectures, between 1816, by which time his early discipleship to Hartley's associationism was over and the Kantian influence had been well digested, and 1834, the year of his death.[4] My aim is to provide an account, at once briefer and more comprehensive than any I know to exist, of the part of Coleridge's thought that he was willing and able to commit himself to publicly.

I should perhaps note that my analysis of the philo-

[2]"By temperament and education, Coleridge is a traditional idealist. The whole bent of his mind led him to Plato and Platonism, to the English Platonic tradition and to the new German idealism which he felt to be deeply akin with the older thought" (*Ibid.*, pp. 66–67).

[3]Coleridge himself was of course responsible for perhaps the most famous statement on the incompatibility of the two great metaphysical traditions. "Every man is born an Aristotelian or a Platonist. I do not think it possible that any one born an Aristotelian can become a Platonist; and I am sure no born Platonist can ever change into an Aristotelian. . . . *Table Talk*, in *The Complete Works*, VI, 336.

[4]The important texts are thus *The Statesman's Manual* (1816), the second *Lay Sermon* (1817), the *Biographia Literaria* (1817), the *Preliminary Treatise on Method* (1818), the final version of *The Friend* (1818), *Aids to Reflection* (1825), and *On the Constitution of the Church and State* (1830), together with the reports of the lectures on Shakespeare and the philosophical lectures of 1818. I am confining myself to what George Whalley has called Coleridge's "public" system, in order to avoid the temptation so easily yielded to of picking and choosing isolated passages from manuscript material. See Whalley's "Coleridge Unlabyrinthed," *University of Toronto Quarterly*, XXXII (1963), 325–45.

sophical structure of Coleridge's thought was originally developed before the publication of three books on his thought, each of which has drawn considerable attention and each of which becomes more intriguing when compared with the others: Norman Fruman's *Coleridge: The Damaged Archangel*, Owen Barfield's *What Coleridge Thought*, and G. N. G. Orsini's *Coleridge and German Idealism*.[5] Barfield heavily emphasizes that thinking is an *act* for Coleridge, that his thinking recognized throughout the relation between the "'two conflicting principles of the FREE LIFE and CONFINING FORM,'" that the "productive power . . . which *in* nature acts *as* nature, is nevertheless 'essentially one (that is, of one kind) with the intelligence, which is a human mind above nature.'" Further, Coleridge's method "demands of us a priori realisation, first, that natural phenomena have an inside that is not itself phenomenal and, secondly, that that 'inside' is . . . the human self in polar counterpoint to the natural world."[6] What is striking in Barfield's book is his initial conscious rejection of the "biographical/comparative" approach and the resultant loving labor devoted to teasing out of Coleridge's works, with a minimum of reference to the German idealists, a system which could much more easily have been described by comparing it with those of Fichte and Schelling. Fruman, on the other hand, marshalls evidence of derivativeness and plagiarism in Coleridge's work going well beyond that previously brought together in any one place. It would seem from Fruman's study that it was not truth in the abstract that was the "divine ventriloquist" speaking through Coleridge but rather a very definite set of works by Kant, Fichte, and Schelling.

G. N. G. Orsini's volume gives a detailed summary of Kant's *Critique of Pure Reason*, and only somewhat less

[5]The reader intrigued by Barfield's consideration of Coleridge's trichotomous logic is encouraged to compare it with J. H. Muirhead's discussion in *Coleridge as Philosopher*.

[6]Barfield, *What Coleridge Thought*, pp. 31, 61, 159.

detailed summaries of Kant's second and third critiques, Fichte's *Wissenschaftslehre*, and Schelling's evolving Transcendental Idealism, in each case carefully reviewing what Coleridge adopted. For Orsini, the central point is not the extent of Coleridge's borrowing, acknowledged or unacknowledged, but how fully in accord with Schelling Coleridge for a time was. "At this time [1818] Coleridge was an absolute or transcendental idealist," writes Orsini, who attributes Coleridge's partial retreat from Schelling to the recognition that the German thinker's Absolute Spirit could not be reconciled with his own belief in the Christian God.[7]

I have been unable to persuade myself that my own quite different attempt to sketch out the ways in which Coleridge's transcendentalist bent worked itself out in various fields of speculation requires modification as a result of these fascinatingly different studies. None explains Coleridge's influence as the leading English opponent of empiricism nor the legacy of purely philosophical problems lying in wait for disciples. Despite the amount of discussion devoted to the philosophical foundations of Coleridge's thought by critics and philosophers of such different emphases and interests as Barfield, Orsini, Fruman, Jackson, Appleyard, Fogle, Boulger, Colmer, Lovejoy, Willey, Wellek, and Muirhead,[8] the present analysis seems to me to take a usefully different approach.

Almost universally, the first step in considering Coleridge's thought has been investigation of the distinction between the Reason and the Understanding. Despite the wearisome length to which this distinction (together with the degree to which Coleridge's formulation of it deviates from Kant's position,[9] and its relation to the Imagination

[7] Orsini, *Coleridge and German Idealism*, p. 219.

[8] For the relevant titles, see the list of volumes cited.

[9] René Wellek's chapter on Coleridge in *Immanuel Kant in England* and G. N. G. Orsini's *Coleridge and German Idealism* are the most penetrating analyses of Coleridge's relationship to Kant. A much simplified, but very handy

and Fancy) has been discussed, not a few commentators have settled for something very close to the substance, if not the spirit, of Carlyle's gibe that Coleridge's distinction amounts to "the sublime secret of believing by the reason what the understanding had been obliged to throw out as incredible."[10] As a summation of Coleridge's later position on religion as set forth in *Aids to Reflection*, this does not, in fact, widely miss the mark. However, it is equally important to remember that the key to understanding Coleridge's political thought is an inversion of Carlyle's comment; in politics, Coleridge tries to demonstrate that the Understanding must be applied to situations and relationships to which the Reason, by definition, is inapplicable. The key to grasping his poetic theory is more radical, the recognition of Coleridge's denial of essentially poetic power to either the Understanding or the Reason, which implies as a corollary the denial of truth-discovering power to the Imagination. Therefore, I believe one must apply very cautiously Basil Willey's comment that for Coleridge "any important thought or distinction in one field must have its counterpart in another, and in every other"; the implications which Coleridge draws from his major distinctions do not always result in the sort of congruence one might expect.[11]

Although interested in politics, literature, theology, and science throughout his life, Coleridge gave his greatest energies to the first three, in succession. His beliefs in each area having solidified thus successively, a final adjustment between the positions taken in each area was never completed. More striking than the resulting minor contraditions in his thought, however, is a consistent set of philosophical difficulties which dogged him in all areas.

---

and helpful outline is to be found in Boulger's *Coleridge as Religious Thinker*, pp. 72–80.

[10] Carlyle, *The Life of John Sterling*, in *Complete Works*, II, 52.

[11] Willey, *Nineteenth Century Studies*, p. 27.

The nature of these difficulties will, I hope, become clear in the course of this survey. At the same time, seeing Kant as having not only answered Hume's skepticism but supplanted the associationism of Locke and Hartley, and as having opened the way to, even if he had not entered upon, knowledge beyond anything attainable by experience, Coleridge's vision of a total system retained a sort of practical consistency. His system might be almost impossible to build on, but it nevertheless seemed to offer a sophisticated refuge from, and a metaphysically impressive challenge to, empiricism.

METHOD AND SCIENCE. In 1817, Coleridge was writing the General Introduction to the *Encyclopaedia Metropolitana*, the general plan of which he had been commissioned to oversee. He was, of course, hardly the man to write a conventional introduction assuring readers of the accuracy, completeness, and convenience of the compilation—what he set forth was an outline of the hierarchy of all divisions of human knowledge, which amounted to a prolegomena to the re-ordering of epistemological theory and philosophical practice. Following Bacon in taking all knowledge for his province and attempting to reduce its relationships to method, Coleridge further determined to condense the statement of method into this brief introduction and, with uncharacteristic economy, succeeded well enough so that, under the title *Preliminary Treatise on Method*, it serves simultaneously to set forth the method to be used in compiling the encyclopaedia and the proper method of pursuing and relating *all* human knowledge.[12]

[12] The *Treatise* must be used with caution since the editor of the *Encyclopaedia* apparently made significant alterations. However, these would appear to have been more in the nature of excision and rearrangement than in the rewriting of individual sentences. The version that appears in *The Friend* omits much

"Method consists in placing one or more *particular* things or notions, in subordination, either to a preconceived *universal* Idea, or to some lower form of the latter; some class, order, genus, or species, each of which derives its intellectual significancy, and scientific worth, from being an ascending step toward the universal."[13] What most matters in Method is attention to "unity" and "progression" in investigation, in short, organicism, as is apparent in Coleridge's choice of Shakespeare to accompany Plato and Bacon as his examples of adepts in Method. For Coleridge, Method is the exploration of relationships. Those relationships absolutely necessary, "predetermined by a truth in the Mind itself,"[14] are called Laws; what objectively exists as a Law is known subjectively as an Idea. Those relationships which are not necessary, which we arrive at by observation and enumeration, which are imperfectly grasped because they are not found in the mind itself, are Theories. Now, although the difference between the Reason and the Understanding is nowhere explicitly developed in the *Treatise*, it clearly underlies the whole distinction between Theory and Idea. It is implied most directly in the explanation that "according to Plato, as well as to Bacon, there can be no hope of any fruitful and secure Method, so long as forms, merely subjective, are arbitrarily assumed to be the moulds of objective Truth, the seals and impresses of Nature."[15] The "forms" here referred to roughly correspond

---

of the more technical explanation, but I find no specific repudiation of positions taken earlier. Indeed, one major alteration introduced in *The Friend* Coleridge later admitted to be a mistake, and his subsequent marginal comments indicate a return to the view expressed in the *Treatise* (see *The Friend*, part 1, ed. Barbara Rooke, *The Collected Works of Samuel Taylor Coleridge*, IV, 459). The *Treatise* has been republished as *S. T. Coleridge's Treatise on Method*, ed. Alice D. Snyder.

[13] Coleridge, *Treatise*, p. 54.

[14] *Ibid.*, p. 4. Cf. the similar passage in *The Friend*, in *Complete Works*, II, 418.

[15] Coleridge, *Treatise*, p. 45.

to both the forms of space and time and the concepts of the Understanding in Kantian terminology. Elsewhere the relationship is made more specific. In *Aids to Reflection*, for instance, generalization is specifically referred to the Understanding, the Reason described as the "source of necessary and universal principles."[16] In the portion of *The Friend* devoted to Method, Coleridge states that "all theory supposes the general idea of cause and effect"[17] (the most important concept of the Kantian Understanding).

In these formulations the essence of Coleridge's departure from Kant is evident. The roles of the Reason and the Understanding are reversed. The necessary and universal operation of the Understanding on sense data had been the guarantee of the necessity of scientific and mathematical laws, axioms, and postulates for Kant; for Coleridge, the Reason is the ground of necessity, finding its certainty within itself. Kant's three "regulative" ever-present Ideas of the Reason (God, the Soul, the World) are replaced by an apparently unlimited number of Ideas which must be discovered in time. It is impossible here to pursue even the most important metaphysical ramifications of Coleridge's transmogrification of Kant. The essential question within

[16] Coleridge, *Complete Works*, I, 247, 251. Coleridge indicates a distinction between "Principles" and "Ideas" in a note in *The Friend*: "By the pure 'reason,' I mean the power by which we become possessed of principles,—the eternal verities of Plato and Descartes, and of ideas, not images—as the ideas of a point, a line, a circle, in mathematics; and of justice, holiness, freewill, and the like in morals" (*Complete Works*, II, 164). However, the exact meaning of the distinction is not clear, and at other times Coleridge seems to want to make the distinction correspond to that between the products of the Speculative and the Practical Reason, or alternatively, to that between Metaphysical and Physical Ideas. Since he at times uses the words interchangeably, however, and both are exclusive products of the Reason, I here regard them as identical.

[17] *Ibid.*, II, 423. The terms Reason and Understanding appear here and there in the version of the *Treatise* Coleridge incorporated into the Second Section of *The Friend*. However, their use there raises more problems than it clears up. Thus, at the beginning of Essay IV, Coleridge indicates that he will discuss the relationship of Method to the Understanding, but by the end of Essay V, we find that we are considering the relation of Ideas of the Reason to Laws of matter. See especially pp. 410 and 423.

his own system, however, is the mode of interaction between the Ideas of Reason and the concepts of Understanding, a question difficult to explore in the *Treatise* because he does not there rely on these terms. But his difficulties appear clearly enough in his distinction between Metaphysical and Physical Ideas. The Idea of a circle is a Metaphysical Idea, the necessity and validity of which requires no reference to experience. But the law of crystallization, to use one of Coleridge's examples, is a Physical Idea and therefore dependent for its accuracy on "the more or less careful observation of things actually existing."[18]

Now to be fair to Coleridge, one can interpret this as meaning that while one does not arrive at an Idea empirically, that one has grasped an Idea and not a chimera can be checked by drawing deductions from it and checking these against observation. Many passages in the *Treatise* and elsewhere support this interpretation. In the *Treatise* he says that, with Bacon "as with us, an *Idea* is an experiment proposed, an experiment is an idea realized."[19] In the Philosophical Lectures we find that "Plato began in meditation, thought deeply within himself of the goings-on of his own mind and of the powers that there were in that mind, conceived to himself how this could be, and if it were, what must be the necessary results and agencies of it, and then looked abroad to ask if this were a dream, or whether it were indeed a revelation from within, and a waking reality."[20] Later, in the same series of lectures, we find, "This therefore is the true Baconic philosophy. It consists in this, in a profound meditation on those laws which the pure reason in man reveals to him, with the confident anticipation and faith that to this will be found to corre-

[18] Coleridge, *Treatise*, p. 10.

[19] *Ibid.*, p. 42.

[20] Coleridge, *The Philosophical Lectures*, p. 186.

spond certain laws in nature."[21] The explanation of this correspondence we find set out directly not in the *Treatise* but in the portion of *The Friend* developed out of the *Treatise*. After earlier arguing, as in his Philosophical Lectures,[22] that the dialogues of Plato are only prolegomena to the higher doctrine, which is ultimately a religious faith, Coleridge returns to the Greek philosopher in explaining "the coincidence between reason and experience; or between the laws of matter and the ideas of the pure intellect." "The only answer which Plato deemed the question capable of receiving, compels the reason to pass out of itself and seek the ground of this agreement in a supersensual essence, which being at once the ideal of the reason and the cause of the material world, is the pre-establisher of the harmony in and between both. Religion therefore is the ultimate aim of philosophy, in consequence of which philosophy itself becomes the supplement of the sciences."[23]

In the *Treatise* as a whole, this distinction between Metaphysical and Physical Ideas is not kept entirely clear from the distinction between Idea and Theory. We find that when we descend from Coleridge's "Pure Sciences" of Grammar, Logic, Mathematics, Metaphysics, Morals, and Theology, which "embrace solely relations of Law," to those sciences which deal with the external world, "theory is immediately introduced."[24] But the same distinction seems to apply to the difference between Metaphysical Ideas, which "relate to the essence of things as possible," and those

[21] *Ibid.*, p. 333.

[22] *Ibid.*, pp. 176–77.

[23] Coleridge, *Complete Works*, II, 422. Cf. Coleridge's reference to the necessity of "the one great Being whose eternal reason is the ground and absolute condition of the ideas in the mind, and no less the ground and the absolute cause of all the correspondent realities in nature" (*Philosophical Lectures*, p. 334).

[24] Coleridge, *Treatise*, p. 58.

things "actually existing and cognizable by our faculties."[25] In other words, it is very difficult to see the difference between a Physical Idea and a Theory, or feel sure that Coleridge kept this distinction clear in his own mind. At times he speaks as though observation initiates the Reason's formulation of Physical Ideas. For instance, Coleridge gives as an example of an important discovery of an Idea of Nature "the moment, when Columbus, on an unknown ocean, first perceived that startling fact, the change of the magnetic needle!"[26] If one goes outside the *Treatise* to *Aids to Reflection*, one finds a definition of the Speculative Reason as the "power by which we . . . draw from particular and contingent appearances universal and necessary conclusions,"[27] which would seem to be exactly what Columbus did. It is hard to know why such an act of interpreting a physical fact is not to be referred to the Understanding. Coleridge's belief in God gave him a ground for explaining the correspondence of the evidence of the senses as interpreted by the Understanding and the Ideas of the Reason (the parallel with Descartes, the Cambridge Platonists, and Continental rationalism is evident). But he remained unable to set forth the manner in which the mind is able to move from one to the other, in which a transition is effected between the Ideas of the Reason and the concepts of the Understanding.

Since the word "Reason" is avoided in the *Treatise*, one might come to the conclusion that the Ideas discussed there were not at all the same as the Ideas of the Reason Coleridge speaks of elsewhere were it not that in the concluding pages we find that "at the head of all Pure Science

[25] *Ibid.*, pp. 9, 10. Cf. also paragraphs 6, 7, and 8 on pp. 4 and 5 and paragraphs 8 and 9, p. 55.

[26] *Ibid.*, p. 15. See also the whole of paragraph 7, p. 17.

[27] Coleridge, *Complete Works*, I, 251. Cf. pp. 261–62 where "the sciential reason" is described as "the faculty of concluding universal and necessary truths from particular and contingent appearances."

stands Theology, of which the great fountain is Revelation," and the entire structure of theology, we know, depends for Coleridge on a structure of the Ideas of the Reason. Moreover, the connection of the *Treatise* with other of Coleridge's works of contemporary and later date reassures one that the *Treatise* is not eccentric but stands near the center of the system. The view there developed that both metaphysics and morals lead on to theology looks toward the structure of *Aids to Reflection* (1825) and back to the conclusion of the *Biographia Literaria* (1817). A modified version of the *Treatise* was made the capstone to the 1818 collected version of *The Friend.* The references to Shakespeare in the *Treatise* parallel important points in the contemporary lectures on Shakespeare; Coleridge's Method is Shakespeare's "organicism." And an explanation of Ideas greatly condensed from the *Treatise* appears as part of the introductory essay of *Church and State* (1830).[28]

In summary, one may say that the *Treatise* avoids the explicit problem of the interaction of Understanding and Reason while implicitly raising the problem in a particularly acute form: the ground of the correspondences between the Ideas of the Reason and experiences as produced by the Understanding may be God, but what intelligible formulation of the relation of the Ideas of theology to the Idea of gravitation and thence to those "imperfect theories" of gravitation Coleridge notices is possible for the human mind?[29] In assuming the existence of an apparently unlimited number of Ideas of the Reason and transferring the quality of necessity from concepts of the Understanding to those Ideas, Coleridge created difficulties that reappear in every area of thought he entered. Ultimately, Coleridge seems to have been less interested in working out how Method aids the inquiry into Natural Science than in presenting Method (i.e., emphasis on the

[28] *Ibid.*, VI, 31.

[29] Coleridge, *Treatise*, p. 58.

Reason and, in the development of the argument of the *Treatise* in *The Friend*, on the Will) as the way to cultivation, that is, religious insight, as opposed to civilization, or the ability to manipulate the external world for man's gratification.[30]

GOVERNMENT AND POLITICS. The discussion of Coleridge's theory of politics or government can begin by focusing on the same problem in a different form. Nothing is more likely to mislead the reader coming to *On the Constitution of the Church and State According to the Idea of Each* than the general notion that Coleridge is using "Idea" in a reasonably Kantian sense. In Coleridge's Platonized Kantianism, Reason generally figures as the source of principles which are ideal in that they are not the result of experience, i.e., the application of concepts to the products of the senses. Reason, as he puts it in *Aids to Reflection*, is the faculty which "in all its decisions appeals to itself as the ground and substance of their truth."[31] Since Coleridge seems to follow Kant in seeing time as a form applied to sense impressions prior to the imposition of concepts, and thus as a condition only of experience, the principles of the Reason should be timeless. They represent the ultimate goals of the processes of the Understanding, but they can never be known, that is, experienced. Thus, in the explanation of Ideas that opens *Church and State*, Coleridge specifically distinguishes the Idea from the concept, which "consists in a conscious act of the understanding."[32] Now "Ideas" of the Church and the State are, Coleridge carefully explains, not concretely realized in experience. So far

[30] See especially *Complete Works*, II, 452–57.

[31] *Complete Works*, I, 246.

[32] *Ibid.*, VI, 31.

they are "ideal." They are, however, in practice discovered by examining the history of the English Church and State and are thus hardly timeless Kantian principles of the Reason, since they are the products of temporal human choices.

Nor can the broader meaning of "Idea" which is developed in the opening of the *Treatise on Method* include the Ideas of Church and State. For there an Idea is said to be the subjective formulation of an objective law which *must be*. The Idea of an ever-originating Social Contract, which Coleridge discusses early in *Church and State*, may be a good example of the Idea as defined in the *Treatise* (he argues that all men seem to assume a vaguely recognized Idea[33] of reciprocal duties between citizen and state), but the Ideas of the Church and State as Coleridge formulates them are clearly the result of analyzing what *is* and thus, to use the language of the *Treatise*, Theories which yield images, not Laws which yield Ideas.

In sum, one must keep clearly in mind Coleridge's own parenthesis in his definition of the "Idea" in *Church and State*: "By an idea I mean (*in this instance*) that conception of a thing, which is not abstracted from any particular state, form, or mode, in which the thing may happen to exist at this or at that time; nor yet generalized from any number or succession of such forms or modes; but which is given by the knowledge of its ultimate aim."[34] As is the case with the Physical Ideas of the *Treatise*, it is hard to see why such an Idea as described in the preceding quotation is not simply a product of the Understanding.

The Idea of the State as a balance of power between the three estates—the landowning, the mercantile, and the Church—is thus machinery for conforming to what is ul-

[33] That an Idea may be either distinct or no more than "a vague appetency towards something which the Mind necessarily hunts for" is specifically stated in the *Treatise*, p. 6.

[34] Coleridge, *Complete Works*, VI, 30 (italics mine).

timately an Idea in the more usual Coleridgean sense of the term: the principle that men must be treated as ends, not means. The manner in which the balance is maintained and the manner in which the National Church is administered so as to perform its duty are subordinate parts of the machinery, parts that may, to some extent, be tinkered with. It is perhaps because he felt it so important to preserve the basic plan of this machinery, to guard against its being consigned to the scrap heap and replaced by another model, that Coleridge invests it with an aura of finality through the use of the term "Idea." Coleridge would of course have objected to my terminology—"tinkering around" with the machinery, adjusting a lever here, adding a set of gears there was what he accused the utilitarians of doing. Nevertheless, although Coleridge's argument in the *Constitution of the Church and State* sounds as though it proceeds directly from principles given by the Reason, it is actually entirely consonant with Coleridge's position in *The Friend* in which, denying that government takes its origin in the Reason of man, he argues that "every institution of national origin needs no other justification than a proof, that under the particular circumstances it is expedient."[35] The Reason gives the ultimate goal—the maxim derived from Kant's Practical Reason that men should be treated as ends not means—but the Understanding, the organ expressly intended to calculate prudence and expedience, determines, under the circumstances given it at a particular time, how best to attempt to approximate that goal.[36]

To the reader coming for the first time to this discussion of government as an exercise in the art of the expedi-

[35] *Ibid.*, II, 163.

[36] Reason would seem to apprehend directly, as a Principle, that men must be treated as ends, but Reason is the ground of the Principle in another way: "Every man is born with the faculty of reason. . . . Hence the sacred principle, recognized by all laws, human and divine, the principle indeed, which is the ground-work of all law and justice, that a person can never become a thing, nor be treated as such without wrong" (*Complete Works*, II, 175).

ent, Coleridge will seem to be contradicting his own strictures on the utilitarians. But his attack on the utilitarians will be found directed, on the one hand, against their attempt to apply immutable principles directly and, on the other, against their assumption that only man's self-interest may be appealed to. They thus combine the errors of both the theories of government he attacks in *The Friend* as alternative to his own: those of Hobbes and Rousseau. That his rejection of systems of government which attempt to base themselves on reason as "the power by which we become possessed of principles"[37] is directed against the utilitarians equally with Rousseau becomes clear in his summary of the beliefs of those who would found government on reason alone.

> Each man is the best judge of his own happiness, and to himself must it therefore be intrusted. Remove all the interferences of positive statutes, all monopoly, all bounties, all prohibitions, and all encouragements of importation and exportation, of particular growth and particular manufactures: let the revenues of the state be taken at once from the produce of soil; and all things will then find their level, all irregularities will correct each other, and an indestructible cycle of harmonious motions take place in the moral equally as in the natural world. The business of the governor is to watch incessantly, that the state shall remain composed of individuals, acting as individuals, by which alone the freedom of all can be secured. Its duty is to take care that itself remain the sole collective power, and that all the citizens should enjoy the same rights, and without distinction be subject to the same duties.[38]

Coleridge argues that although the Reason gives the principles which the Understanding is to apply, "this, however, gives no proof that reason alone ought to govern and

[37] *Ibid.*, II, 164.

[38] *Ibid.*, II, 183–84.

direct human beings, either as individuals or as states. It ought not to do this, because it can not. The laws of reason are unable to satisfy the first conditions of human society." Thus, although on one hand it is to "property . . . and to its inequalities" that "all human laws directly or indirectly relate, which would not be equally laws in the state of nature," nevertheless "it is impossible to deduce the right of property from pure reason."[39]

There is plenty of reference to the Reason in Coleridge's political discussions, but he skirts the question of the interaction between the principles of the Reason and the Understanding's task of grappling with the practical problems of government, placing his emphasis here on the role of the latter faculty. In the absence of a system of mediation between the Reason and the Understanding, Coleridge finds it impossible to formulate a program. In the *Lay Sermon Addressed to the Higher and Middle Classes*, for instance, Coleridge states the negative aims of the state to be the preservation of "its own safety by means of its own strength, and the protection of person and property for all its members." The positive ends are "to make the means of subsistence more easy to each individual," "to secure to each of its members the hope of bettering his own condition or that of his children," and "the development of those faculties which are essential to his humanity, that is, to his rational and moral being."[40] Few reformers could ask for more, at least in terms of generally stated goals, than these objectives. But how should the state try to gain them? Only by an appeal to the conscience. "All reform or innovation, not won from the free agent by the presentation of juster views and nobler interests, and which does not leave the merit of having effected it sacred to the individual proprietor, it were folly to propose, and worse than folly to at-

[39] *Ibid.*, II, 184–85.

[40] *Ibid.*, VI, 216.

tempt."[41] Coleridge went so far as to write in 1818 in favor of Peel's Factory Acts to protect children in the cotton mills, and he closes the sermon with the exhortation that "our manufacturers must consent to regulations." But even though he can see the need for certain external restraints on the commercial spirit, he does not specifically formulate these here or elsewhere, and the landed interest can only be admonished to "regard their estates as secured indeed from all human interference by every principle of law, and policy, but yet as offices of trust, with duties to be performed. . . ."[42] The problem of reducing the Ideas of the Reason, "predetermined by a Truth in the Mind itself," to formulas applicable to the England of the time and translatable into statutes would appear to have proved insurmountable; Coleridge reproduces the traditional idealist solution: the world can only be made better by making individual men want to live in accord with the ideal.[43]

Religion and Morality. René Wellek's analysis of Coleridge's distinction between Reason and Understanding supports Carlyle's epigram: Coleridge "simply desires the breakdown of human Intelligence in order to substitute pure Faith."[44] Such a sweeping summary goes too far, but the gulf between the world of political action and

[41] *Ibid.*, VI, 217.

[42] *Ibid.*, VI, 225. Similarly, in the essay "On the Slave Trade" for the *Watchman* (25 March 1796), rptd. in *The Collected Works of Samuel Taylor Coleridge*, II, 130–40, Coleridge's formula for ending the slave trade is to refrain from using rum and sugar.

[43] Cf. "It is only to a limited extent that laws can be wiser than the nations for which they are enacted" (*Complete Works*, VI, 121).

[44] Wellek, *Immanuel Kant in England*, p. 91.

that of religious belief and private morality is a real one in Coleridge's thought, one which rises out of the distinction between Reason and Understanding. As early as 1798, according to Hazlitt's well-known report of one of the sermons, Coleridge was insisting on the opposition between the spirit of the world and the spirit of Christianity, a point specifically made in and essential to the argument in *The Constitution of the Church and State.*[45] There, the Christian Church is described as the opposite of all realms, of the World and its evils.[46] Coleridge is saying more here than that Christianity is opposed to "worldliness" or to excessive concern for worldly success, or, simply, to evil. For it is opposed even to the National Church, a piece of machinery which, on the imperfect level of the ordinary world, is entrusted not only with balancing the commercial and landed interests, but positively opposing evil by combating ignorance and relieving misery.

The belief in God which is the starting point of the theology of the Christian Church cannot, according to Coleridge, be grounded in either philosophical argument or appeal to history. His arguments in *Aids to Reflection* for the inadequacy of the Understanding to arrive at a proof of God's existence make use of Kant, of course, but more direct (and less obscured by questions of the exact use to which Coleridge put Kantian terms and arguments) is his presentation of this point in his philosophical lectures of 1818. The whole direction of those lectures is toward showing the limits of philosophy and establishing Christianity as its "proper supplement." Thus, in a typical passage from the seventh lecture he argues that the great moral truths "show a fitness in the human mind for religion, but

[45] J. D. Campbell, *Samuel Taylor Coleridge: A Narrative of the Events of His Life*, p. 82.

[46] Coleridge, *Complete Works*, VI, 98. See also the similar comments in *Aids to Reflection* (*Complete Works*, I, 126).

the power of giving it is not in the reason; that must be given as all things are given from without, and it is that which we call a revelation. And hence it is that I have ventured to call Christianity the proper supplement of philosophy—that which, uniting all that was true in it, at the same time gave that higher spirit which united it into one systematic and coherent power."[47]

The four intentions of *Aids to Reflection* are given by Coleridge in his preface in an ascending order, which suggests the manner in which each point is to be built on the previous ones. These intentions are to (1) "direct the reader's attention to the value of the science of words," which will lead to the second intention, and (2) to "establish the distinct characters of prudence, morality, and religion"; that distinction leads on to (3) the setting forth of "the momentous distinction between reason and understanding," and thence to (4) the final point, the exhibition of "a full and consistent scheme of the Christian Dispensation," which will show that the mysteries of the Christian religion are "reason in its highest form of self-affirmation."[48]

It is helpful to trace in bare outline the course of Coleridge's argument. After the introductory aphorisms, emphasizing the importance of reflection, Coleridge devotes a section to four "Prudential Aphorisms" in which he grants a great many of the principles of utilitarian morality, but only as they apply to the lowest level of religious thought. Yes, says Coleridge, "in all our outward conduct and actions . . . the dictates of virtue are the very same with those of self interest. . . . For the outward object of virtue being the greatest producible sum of happiness of all men, it must needs include the object of an intelligent

[47] Coleridge, *Philosophical Lectures*, pp. 233–34. See also p. 224: "As in truth philosophy itself is nothing but mockery unless it is considered the transit from paganism to religion."

[48] Coleridge, *Complete Works*, I, 114–15.

self-love, which is the greatest possible happiness of one individual." Or again, "If then the time has not yet come for anything higher, act on the maxim of seeking the most pleasure with the least pain. . . ."[49] But, although virtue leads toward happiness, the attempt to make oneself happier, even to make others happier, is not virtue. Coleridge later gives an analogy: "Without kind offices and useful services, wherever the power and opportunity occur, love would be a hollow pretense. Yet what noble mind would not be offended, if he were thought to value the love for the sake of the services, and not rather the services for the sake of the love."[50]

Coleridge then gives a section of "Moral and Religious Aphorisms" based on the definition he had given of morality in Aphorism XXX of his "Introductory Aphorisms": "What the duties of morality are, the Apostle instructs the believer in full, comprising them under the two heads of negative and positive; negative, to keep himself pure from the world; and positive, beneficence from loving-kindness, that is, love of his fellowmen (his kind) as himself."[51] The third and the longest portion of the volume is made up of aphorisms concerning "Spiritual Religion," the whole basis of which is found in Coleridge's comments to the first two "Aphorisms of that which is Indeed Spiritual Religion."[52] These aphorisms, like many throughout the volume, are drawn from Archbishop Leighton, but both, and especially the second, function primarily as texts for Coleridge to dilate on.[53] The first sentence of Aphorism I—"Where, if not

[49] *Ibid.*, I, 141–42.

[50] *Ibid.*, I, 144.

[51] *Ibid.*, I, 133.

[52] The word "Indeed" is here intended to emphasize the main point of the brief group of "Aphorisms of Spiritual Religion," that "spiritual" means "according to the Reason."

[53] Coleridge's "advertisement to the first edition" explains that the works began as a selection from the writings of Archbishop Leighton.

in Christ, is the power that can persuade a sinner to return, that can *bring home a heart to God*?"[54] makes clear that Coleridge is speaking to those who accept the particular Christian doctrines as given by divine revelation.

The goal Coleridge sets for himself, as the whole work makes clear, is to give guides for the reasonable contemplation of those doctrines, to guard the contemplator against being led into speculative swamps. "It is the office . . . of reason, to bring a unity into all our conceptions and several knowledges," and this is possible "only on the assumption or hypothesis of a One as the ground and cause of the universe . . . which . . . is the subject neither of time nor change."[55] Coleridge here is staying within Kantian bounds, stopping short of attributing necessity to the Idea of God. The step from assuming God to finding unquestioning faith in his existence requires Coleridge's distinction between the Practical and the Speculative Reason, a distinction suggested by but not reducible to Kant's distinction between the Pure and the Practical Reason. By the Practical Reason Coleridge means "the power of proposing an ultimate end, the determinability of the will by ideas."[56] Religious belief requires the assent of the Will no less than the Reason. "If there be aught spiritual in man the Will must be such."[57] The Will is guided by the Reason (thus functioning as the Practical Reason), but the result of willing in conformity with Reason is assurance about truths which cannot be derived from Reason.[58]

Moreover, as Coleridge sets forth the argument in brief outline in the *Biographia*, until the Will is determined to

[54] Coleridge, *Complete Works*, I, 205.

[55] *Ibid.*, I, 210–11.

[56] *Ibid.*, I, 261.

[57] *Ibid.*, I, 192.

[58] Cf. "Now what the telescope is to the eye, just that, faith (that is the energies of our moral feelings) is to the reason" (*Philosophical Lectures*, p. 269).

act in accordance with religious truth by the joint persuasions of all the faculties, Reason can be no more than Speculative.[59]

> The question then concerning our faith in the existence of a God, not only as the ground of the universe by his essence, but as its maker and judge by his wisdom and holy will, appeared to stand thus. The sciential reason, whose objects are purely theoretical, remains neutral, as long as its name and semblance are not usurped by the opponents of the doctrine. But it then becomes an effective ally by exposing the false show of demonstration, or by evincing the equal demonstrability of the contrary from premises equally logical. The understanding mean time suggests, the analogy of experience facilitates, the belief. Nature excites and recalls it, as by a perpetual revelation.[60]

The same is true of the doctrines of revealed religion. The "safety-lamp for religious inquirers . . . [is] the principle, that all revealed truths are to be judged of by us, so far only as they are possible subjects of human conception, on grounds of practice, or in some way connected with our moral and spiritual interests."[61] Thus, to believers the doctrine of Election "is a hope, which if it spring out of Christian principles, be examined by the texts and nourished by the means prescribed in Scripture, will become a lively and an assured hope, but which can not in this life

[59] Cf. pp. 224, 225 of the *Philosophical Lectures* on the importance of the Will to true religion.

[60] Coleridge, *Biographia Literaria*, in *Complete Works*, III, 297. The reference to the Reason "evincing the equal demonstrability of the contrary from premises equally logical" is of course from Kant's antimonies. Cf. "Reason is the power of universal and necessary convictions, the source and substance of truths above sense, and having their evidence in themselves. . . . Contemplated distinctively in reference to formal (or abstract) truth, it is the Speculative Reason; but in reference to actual (or moral) truth, as the fountain of ideas and the light of the conscience, we name it the Practical Reason" (*Complete Works*, I, 241–42).

[61] Coleridge, *Complete Works*, I, 215.

pass into knowledge, much less certainty of fore-knowledge."[62] Though the existence of a God with traditional Christian attributes cannot be "proved," the existence of that God is established "for every mind not devoid of all reason, and desperately conscience-proof" by an inner revelation which consists in the mutally supporting evidence of all the faculties.[63]

Such a position would seem to leave little for Reason to do and occasion little need for the insistence on the difference between the Reason and the Understanding. But once grounds for faith in God have been set out, Reason can be regarded as proceeding directly from God. By Aphorism VIII, Coleridge has gone beyond the Kantian restrictions on Reason implied in his comment on Aphorism II: Reason now becomes synonymous not only with Leighton's "faith" but with the "Divine Spirit."[64] The Reason becomes "even the light that lighteth every man's individual understanding, and this maketh it a reasonable understanding" (so far, a statement which might be taken as a highly metaphorical version of Kant) and "*an influence from the Glory of the Almighty*, this being one of the names of the Messiah, as the Logos, or co-eternal Filial Word."[65] There's an end of Kant's whole structure. Reason, which even in Coleridge's treatment of politics and aesthetics threatens to burst its Kantian grounds, becomes here, in a formulation taken from Hooker, "direct aspect of truth, an inward beholding, having a similar relation to the intelligi-

[62] *Ibid.*, I, 214.

[63] *Ibid.*, I, 221. Cf. "By the mere power of reasoning no man ever yet arrived at God, at that Being given by his conscience and his moral being" (*Philosophical Lectures*, p. 209).

[64] It is important to remember that not only did Coleridge express the view that Kant had meant more "by his *Noumenon*, or Thing in itself, than his mere words express" (*Biographia Literaria*, in *Complete Works*, III, 258), but he similarly argues that the whole of Plato's doctrine was never committed to the world (see *Philosophical Lectures*, pp. 165, 177).

[65] Coleridge, *Complete Works*, I, 242.

ble or spiritual, as Sense has to the material or phenomenal."[66] (The same sort of maneuver in which a Kantian position is taken and then immediately expanded beyond the bounds of Kant's system occurs in Essay V of the "First Landing Place" in *The Friend*. "Thus, God, the soul, eternal truth, &c., are the objects of reason [orthodox so far, except for the &c.]; but they are themselves reason." This is unabashed post-Kantian German Idealism.)[67] Coleridge will continue to use formulations that *can* be interpreted so as not to be incompatible with Kant, but his whole intent in the Reason/Understanding distinction leads beyond these. This indeed it must do to validate the method set forth in the *Treatise* on the one hand and establish the validity of revealed religion on the other hand. He is now prepared, as he says in his "Reflections Introductory to Aphorism X," to present "the so-called mysteries of Faith, that is, the peculiar tenets and especial constituents of Christianity, or religion in spirit and in truth."[68] All this developed, he can, in the short Aphorism XII, dismiss Paley as "not a moralist." How much his whole structure is directed against Paley is clear from the Conclusion. This is called a "dialogue," although, consisting of a two-sentence question and a twelve-page reply, it is so only in that peculiarly Coleridgean sense which would have been familiar to his visitors at Highgate. Paley is the perfect foil, a Christian whose position opposes Coleridge's at almost every point. Paley has confused necessary distinctions and has been led to use language sophistically through his failure to distinguish between prudence and morality and between "proofs" of Christianity and the assurance that can only come from

[66] *Ibid.*, I, 246.

[67] *Ibid.*, II, 144–45.

[68] *Ibid.*, I, 265. The mysteries on which Coleridge concentrates are Original Sin, Atonement, and Justification; these mysteries, he is now prepared to show, are, as he suggests in his Preface, "reason in its highest form of self-affirmation" (*Complete Works*, I, 115).

within. Both errors are of course the result of failure to discriminate between Reason and Understanding.

In the area of religion, the problem of relating the Ideas of the Reason to the concepts of the Understanding is not prominent. The question Coleridge attacks there is not how to make theological ideas relevant to daily life but how to assure ourselves of the validity of the theological Ideas, and Coleridge bases his argument on the insufficiency of the Understanding which forces one to look to the Reason. The real problem here is accepting the way the insufficiency of the Reason in the Kantian sense is somehow made to generate, or else perhaps cause us to look to, an even higher Reason, "a spiritual organ" as distinguished from the organ by which "we possess the ideas of the necessary and the universal."[69]

Even here, however, Coleridge does not altogether escape from his difficulties in bridging the chasm between Reason and Understanding, for morality, an area which is contiguous to and for Coleridge largely overlaps religion, becomes almost a no-man's land.[70] The word itself appears often enough, but it is significant that only a very brief and relatively unenlightening section is devoted to *moral* aphorisms in *Aids to Reflection*, and even that is entitled "Moral and Religious Aphorisms." It is also significant that in the scheme set forth in the last aphorism of the Introductory section of the *Aids to Reflection*, Coleridge finds that the moral corresponds to the heart and conscience—much more shadowy faculties than the Reason, Under-

[69] *Ibid.*, II, 146. (I here make use of the language Coleridge employed in *The Friend.*) René Wellek (*Immanuel Kant in England*, p. 105) comments perceptively on the "two reasons" developed by Coleridge, though it seems to me that he errs slightly in equating either wholly with Kant's Reason. The fact is that though Coleridge does use the term Reason at times in a purely Kantian sense, he is always ready to transcend it and does so in a variety of ways and degrees.

[70] Morality also of course overlaps politics, causing similar problems to arise.

standing, Imagination, or Will.[71] The fact is that morality is almost totally subsumed under religion for Coleridge.[72] Man's moral promptings lead him to religious faith, which in turn begets a true morality. Here is one of Coleridge's most significant departures from Kant; the German philosopher had of course gone far to found morality on an ethical principle independent of religious belief. The subordination of morality to religion is made explicit, for instance, at the end of the attack on Paley and utilitarian ethics in Essay XV of the First Section of *The Friend.* Coleridge is seeking to prove that the general consequences of an act cannot be the proper criterion of the morality of particular actions, that the motive, not the consequence, is all important. In answer to the argument that the utilitarian view has reference to the action, not its agent, Coleridge answers: "The character of the agent is determined by his view of the action: and that system of morality is alone true and suited to human nature, which unites the intention and the motive, the warmth and the light, in one and the same act of mind. This alone is worthy to be called a moral Principle. Such a Principle . . . is to be found unalloyed and entire in the Christian system, and is there called faith."[73] Coleridge describes the First Section of *The Friend* as having "for its express object the principles of our duty as citizens, or morality as applied to politics." That section begins with five essays arguing that the proper system of political justice is that "under which the human being may be con-

[71] Coleridge, *Complete Works*, I, 134.

[72] In the *Biographia Literaria*, the whole relationship is summed up in Coleridge's reference to religion "as both the cornerstone and key-stone of morality" (*Complete Works*, III, 297).

[73] Coleridge, *Complete Works*, II, 296. Cf. "That the maxims of a pure morality, and those sublime truths of the divine unity and attributes, which a Plato found hard to learn and more difficult to reveal; that these should have become the almost hereditary property of childhood and poverty, of the hovel and the workshop; that even to the unlettered they sound as common-place; this is a fact which must withhold all but minds of the most vulgar cast from undervaluing the services even of the pulpit and the reading desk" (*Complete Works*, VI, 70–71).

sidered, namely, as an animal gifted with understanding, or the faculty of suiting measures to circumstances" and according to which "every institution of national origin needs no other justification than a proof, that under the particular circumstances it is expedient."[74] But the entire section builds up to Essay XV, which is written to establish, in the words of the Table of Contents, that the "doctrine of general consequences as the best criterion of the right and wrong of particular actions [is] not tenable in reason, or safe in practice" and ends in the appeal to the Christian faith. Moreover, when Coleridge returns to the matter at the beginning of the first essay of the Second Section, he raises the question of "whether morality can be said to have any principle distinguishable from religion, or religion any substance divisible from morality."[75] The answer, which the entire section digressively establishes, is that it cannot.

How the Ideas of the Reason, whether taken in the limited Kantian sense or expanded to Christian revelation, are to be applied by the Understanding so that expedience is to be judged without reference to the calculations of the consequences of particular measures remains obscure. Neither does Coleridge's apparent subsumption of the Reason under revealed Religion lessen the difficulties already noticed in his political thought. The obscurity on this point is not lightened by *The Statesman's Manual*, the avowed purpose of which is to establish, according to its subtitle, that "the Bible [is] the best guide to political skill and foresight." What light attention to "the latter period of the reign of Solomon, and to the revolutions in the reign of Rehoboam, his successor," might cast "on the present state of public affairs in this kingdom, or on the prospective measures in agitation respecting our sister island"[76] remains a matter of conjecture, its translation into specific measures

[74] *Ibid.*, II, 163.

[75] *Ibid.*, II, 376.

[76] *Ibid.*, I, 439.

a mystery. Just how the learned are "to apply their powers and attainments to an especial study of the Old Testament as teaching the elements of political science"[77] does not, unfortunately, appear.

However, as we have already seen, the real thrust of Coleridge's political thought is summed up in a single sentence from the second *Lay Sermon*: "Let us become a better people, and the reform of all the public (real or supposed) grievances, which we use as pegs whereon to hang our own errors and defects, will follow of itself."[78] Coleridge here follows the parallel thrusts of philosophical idealism and protestant theology to insist that the path toward improvement in the human condition is through each individual's struggle for perfection. To live as though a member of an ideal kingdom of ends or to live by God's grace as one redeemed from sin is to recognize that it is much more important that each individual will the right than that each individual be governed rightly. "The universal necessary laws, and pure ideas of reason, were given us, not for the purpose of . . . enabling us to become national legislators; but that, by an energy of continued self-conquest, we might establish a free and yet absolute government in our own spirits."[79]

But if men are to will the right they must look to the guidance of religion—specifically, of course, for Coleridge, the National Church. Chapter VII of *Church and State* provides a kind of compendium of the things Coleridge deplores: the fading discipline of the church, the separation of education from the supervision of the church, the reduction of ethics to "a digest of the criminal laws, and the evidence required for conviction under the same," "the tillers of the land paid by poor rates, and the remainder of the population mechanized into engines for the manufactory

[77] *Ibid.*, I, 450.

[78] *Ibid.*, VI, 225.

[79] *Complete Works*, II, 171.

of new rich men," "the mechanico-corpuscular theory raised to the title of the mechanic philosophy," the degradation of meaning in the word "Idea," "a state of nature, or the Ou ran Outang theology of the origin of the human race, substituted for the first ten chapters of the Book of Genesis," "the guess-work of general consequences substituted for moral and political philosophy." These aversions, among others less specifically stated, illustrate how directly he opposes the doctrines and policies of the empiricists. True to the transcendentalist syndrome, he finds right education "for the rulers and teachers of a nation" indispensable but the hope of making general a scientific or systematic knowledge folly. What he opposes to the concrete policies of the empiricists is simply a sound state of religion.[80]

The relationship between religion and morality, and Coleridge's rejection of utilitarian ethics because religious precept and divine grace provide a way out of the demands of man's selfish nature and the difficulties of knowing what actions will lead to happiness is given in capsule form in one of Coleridge's Philosophical Lectures: ". . . it is very absurd to make that to be the principle of regulation which is to be the thing grounded. . . . There is no man, not even a madman, but wishes to be happy in some way, but unfortunately every man wishes it according to his passion at the moment. . . . No man doubts every sentient being must seek for a pleasurable sensation and avoid a painful sensation, but what has this to do with morality?" Coleridge concludes that "there are in short but two systems possible that have an essential difference; the one is that virtue is the *means*—the other that it is an absolute *end*. To take virtue as a precept in order to render it a nature, this is the true problem of all true philosophy. Then comes history and the most important comment on history—self-knowledge, which acknowledges the truth of this position and

[80] *Ibid.*, VI, 63–67.

the moral necessity, but at the same time its impracticability by human nature unaided."[81] Thus the necessity of religious faith.

EDUCATION. The above summaries of the relations between Coleridge's metaphysical beliefs and his views on government and religion have already set out the foundations of his somewhat curiously general views on the proper role of education. Reform and innovation in society are to be gained primarily, if not solely, by "the presentation of juster views and nobler interests," or, in an alternative formulation, "reform of all the public grievances" waits on our decision to "become a better people."[82] Moral education thus becomes the sole basis of improvement not only of the individual but of society. And inasmuch as morality in its highest form becomes identical with religion, the responsibility for education throughout England should fall on the National Church. The members of the third estate, the National Church or National Clergy, are not only to serve as "the fountain head" of knowledge, but, as parish priests, "not to leave even the smallest integral part or division [of the country] without a resident guide, guardian, and instructor," and "to diffuse through the whole community, and to every native entitled to its laws and rights that quantity and quality of knowledge which was indispensable both for the understanding of those rights, and for the performance of the duties correspondent."[83] Because they may be expected to have most fully developed that Reason which arrives at the Ideas on which science is based, as

[81] Coleridge, *Philosophical Lectures*, pp. 215–16.

[82] See pp. 59 and 69 above.

[83] Coleridge, *On the Constitution of Church and State*, in *Complete Works*, VI, 52.

described in the *Treatise on Method*, and the higher Reason, which *Aids to Reflection* tells us is "an influence from the Glory of the Almighty," the clergy are those fittest to perform this function. In the 1818 edition of *The Friend*, the education of children with the right Method in view (recognizing that "all true and living knowledge proceed[s] from within") is the only path to cultivation rather than mere civilization, to cultivation that is, of "the truly human in human nature."[84]

The suggestion which here occurs that there is a basic reservoir of good in human beings (sustained there by the glimmering, however fitful, of the Ideas of the Reason) is usual both in transcendentalists as a whole and in Coleridge. In the "Answer to Mathetes" (written by Wordsworth, but obviously endorsed by Coleridge) in the 1818 *Friend*, the assumption by "Mathetes" that uncorrupted children and youths are intrinsically drawn to the good and noble is unquestioned. Therefore, the chief means of protection from the seductions of evil for "pure and high-minded youth" is self-examination. For instance, "Knowing that it is my duty, and feeling that it is my inclination, to mingle as a social being with my fellow-men; prepared also to submit cheerfully to the necessity that will probably exist of relinquishing, for the purpose of gaining a livelihood, the greatest portion of my time to employments where I shall have little or no choice how or when I am to act; have I, at this moment, when I stand as it were upon the threshold of the busy world, a clear intuition of that pre-eminence in which virtue and truth (involving in this latter word the sanctities of religion) sit enthroned above all denominations and dignities which, in various degrees of exaltation, rule over the desires of men?"[85]

Coleridge provides no detailed suggestions for the awakening of the Ideas of the Reason or habituation of

[84] Coleridge, *Complete Works*, II, 452.

[85] *Ibid.*, II, 365.

children and youths to the requirements of his Method. But brief passages tell us of two great dangers. One is the rise of the Lancastrian schools, "pernicious" schools that teach "those points only of religious faith, in which all denominations agree: rather than the tenets of the Church of England."[86] The other is the pressure to sunder National Education from all religion and from the superintendence of the National Clergy. The result anticipated from the second threat is as follows:

> Education is to be reformed, and defined as synonymous with instruction. The axiom of education so defined is—knowledge being power, those attainments, which give a man the power of doing what he wishes in order to obtain what he desires, are alone to be considered as knowledge, or to be admitted into the scheme of national education. The subjects to be taught in the national schools are to be—reading, writing, arithmetic, the mechanic arts, elements and results of physical science, but to be taught, as much as possible, empirically. For all knowledge being derived from the senses, the closer men are kept to the fountainhead, the more knowing they must become.
>
> Popular ethics consist of a digest of the criminal laws, and the evidence requisite for conviction under the same: lectures on diet, on digestion, on infection, and the nature and effects of a specific virus incidental to and communicable by living bodies in the intercourse of society.[87]

Although he several times announced his intention of

[86] Coleridge, *Statesman's Manual*, in *Complete Works*, I, 444. Joseph Lancaster, a Quaker schoolmaster, and Andrew Bell, one-time superintendent of the Madras orphan asylum, were, from their separate experiences with the monotorial (mutual instruction) system, convinced of the efficacy of a national system of voluntary education conducted on such a system. Bell's included the teaching of Church of England doctrines; Lancaster's limited itself to doctrines common to all Christian denominations. Coleridge had some reservations about Bell's approach but in general expressed approval for it.

[87] Coleridge, *On the Constitution of Church and State*, in *Complete Works*, VI, 62.

treating education systematically, this was one of those promises Coleridge never fulfilled. Clearly he feared the utilitarians at the gates of pedagogical practice, but we do not know precisely what he would oppose to them. Given the paucity of evidence in his published statements, I should like to look beyond these, specifically to the *Bristol Gazette* account of Coleridge's lecture on "The New System of Education" of 18 November 1813 in which he condemns just the sort of system under which James Mill was at that moment educating his son John Stuart.

> The Lecturer concluded with recommending an observance of the laws of nature in the Education of Children; the ideas of a child were cheerful and playful; they should not be palsied by obliging it to utter sentences which the head could not comprehend nor the heart echo; our nature was in every sense a *progress*; both body and soul.[88]

THE POETIC IMAGINATION. The difficulty in relating the metaphysical assumptions expressed in Coleridge's view of the distinctive functions of the faculties of the mind to his beliefs about the nature of poetic creation is that in those statements from the *Biographia Literaria* which are generally taken as the central expression of his theory of poetry, the creative process is presented not in terms of the Reason and the Understanding but in terms of the Imagination and Fancy.[89] It is true that in gathering together those "transcendental swim-bladders" which Coleridge deemed necessary to float his theory, the differences between the Reason and the Understanding are ex-

[88] See Alice D. Snyder, *Coleridge on Logic and Learning*, p. 46.

[89] Coleridge was discussing this distinction as early as January 1804, according to E. K. Chambers, *Samuel Taylor Coleridge: A Biographical Study*, p. 178.

plicitly mentioned in Chapter X, but just when it seems that Coleridge is going to close with the grounds of the distinction between the Fancy and the Imagination (the existence of these two faculties having already been touched on in one way or another in Chapters IV, V, and VII), the argument is deflected. That Coleridge found the struggle to ground the difference between the Imagination and Fancy in the faculties of the mind to be one of those unpleasant duties that paralyzed his energies is clear, we should remind ourselves, from the nature of the digressions that intervene between Chapter IV, in which the distinction is portentously introduced, and Chapter XIII, in which it is finally hurriedly served up. In *The Friend*, or *Aids to Reflection*, or *On the Constitution of the Church and State*, Coleridge's circuitous mode of progression is at times maddening, but his digressions, though we may deny the strict necessity of their existence, generally prove their relevance to the patient reader. Here the digressions, particularly in Chapters X and XII, are not pertinent. Casting about for a fresh start which will not take him through the whole of Platonic and Neo-Platonic philosophy or through Kant's three Critiques yet which will link up with the denial of the passive associationism of Locke and Hartley served up in Chapters V, VI, VII, and VIII, Coleridge, in the notorious Chapter XII, tries to construct a shortcut out of Schelling. Coleridge's major error in using Schelling was not the failure to provide appropriate quotation marks and footnotes but the failure to realize that in using Schelling he was drawing on the development of German Idealism too far downstream from the Kantian source he had used as a means of organizing his own position. Whether he began to find the pantheistic tendency of Schelling's doctrines subversive of his own beliefs, or, accepting Schelling's position, nevertheless began to recognize its inutility to the task at hand, by the ninth and tenth theses, which bring him to the point where he is able to say, "We proceed from the SELF, in order to lose and find all self in

GOD,"[90] he must have seen that he was little closer to his goal in the *Biographia*.[91] In Chapter XIII, he tries to get back to Kant but gives it up in his famous letter to himself setting forth the reasons for breaking off this disquisition. The Imagination and Fancy we are asked to consider in his brief Delphic summary of his theory of poetry remain *non sequiturs*, although in the following chapters on Wordsworth (and as late as the pronouncements recorded in *Table Talk*), Coleridge clings to the terms.

The existence of the distinction was to be continually asserted; the explanation of its ultimate grounds continually deferred. A speech from Peacock's *Nightmare Abbey* by Mr. Flosky hits rather brutally home. "This distinction between fancy and imagination is one of the most abstruse and important points of metaphysics. I have written seven hundred pages of promises to elucidate it, which promise I shall keep as faithfully as the bank will its promise to pay."

Many have been the attempts to clarify the relations between the two pairs of terms. The first accommodation which suggests itself to most readers of Coleridge is the equation of Understanding with Fancy, and Reason with Imagination. But clearly the Reason, as the faculty which provides principles, seems hardly identical with the faculty which "dissolves, diffuses, dissipates, in order to re-create." The list of faculties which Coleridge gives at the end of Chapter XII is hardly helpful, because although it assigns certain attributes to each faculty, it does not clearly indicate the relations between them. Since Coleridge nowhere explicitly states the relationship between Reason, Understanding, and Imagination, perhaps it will not be amiss to follow Coleridge's early editors (and Shawcross[92]) in con-

[90] Coleridge, *Complete Works*, III, 348.

[91] G. N. G. Orsini interprets the breaking off at this point as Coleridge's recognition that Schelling was leading him too far away from the Christian conception of Deity (*Coleridge and German Idealism*, pp. 214–15).

[92] Coleridge, *Biographia Literaria*, ed. J. Shawcross, I, lviii*ff.* It will be

sidering the relation set forth by Kant as a clue. Kant distinguishes between three forms of the Imagination. The Productive Imagination is what makes possible the synthesis of simultaneous sense impressions in the Understanding. The Reproductive Imagination makes it possible for the mind to relate the experience that it is deriving at any one time from the senses (under the forms of space and time and under the concepts imposed by the Understanding) with past experiences. It operates under the laws of association. (These seem to be the interpretations offered by most of Kant's commentators; unfortunately, this is a point of considerable obscurity in Kant's system.[93]) It seems clear, however, that both the Productive and Reproductive Imagination are faculties subordinate to and in the service of the Understanding. The Aesthetic Imagination, however, is free from direct bondage to the immediate data of the senses, from the strict rules of the Understanding, which determine the application of concepts to experience, and from the rules of association. Thus, says Kant, in employing the Aesthetic Imagination "we feel our freedom from the law of association which attaches to the empirical employment of the imagination." Moreover, "the [Aesthetic] imagination . . . is creative, and it sets in motion the faculty of intellectual Ideas, namely, Reason." "In a word, the aesthetic Idea is a representation of the imagination

---

apparent to those acquainted with Shawcross's classic Introduction that I find in the *Biographia* less of a Schelling-like extension of the power of both the Primary and Secondary Imagination. It seems to me that in terminating his development of Schelling's position in the midst of Chapter XIII, Coleridge was drawing back from just such extensions. The relationship between Fancy and Imagination and Kant's Reproductive and Productive Imaginations was of course suggested by Coleridge's earlier editors (see the first note, *Complete Works*, III, 364).

[93] See, for instance, A. C. Ewing's *A Short Commentary on Kant's Critique of Pure Reason*, pp. 91–94, and Norman Kemp Smith's *A Commentary on Kant's Critique of Pure Reason*, pp. 264–65, for an outline of some of the problems. See also Heinrich W. Cassirer, *A Commentary on Kant's Critique of Judgment*, pp. 218*ff.*

which becomes associated with a given concept. In making free use of it, the imagination connects it with such a manifold of partial representations as makes it impossible to find a definite expression for it which could be signified by a determinate concept. Thus, it becomes possible to add in thought to a concept much that cannot be expressed in language; and when we feel this our faculties of knowledge are enlivened, and language, as a mere thing of the letter, is connected with the spirit (*Geist*)."[94]

This Aesthetic Imagination is very like Coleridge's secondary imagination, while his primary imagination can be seen as the counterpart of Kant's productive imagination, actively creating the "experience" on which the Understanding acts. The extent to which Coleridge was attempting to model his argument directly on Kant is likely to remain a moot point, especially since he also knew some of the transformations the Kantian system had undergone in the hands of Schelling and Fichte. (The words "repetition in the infinite mind of the eternal act of creation in the Infinite I AM" can be read as equivalent to Fichte's ego positing the non-ego; G. N. G. Orsini goes further and identifies the activity with Schelling's "Productive intuition" so that, writes Orsini, it "might be called the cosmic Imagination.")[95] However, the whole of Coleridge's treatment of the imagination is in consonance with Kant's development of the three forms of the Imagination. For instance, toward the end of Chapter V of the *Biographia* we find Coleridge approving Aristotle's formulation of the doctrine of association: "In association then consists the whole mechanism of the reproduction of impressions, in the Aristotelian Psychology. It is the universal law of the passive fancy and mechanical memory. . . ."[96] Fancy would seem to corre-

[94] *Critique of Judgment* (Berlin edition), pp. 314–16, as translated by H. W. Cassirer, *A Commentary*, pp. 281–82.

[95] Orsini, *Coleridge and German Idealism*, p. 223.

[96] Coleridge, *Complete Works*, III, 221–22.

spond to the Reproductive Imagination, which Kant also states to be governed by association. The two powers, one active and the other passive, between which, according to Coleridge, the Imagination (in this case Kant's Productive Imagination) mediates I take to be sensibility and Understanding, and the "superior degree of the faculty" to which "in common language, and especially on the subject of poetry," we give the name Imagination to be the Aesthetic Imagination.[97]

In view of the difficulties experienced by twentieth-century commentators who have before them the whole of Kant's works and the benefit of over a hundred years of study of the Kantian system by careful scholars, it is not surprising that Coleridge found it difficult to make clear to his readers (and very likely to himself) the exact relationship of the Imagination to the other faculties of the mind.[98] The conjectural relationships supposed between Kant's three functions of the Imagination and Coleridge's Fancy, Primary Imagination, and Secondary Imagination can of course be objected to on the grounds that some of Coleridge's comments on these faculties are incompatible with Kant's. But this is simply to say what we knew before, that Coleridge did not follow Kant strictly.

However, it is extremely important that the student of Coleridge be clear that the Imagination is not the same as the Reason.[99] For, as has frequently been noted, Coleridge was dissatisfied with the limits Kant had put on the Rea-

[97] *Ibid.*, III, 237.

[98] In his commentary to the *Critique of Pure Reason*, p. 94, A. C. Ewing explicitly points out the difficulty of reconciling all of Kant's statements about the Productive and Reproductive Imaginations with the treatment of the Aesthetic Imagination in the *Critique of Judgment*.

[99] As Appleyard points out in his excellent *Coleridge's Philosophy of Literature*, an incisive analysis of the development of Coleridge's thought from the years of his allegiance to Hartley forward, Coleridge himself for a long time confused his attempt to get beyond associationism through his theory of the Imagination and his attempt to account for man's knowledge of God through the distinction between the Reason and the Understanding. See especially pp. 250*ff*.

son, and, as we have seen, in his hands it developed into the faculty that, on the one hand, is the source of all necessary and universal laws and, on the other, opens up for us the whole religious experience. In this second function it pierces the veil and gives us an assurance which, not the same as the knowledge derived from the Understanding, is yet more certain. It thus reveals to us certain things that are in Kant's terminology "transcendent," that is, not possible objects of experience. Now Coleridge's Imagination does not do this. One is at first surprised; the whole romantic yearning for a kind of mystical transcendence and the insistence on the power of poetry associated with Coleridge and Wordsworth leads one to expect the Imagination to be the faculty that allows us to "see into the heart of things." But such is not the case: in the whole of Coleridge's discussion of Wordsworth's poetry in the *Biographia Literaria*, for instance, though he frequently speaks of the Imagination, he never assigns to it more than the power to unify "organically." Coleridge tells us in a lecture of 1818 that Beaumont and Fletcher, employing what I take to be the Fancy, worked "just as a man might fit together a quarter of an orange, a quarter of an apple, and the like of a lemon and of a pomegranate, and make it look like one round diverse coloured fruit."[100] Presumably, the Imagination would fuse the four, working organically just as a master gardener who successfully grafts them together. The resulting fruit (perhaps to be called an oraplepom?) is a fitting emblem of the working of the Imagination. But the oraplepom, whether merely "imagined" in Coleridge's sense or actually created in the garden, is no revelation of any transcendent truth.[101] That a poem proposes as its "*immediate* object pleasure, not truth" thus is in need of little

[100] *Coleridge's Miscellaneous Criticism*, ed. T. M. Raysor, pp. 42–43. The passage goes on to contrast such a mode of working with that of Shakespeare, who evolved "the germ within by the imaginative power according to an idea."

[101] Meyer Abrams is one of the few critics who make this point unequivocally: "Coleridge," he says, "does not make special cognitive claims for poetry" (*The Mirror and the Lamp*, p. 314).

explanation; the primary object *is* pleasure and delight. It may offer truth, as does Wordsworth's poetry, but the truths it offers are not revelations of Reason; at most they may prepare one to regard the world as other than fixed and dead and thus lead beyond slavery to the Understanding.

It is true that in the *Statesman's Manual*, written in 1816 as Coleridge was struggling with the printing of the *Biographia*, there is evidence of a desire to extend the power of the Imagination. There, the "histories and political economy of the present and preceding century," products of the "unenlivened general understanding," are contrasted with Scriptural history, the product of the Imagination as a "reconciling and mediatory power, which incorporating the reason in images of the sense . . . gives birth to a system of symbols, harmonious in themselves, and consubstantial with the truths of which they are the conductors."[102] This leads Coleridge on to his well-known distinction between allegory, the "translation of abstract notions into a picture-language," and symbol, "characterized by a translucence of the special in the individual, or of the general in the special, or of the universal in the general; above all by the translucence of the eternal through and in the temporal."[103] Juxtaposing these two passages, we see Coleridge making Imagination the mediator between Reason and sense-images (rather than between the senses and the Understanding, where Kant, and elsewhere he himself, placed it). Imagination becomes here the symbol-creating faculty, the faculty that performs the mediation between individual, general, and universal, between eternal Ideas and the senses.[104] But even this almost cer-

[102] Coleridge, *Complete Works*, I, 436. See also the final paragraph of Appendix E to the *Statesman's Manual* (*Complete Works*, I, 484).

[103] *Ibid.*, I, 437.

[104] The same idea is present in the fragment "On Poesy or Art," which may or may not have formed a part of the lectures of 1816. See the note on this fragment in the Shawcross edition of the *Biographia Literaria*, II, 317.

tainly Schelling-influenced position, though it gives a high function to art, fails to solve the problem of making transitions between the Reason and the Understanding.

Development of this position would have given the Imagination that power which it would have to have to make poetry, and all art, a means of reaching beyond phenomena to the transcendent. But Coleridge does *not* develop it further, here or elsewhere in his public writings, and it is an error, I submit, to try to interpret his other published works in terms of the two paragraphs from the *Statesman's Manual* which sketch this view. It may have lain behind Coleridge's thought in all his writings here examined, but his failure to develop the position and relate it to his thought in other areas argues that for some reason he did not find it finally satisfactory. It is, after all, only the symbols of Scripture—the revealed word of God as understood by pious men—which he is specifically discussing in the *Statesman's Manual.* As Appendix B to the *Manual* makes clear, "Reason" here is already becoming the "Higher" Reason he would employ in *Aids to Reflection.*[105]

Coleridge's usual interpretation of the role of art is implied in the discussion of Shakespeare in the *Treatise* and corresponding portion of *The Friend*, and developed more precisely in the fragment of Lecture XIII of the 1818 lectures on literature entitled "On Poesy or Art." The latter has, I think, been frequently misinterpreted as assigning a higher role to the Imagination than Coleridge intended.[106] But what is specifically argued is that art is "the union and reconciliation of that which is Nature with that which is exclusively human" and that this is accomplished through the artist's acquisition of "living and life-producing Ideas, which contain their own evidence and in that evidence the certainty that they are essentially one with the germinal

[105] See especially *Complete Works*, I, 460*n*.

[106] As, for instance, in Margaret Sherwood's stimulating but, I think, not wholly tenable *Coleridge's Imaginative Concept of the Imagination*.

causes in Nature."[107] The true artist refers constantly to the realm of Reason, the source of Ideas, rather than to the Understanding, the source of conceptions, and thus produces imitations rather than copies. However, poetry and art are not the means to the discovery of Ideas, for the artist must acquire his grasp of Ideas *before* he creates the object of art. As is clear from the *Treatise* and the relevant portions of *The Friend*, Shakespeare is able to create organically because he is in possession of Method and the necessary germinal Ideas. Nothing in "On Poesy or Art" insists even that art is the means of revealing Ideas to others, although it implies that contemplation of art may help free one from bondage to the Understanding.

Another way of understanding what Coleridge appears to have been attempting to do emerges from a comparison with Addison's essays on "Pleasures of the Imagination." Ernest Tuveson's *The Imagination as a Means of Grace* sets out various ways in which those who felt that Locke's theory was inadequate for the explanation of moral and aesthetic experience tried to extend his concept of the mind. If poetry were regarded as addressed to a faculty that had no cognitive power, and as providing not knowledge but a subjective feeling of pleasure, it could be regarded as autonomous, and not merely a by-product of association. To regard poetry, and art in general, as having no purpose but to provide pleasure would have been too long a step toward art for art's sake, but the pleasure one feels in all beauty, including art, could be interpreted as providing a means of bringing man closer to God. That, essentially, is the explanation of the pleasures of the imagination which Addison gives. As Tuveson summarizes it, "Aesthetic experience is identified as a means of grace, in the sense that one area of sensuous experience is designed to produce, directly, a spiritual effect."[108] It reconciles man to a Lockian

[107] *Coleridge's Miscellaneous Criticism*, pp. 206, 210.

[108] Tuveson, *Imagination as a Means of Grace*, p. 95.

universe by assuring him that there is something beyond it. Nor is the manner in which Addison's artist is a "second maker under Jove" much different from Coleridge's poet employing the secondary imagination. None of this is far from Coleridge's view of the function of poetry and the poetic imagination, though, as we have seen, he seems, especially during the years when he wrote the *Biographia* and the *Statesman's Manual*,[109] to have yearned toward a theory that would have given the Imagination a kind of higher cognitive power and thus avoided the separation of the good, true, and beautiful by the sundering of the faculties through which these are apprehended.

WHAT I TAKE TO BE the core of Coleridge's philosophical problems in the works published between 1816 and 1834 can be formulated in another way. Despite all his concern with the subject of language, in one sense at least the problem lies precisely in language: how is truth to be communicated? If the highest and most important truths are known only by the Reason and yet the Ideas of the Reason are finally such as may be neither defined nor conceived, the problem of communication becomes acute. As I have tried to indicate, Coleridge appears to have hoped that the poetic Imagination was a means of translating the Ideas of the Reason into images that might be grasped by the Understanding, but he drew back. Possibly he recollected that neither he nor Wordsworth had succeeded in

[109] Coleridge's position in 1814, which he apparently had not repudiated in 1834 (see Shawcross's notes to the essays on the Principles of Genial Criticism in his edition of the *Biographia Literaria*, II, 304–5), is presented in series of essays entitled "On the Principles of Genial Criticism" published in *Felix Farley's Bristol Journal.* Here he is concerned primarily with distinguishing the agreeable and the beautiful, the second depending on intuitive response, not the laws of association. This doctrine is inflated into the high-flown statements on poets, poetry, and the imagination in the *Biographia Literaria.*

expressing in poetry what he now was seeing as the highest truths. Where, except in the Scriptures, was the evidence that poetry translated the Anglican Christianity that he was coming to regard as identical with Reason into more directly graspable forms? By 1817, the insufficiency of the poetic Imagination seems to have been clear to Coleridge, and no other way of communication suggested itself. In endeavoring to push beyond the limits Kant had placed on the Reason, he found himself exploring a land from which no accurately descriptive reports could be sent back. He could only say—come and see for yourself.[110]

The problem of communication hung over Coleridge in another way. His very allegiance to organicism and unity constantly tripped him up. A truly comprehensive view of human knowledge and value, such as he had indicated the need for in the *Treatise on Method*, must, as he there argues, begin with the first and highest principles and then trace the ramifications of these principles through all areas of human concern. Having found that neither Locke nor an unmodified Kant provided a usable basic structure, Coleridge was faced with producing an alternative of his own, the labor of which would still give him only a starting-point for the larger system he wished to develop—Kant, it should be remembered, presented his three Critiques as the *beginning* of a philosophical system. He was of course perfectly aware of this, as his attempts to get on with the Magnum Opus testify,[111] but to begin *ab ovo* was too much a demand on one whose ideas, at middle age, were still developing. How the mind could move from constitutive, necessary, and ultimately Divine Ideas to political and moral formulations in the Understanding remained as un-

[110] Coleridge, *Complete Works*, I, 233.

[111] Hazlitt's scornful but shrewd remark that *The Friend* was "an enormous title-page . . . an endless preface to an imaginary work" penetrates to the core of the problem, the imaginary work being of course the projected Magnum Opus; Hazlitt, *The Complete Works*, VII, 115.

solved as how it could move from facts assimilated in the Understanding to Physical Ideas in Science.

Coleridge could have abandoned himself to the production of finished essays on individual fragments of the whole. But his desire to explore and exhibit all the interrelationships of a total system grounded on necessary principles forbade that. The paradoxical result was that in his dissatisfaction with anything short of an organically unified view he was forced into the production of fragments. Some of these only imply, others incompletely sketch, the metaphysical beliefs that lie behind the subtleties there discussed.

The following dialogue in *Nightmare Abbey* between Listless and Flosky hardly exaggerates the reputation for lack of coherence that Coleridge to some extent came to deserve.

> Mr. Listless.—Tea, late dinners, and the French Revolution. I cannot exactly see the connection of ideas.
>
> Mr. Flosky.—I should be sorry if you could; I pity the man who can see the connection of his own ideas. Still more do I pity him, the connection of whose ideas any other person can see. Sir, the great evil is, that there is too much commonplace light in our moral and political literature; and light is a great enemy to mystery, and mystery is a great friend to enthusiasm. Now as the enthusiasm for truth is an exceedingly fine thing, as long as the truth, which is the object of the enthusiasm, is so completely abstract as to be altogether out of the reach of the human faculties. . . .

Coleridge did not, however, take delight in fabricating mysteries. In the *Treatise on Method*, Coleridge describes the mark of a "man of superior Mind" as the subordination of his thought to Method; this we are to perceive "in the unpremeditated and evidently habitual arrangement of his words, flowing spontaneously and necessarily from the clearness of the leading Idea; from which distinctness of mental vision, when men are fully accustomed to it, they obtain a habit of foreseeing at the beginning of every instance how it is to end. . . ."[112] It is easy to smile at the difference between the impression which, according to Coleridge, the methodical mind offers, and the impression Coleridge's prose often gives, though few would charge Coleridge with having a mediocre mind. The real problem was that Coleridge failed to follow the order of development he himself prescribed for the *Encyclopaedia Metropolitana*, and he is thus unable to refer the reader of his essays on politics, aesthetics, or religion back to basic principles established in earlier writings. Coleridge's habit of promising readers that certain points will be made clear in the future is just the practice he enjoined the editors of the *Metropolitana* to eschew.

Unable to begin from the beginning, he begins anywhere. Shakespeare's plays, Wordsworth's poems, Leighton's aphorisms, a page of another's philosophical or religious work lying before him, any point of departure will do, and once given a text on which to bring to bear some part of the system he was revolving in his mind, he becomes eloquent. His brilliance as a commentator results from his constant philosophical endeavors: almost any text on which he focuses will strike sparks from some portion of the vast structure of thought he was never able, at least in the works he published, to reduce to complete order. That Coleridge's total system remained inchoate and his mode of presenting it uninviting perhaps explains the little "direct philosophical influence" on succeeding generations that J. H. Muirhead, a commentator most sympathetic to Coleridge and to what I here call the transcendental cast of mind, discusses in the conclusion to *Coleridge as Philosopher*.[113]

But while both technical philosophers and thinkers

[112] Coleridge, *Treatise*, pp. 13–14. See also the slightly different formulation in *The Friend* (*Complete Works*, II, 409).

[113] Muirhead, *Coleridge as Philosopher*, p. 257.

concerned with theories of government and the practicalities of political science found Coleridge more irritating than provocative, the excellence of his best poetry, the importance of the English Romantic movement announced in *Lyrical Ballads*, and the interest in the Wordsworth-Coleridge relationship kept the *Biographia Literaria* and its celebration of the power of the imagination before the literary world. Seemingly, the first volume of the *Biographia* certified that a unique power lay in the literary imagination, which was opposed to the tedious and trivial understanding wielded by empiricists. Similarly, the *Aids to Reflection* and the *Confessions of an Inquiring Spirit*, which almost might have been an appendix to the *Aids*, kept Coleridge before religious thinkers. Julius Hare and F. D. Maurice at Cambridge and both Thomas Arnold's broad churchmanship and certain aspects of the Oxford Movement he so bitterly opposed reflect his influence. (The leather-bound, gold-stamped volume reprinting the *Aids* and *Confessions* given as first prize at the Midsummer Examination at Culham College, Oxford, in 1884, that has found its way into my library strikes me as a monument to such continuing esteem.) Basil Willey has eloquently reviewed the importance of Coleridge's arguments that faith is arrived at by a convergence of evidence, that religious belief only deepens into faith as it is tried, that given the power of Reason as defined in the *Aids to Reflection*, one need not accept every word in the Bible as divinely inspired but may, once faith is attained, read it with the same discrimination as any other book. The foreshadowings of writers as different, and as significant, as Newman and Arnold is evident. And, in Willey's words, "in demonstrating that Christianity could and must be disengaged from the millstone of fundamentalism he was in effect producing a blue-print for all possible future defences of the faith."[114]

[114] Willey, *Nineteenth Century Studies*, p. 40.

III

James Mill

T

HE BASIS of Coleridge's system of thought is best seen in the *Treatise*; there we find him working from definitions of Ideas and Laws to the construction of an ordered hierarchy of the fields of human knowledge. The basis of James Mill's system of thought is best seen not in his early writings but in the two-volume *Analysis of the Phenomena of the Human Mind*, where we find him working from an analysis of sensation to a "theory of the Human mind."

Behind Mill's analysis, of course, are the cardinal principles of Jeremy Bentham. When Bentham came to set out a simple and convincing statement of the principle of utility as the foundation of the system set forth in *Principles of Morals and Legislation*, he offered a famous formulation. "Nature has placed mankind under the governance of two sovereign masters, *pain* and *pleasure*. It is for them alone to point out what we ought to do, as well as to determine what we shall do. On the one hand the standard of right and wrong, on the other the chain of causes and effects, are fastened to their throne."[1] For the purpose of

[1] *The Works of Jeremy Bentham*, I, 1.

his argument, this is undoubtedly the clearest, most effective beginning. Logically, however, a more basic principle or belief lies behind it: the empiricist principle that there is no source of knowledge other than experience and that generalizations from experience and subsequent deductions from the resulting generalizations are the only valid means of ordering or understanding that experience. Bentham's insistence that the adversaries of utility have nothing to depend on but the principle of "sympathy and antipathy" is not merely the supporting argument it appears to be but the necessary denial of all other sources of knowledge which justifies the deduction of man's guiding principle from experience. "Moral sense," "common sense," "rule of right," "fitness of things," "natural equity," and "good order" are all dismissed as phrases reducible to an appeal to personal preference and opinion, as are all doctrines of innate ideas, revelation, or transcendent faculties of the mind. Three principles, the empiricism that denies all other sources of knowledge, the principle of utility (which is a generalization from experience), and the faith in ordinary logic demonstrated throughout the conduct of Bentham's argument are, then, the root-principles of Bentham's system.

In addition, a fourth principle almost as important as the first three is drawn both from experience and from the whole Lockian argument—the self-regarding nature of all men. Hear Locke: "*Self* is that conscious thinking thing,—whatever substance made up of . . . which is sensible or conscious of pleasure and pain, capable of happiness or misery, and so is concerned for itself, as far as that consciousness extends."[2]

Mill is faithful to these principles although he modifies and extends them in significant ways. First, his use of them is linked much more directly to associational psychology. Bentham assumes that the operation of the mind is something like that explained by Locke and Hartley, but,

[2]Locke, *Essay Concerning the Human Understanding*, I, 458.

somewhat surprisingly, he gives very little examination to the way the mind functions. Mill, on the other hand, seems to have realized that Bentham's application of empiricist method required a more thorough explanation of the processes of human thought. Presuming associational psychology as adapted from Hartley by Priestley to be adequately grounded in experience, he interweaves his version of it closely with the principle of utility. Second, Bentham had applied his greatest happiness principle primarily to the theory of legislation rather than conduct in general. James Mill's exploration of the ramifications of associational psychology allowed him to widen the field of utilitarian thought. Third, Mill's thought is colored by his greater pessimism. Bentham never blinks the amount of unavoidable pain in the world, but Mill's insistence on the limited materials of pleasure available for sharing among the total society at any given time gives a much less optimistic cast to his thought. The classical economists' preoccupation with the inadequacy of the wage fund to meet the demands on it is paralleled by Mill's preoccupation with the inadequacy of what might be called the pleasure-fund. To the concern for the paucity of nature's fruits in comparison to humankind's desires was added the Malthusian spectre. From the time of the publication of Malthus's *An Essay on the Principle of Population* (1798), economic, political, and ethical theory was haunted by the impossibility of providing even subsistence for a "geometrically expanding" population. Purely theoretical speculation on the matter was constantly reinforced by the actuality of the hopeless poor crowded into the cities. "It is hardly too much to say," writes W. R. Sorley, "that the prospect weighed on the social mind of the nineteenth century like a nightmare."[3]

On the one hand, the trenchancy of Mill's writing and his ability to pull together material bearing on a particular question from various areas of Bentham's writing made his

[3] Sorley, *A History of British Philosophy to 1900*, p. 233.

presentation of utilitarian/empiricist thought more influential than Bentham's. However, the combination of his pessimism and associationism modify Bentham in ways that are both interesting in themselves and significant for an understanding of nineteenth-century empiricist thought.

THE ASSOCIATIONAL BASIS. Coleridge, once he has rejected associationism and embraced the view that the Idea both organizes our experience and reflects a permanent, transcendent world pattern, concentrates on exhibiting this dual nature, never looking closely into what we mean by "experience." Mill, taking for granted that everything in the mind arises directly out of experience, begins *The Analysis of the Phenomena of the Human Mind* with an examination of the eight kinds of sensation through which all of the mind's contents are introduced to it: smell, hearing, sight, taste, touch, sensations of disorganization (for instance from disease), feelings that accompany the action of muscles, and sensations in the alimentary canal. In Chapter II, the full empiricist direction of the argument becomes clear. "It is a known part of our constitution," says Mill, "that when our sensations cease, by the absence of their objects, something remains."[4] That residuum, the "copy," "image," or "trace" of the sensation, is the Idea. "We have two classes of feelings; one, that which exists when the object of sense is present; another, that which exists after the object of sense has ceased to be present."[5]

Mill is now in a position to explain the mechanism underlying the association of ideas, the general law of which is that "our ideas spring up, or exist, in the order in which

[4] James Mill, *Analysis of the Phenomena of the Human Mind*, I, 51.

[5] *Ibid.*, I, 52.

the sensations existed, of which they are copies."[6] He clarifies this law by (1) a definition of "order," which includes the "synchronical" (simultaneous) as well as the successive, (2) the explanation that ideas may be excited either by sensations or other ideas, and (3) an examination of the causes of the different degrees of vividness found in sensations, similar differences found in ideas, and differences in strengths of associations. By this point Mill has set out all the processes he needs to explain the complex phenomena of the human mind. Simple ideas associated in sensation lead to more complex ideas, as in our ideas of objects (a rose, a brick, a horse); more complex associations make up our ideas of extension, space, time, and movement. Thought is the successive appearance of a train of associated ideas.

To follow Mill through the twenty-one chapters of the *Analysis* would be tedious. The essential points of Mill's scheme emerge clearly enough from the chapters on "Naming," "Classification," "Belief," "Names which Require Special Explanation," and "The Will," under which innocuous-seeming rubrics the reader unfamiliar with the history of philosophy will be surprised to find doctrines of considerable importance. For instance, the importance of "Naming" (that is, of language) is made clear at the beginning, where appears the following significant paragraph:

> We cannot recall any idea, or train of ideas, at will. Thoughts come into the mind unbidden. If they did not come unbidden, they must have been in the mind before they came into it; which is a contradiction. You cannot bid a thought come into the mind, without knowing that which you bid; but to know a thought is to have the thought: the knowledge of the thought, and the thought's being in the mind, are not two things but one and the same thing, under different names.[7]

[6] *Ibid.*, I, 78.

[7] *Ibid.*, I, 130.

If we cannot recall ideas at will, neither can we recall trains of ideas. "A train of ideas may have passed in our minds corresponding to events of great importance; but that train will not pass again, unvaried, except in very simple cases, without the use of *expedients*."[8] The major expedient Mill has in mind is language. "By the power . . . which we have over the occasions of our sensations [that is, by the use of language], we can make sure of having a train of sensations exactly the same as we have had before."[9] This view of language as the system of sensible objects which makes possible control over our trains of ideas, for our own use, as well as for communication, is one of Mill's additions to Bentham that proves to have great importance.

In the discussion of "Classification" arises the occasion for the book's first direct attack on the Platonic doctrine of the Idea. Mill's explanation of the origin of transcendental Ideas in man's need to classify (which follows Bentham's) is as follows:

> The opinion, that the particulars in which the individuals of a class agree were distinct Objects of the Mind, soon made them distinct EXISTENCES; they were the Essence of things; the Eternal Exemplars, according to which individual things were made; they were called UNIVERSALS, and regarded as alone the Objects of the Intellect.[10]

After quoting passages from James Harris and the Cambridge Platonist Ralph Cudworth that present the transcendental argument for the existence of inimitable, eternal, and necessary entities, archetypes, or Ideas, Mill gives his own explanation of classes of things, an explanation that requires the invoking of no immutable essences:

[8] *Ibid.*, I, 131.

[9] *Ibid.*, I, 132.

[10] *Ibid.*, I, 251.

> Man first becomes acquainted with individuals. He first names individuals. But individuals are innumerable, and he cannot have innumerable names. He must make one name serve for many individuals. It is thus obvious, and certain, that men were led to class solely for the purpose of economizing in the use of names.[11]

"Belief" Mill defines as an instance of "indissoluble association"—in those cases in which association is so strong that we are unable to break the association (which may exist between sensations, between ideas, or between one or more sensations and one or more ideas), we are said to believe. In the chapter titled "Some Names which Require a Particular Explanation" we find that space may be defined as the association of all the ideas included in the terms "infinitely extended" except that of "resistance." That is, the idea of extension arises out of "the muscular feelings in what we call the motion of parts of our own bodies,"[12] associated with the resistance in individual objects (the idea of limit is already removed by the term "infinitely"), and one is left with the complex idea we name space. Time sums up the associations of Pastness, Presentness, and Futureness. Thus, the "indissoluble associations" contained in the idea of Time are Infinity and Succession, or infinite successions of antecedents and infinite successions of consequences. Perhaps the most remarkable of Mill's definitions and explanations is that of the will. He is at pains to present the case that our muscle movements, which lie at the base of all action, are responses to ideas, and that, therefore, "the power of the will is not immediate over the muscle, but over the Idea."[13] What happens, says Mill, is that the idea of a pleasure (or a pain to be avoided) initiates a train of associated ideas

[11] *Ibid.*, I, 260.

[12] *Ibid.*, I, 92.

[13] *Ibid.*, II, 348.

leading to the idea of action and that if this train is not cancelled out by stronger opposing ideas called up in the process of pursuing this train, the idea of the action initiates the action which, it is assumed, will lead to the pleasure. The will thus becomes nothing more than the process of association.

Necessary to the completion of Mill's theory is a consideration of the causes of the ideas of pleasure and pain that set going the trains of association which lead to action. Mill rather summarily resolves the principal causes of pleasure into Wealth, Power, and Dignity, and the principal causes of pain into their opposites: Poverty, Impotence, and Contemptibility. He then proceeds to a very significant conclusion:

> One remarkable thing is first of all to be noticed: the three, above named, grand causes of our pleasures agree in this, that they all are the means of procuring for us the Services of our fellow-creatures, and themselves contribute to our pleasures in hardly any other way. It is obvious from this remark, that the grand cause of all our pleasures are the services of our fellow-creatures; since Wealth, Power, and Dignity, which appear to most people to sum up the means of human happiness, are nothing more than means of procuring those services.[14]

In "services" Mill includes all that one man may do to give pleasure to another; friendship, kindness, and family affection are among the causes of pleasure ultimately derived from "services." One's Wealth, Power, and Dignity are not the causes of all services one receives from Fellow-creatures, but they are the prerequisites for so many services that pleasure comes to be associated very strongly with these three causes. Mill's argument here is not well worked out, nor, as it stands, readily defensible. One's understanding of the argument and its validity are somewhat in-

[14] *Ibid.*, II, 207–8.

creased, however, if the phrase "services of our Fellow-creatures" is identified with three of the four "sanctions" or sources of pleasure and pain outlined in Chapter III of Bentham's *Principles of Morals and Legislation*. The political, social, and religious sanctions lead to the granting or withholding of the services of others.

This, then, which Mill calls the Expository part of the Doctrine of the Human Mind, is the base upon which he will build in examining all other areas of human thought and endeavor. For instance, the Practical part of the Doctrine of the Human Mind, he says, ought to be treated in three Books: Logic, Ethics, and Education. The whole foundation thus set forth is unquestionably less ambiguous and easier to interpret than Coleridge's *Treatise*. But the problems that will plague the utilitarian structure built on these foundations are just as clearly visible in the *Analysis* as the problems in Coleridge's system are in the *Treatise*.

The major problem is the passivity of the mind as understood by Mill. One must depend on association for calling up ideas or trains of ideas, for initiating all actions. To be sure, one can turn to the written word in order to have ideas recalled, but only a particular train of associated ideas will lead one to the idea of the action of turning to the written word. There may develop within a man a system of strong associations that will call up the trains of association, and therefore actions, which will be of greatest benefit to him and to society, but the development of these strong associations depends on his experience. One need not become embroiled in debating the existence, or meaning, of "freedom of the will" to see not only that such a position carries important consequences in the interpretation of all human action and thought, but that it will make it difficult to explain discovery, creativity, and initiative, to explain how, in short, man is able to think purposively, to solve problems in any other way than by awaiting fortunate associations.

An interesting example of the problems into which Mill's view of the mind leads him is found in his review of *Essays on the Formation and Publication of Opinions.*[15] Belief, argues Mill, is the result of evidence; "the feeling of the force of evidence, and belief, are not two mental states, they are one and the same state." Therefore, a man is not responsible for his belief, although, Mill goes on to argue, he is responsible for his manner of dealing with evidence, for objectively seeking and giving attention to it. But, unless the mind is more active than it appears to be in the *Analysis*, how is it possible, for instance, "to allow greater weight to the evidence opposite to the affection that it seems to have, and less to that which favors it." Where, in other words, is a mind operating on associative principles to find the means of putting such weights in the scale?

The passivity of the mind also tightly limits the ways in which human action, and therefore human society, can be influenced. When a desire (either a pleasure to be seized or a pain to be avoided) enters the mind, and the resulting trains of association lead to the idea of an act that society regards as immoral or illegal, only collision with another train of ideas, somehow gotten under way by association with one or more ideas in the original train, can derail the process. There appeared to Mill, as will become clear in the examination of his other works, only two means of increasing the strength of those associations which would call up the trains whose ultimate destinations would be in accord with general utility (the greatest happiness of the greatest number), rather than the achievement of selfish, purely personal desires. The first is through a system of government and law that annexes sufficient (and sufficiently sure) pain to cause an association between the anticipated pleasure of an act opposed to the general utility and an even greater anticipated pain. The other is through a process of education that creates and strengthens utili-

[15] *Westminster Review*, VI (1826), 1–23.

tarian associations while minimizing the formation of anti-utilitarian ones.

GOVERNMENT AND POLITICS. The consequences of James Mill's reduction of the will to the associative trains set in motion by human desires is immediately apparent in the essays on Government, Jurisprudence, and Liberty of the Press which Mill contributed to the *Encyclopaedia Britannica*. Bentham's whole empirical system as set forth in the *Principles of Morals and Legislation* remains intact in Mill's essays, but Mill's emphasis on the associative structure of the mind makes certain aspects of it seem even more mechanical.

The essay on Government defines the end of government in the Benthamic formula: "the greatest happiness of the greatest number." For Coleridge, all things end in mystery; for utilitarians, all things end in politics and economics. Mill begins not with premises about the good, the true, and the beautiful, but with a generalization from experience: man's need to labor for his subsistence and pleasure, the law of nature "which is attended by the greatest number of consequences," calls forth government. Much is in the eye of the beholder besides beauty. Paley looked at nature and found a cunningly made cosmic watch; Coleridge found the eternal I Am; Newman found God's creation as tarnished by original sin; Mill, as noted above, finds a banquet at which there is not enough to go around. The very formula "the greatest happiness of the greatest number" becomes less an optimistic program than an attempt to make the best of a bad thing.

Part of the grimness of Mill's thought comes from the limitations of the political economy in fashion at the time. The "iron laws" of economics had none of the properties of the loaves and fishes. Economic laws which produced a wage fund to be fought over like a birthday cake at a party to which too many children had been invited and which transformed present charity into ultimate cruelty were hardly warrants for optimism. But part of the grimness was a result of Mill's associationist psychology. All action being the product of desire, and man's desire being, potentially at least, infinite,[16] no conceivable world could satisfy mankind, certainly not the actual one. Thus, within a few paragraphs of exposition Mill transforms the end of government from a means of creating the "greatest happiness of the greatest number" into a means of making "that distribution of the scanty materials of happiness, which would insure the greatest sum of it in the members of the community, taken altogether, preventing every individual, or combination of individuals, from interfering with that distribution, or making any man to have less than his share."[17] That being the end of government, Mill's formulation of the problem of the best means of government is not surprising: "all the difficult questions of Government relate to the means of restraining those, in whose hands are lodged the powers necessary for the protection of all, from making a bad use of it."[18]

Mill sums up for us, succinctly if perhaps elliptically, the way in which his view of government is grounded in his analysis of the mind: "The positions which we have already established with regard to human nature, and which we assume as foundations, are these: That the actions of men are governed by their wills, and their wills by their desires: That their desires are directed to pleasure and relief from pain as *ends*, and to wealth and power as

[16] One recalls Carlyle's shoeblack who can be made happy only by possession of "God's infinite Universe altogether to himself"; Carlyle's solution to man's insatiability is of course quite different from Mill's.

[17] James Mill, *Essays on Government, Jurisprudence, Liberty of the Press and Law of Nations*, p. 4.

[18] *Ibid.*, p. 5.

the principal means: That to the desire of these means there is no limit; and that the actions which flow from this unlimited desire are the constituents whereof bad Government is made."[19]

His detailed application of these principles to the evaluation of possible forms of government need not be pursued here; it will be enough to recognize that when Mill argues that "in the Representative System alone the Securities for good Government are to be found," he means by "securities" a system that will force the legislator to associate his own best interests with those of his electors, that is, will cause his mind to pursue trains of ideas that identify the achievement of his desires with the achievement of the desires of those he represents. The remaining portion of the essay, a discussion of what portion of the population should elect representatives, pursues another form of the same problem: what distribution of the franchise will most economically but effectively prevent one group in society from taking advantage of others in pursuit of the fulfillment of their desires? All powers must be balanced against equally powerful restraints, for "they who have a fixed, invariable interest in acting ill, will act ill invariably."[20]

Mill's article on Jurisprudence looks to the same premises as the articles on Government and specifically refers to the conclusion of that article. We need not follow Mill through his masterly redaction of the fruits of Bentham's thoughts on the reform of law. Precisely as in Bentham, the great end of Jurisprudence is to prevent undesirable

[19] *Ibid.*, p. 14.

[20] *Ibid.*, p. 29. D. C. Moore has reminded us (*Victorian Studies*, XIII [1969], 5–36) that, as Macaulay pointed out long ago, Mill contradicts this cardinal principle in arguing that the lower class will form its opinion on those of the middle class. But Mill would never have denied that though men may be selfish, their views of the ways in which their desires may be fulfilled are often drawn from others.

acts by attaching punishments, the contemplation of the certainty and severity of which will outweigh the contemplation of the pleasure to come from them. This requires cunning manipulation of the hedonic balance: "If we apply a less quantity of evil than is sufficient for outweighing these motives, the act will still be performed, and the evil will be inflicted to no purpose; it will be so much suffering in waste. If we apply a greater quantity of evil than is necessary, we incur a similar inconvenience; we create a quantity of evil which is absolutely useless. . . ."[21] The securities for the judge are the same as those for the legislator: means must be found of forcing the judge to identify his interests with those of society. Frequent opportunity for turning the legislator out of office is the great security against a legislator's malfeasance; each political idea that passes through the representative's mind must call up the ideas of remaining in or being turned out of office. Publicity is the great security against judicial malfeasance, and, therefore, no opinion expressed about a judge, no facts charged against him on reasonable grounds should be punished as libel. "Allow judges, or allow any men, to frame laws, and they will frame them, if they can, to answer their own purpose."[22]

Mill avoids the specifically associationist vocabulary of the *Analysis of the Human Mind*, but in his exposition it is evident that he is reinforcing Bentham's arguments, as set forth especially in *Principles of Morals and Legislation*, with his own interpretation: law, like government, is concerned with setting up trains of association that cancel out undesirable trains somewhere between the idea of an antisocial pleasure and the act. The ever-present conviction that all men will be rascals if they can, and the constant recognition of the dangers with which any social arrange-

[21] James Mill, *Essays on Government*, p. 19.

[22] *Ibid.*, p. 38.

ment, whatever its end, can produce an overbalance of pleasure, are found equally in Bentham. But the grim sense that there is not enough pleasure to go around stalks through Mill's essay.

For instance, early in the article on Jurisprudence, Mill insists that rights "always import obligations."[23] The reader unfamiliar with the utilitarian tradition is likely to interpret this as if it came from the pen of Coleridge or Carlyle, that is, as stating that those who are given privileges have concomitant responsibilities—that the aristocrat, the landowner, and the industrialist have duties to those beneath them. But Mill's point is quite another: he means that "if one man obtains a right to the services of another man, an obligation is, at the same time, laid upon this other to render those services. If a right is conferred upon one man to use and dispose of a horse, an obligation is laid upon other men to abstain from using him." One man's pleasure is very likely to be another's burden.

The essays on Government and Jurisprudence insist that representative government can be successful only when the electors know as much as possible about the action of their representatives; the press is the great organ of this knowledge. We are thus led to the third of the encyclopaedia articles central to an understanding of Mill's view of government: "Liberty of the Press." Clearly, just censure must be permitted, but no one can know what is a just censure until the evidence for and against it has been presented. Thus one cannot simply forbid unjust censures, and one is forced to conclude "that there is no safety to the people in allowing anybody to choose opinions for them; that there are no marks by which it can be decided beforehand, what opinions are true and what are false; that there must, therefore, be equal freedom of declaring all opinions, both true and false; and that, when all opinions, true and

[23] *Ibid.*, p. 6.

false, are equally declared, the assent of the greater number, when their interests are not opposed to them, may always be expected to be given to the true."[24]

EDUCATION. Whereas Coleridge's comments on education tend to blend into a consideration of the role of the National Church and move thence to the ground of religious belief in the Ideas of the Reason, Mill's much more explicit views on education are closely intertwined with those on government. (Hence the shift in the order in which the major topics are taken up in my two chapters.) Throughout the essays on Government, Jurisprudence, and Freedom of the Press, Mill insists on the education of the people—the "securities" he proposes for insuring that the legislator and the judge act conformably with the interests of the people demand an educated electorate. Only if the people know their own interests can they determine whether legislator or judge is acting for or against their interests, and only when legislator and judge know that the people know their own interests (and will depose those representatives and officials acting contrary to these) will the legislator and judge come to identify their interests with those of the people.

> It is no longer deniable that a high degree of knowledge is capable of being conveyed to such a portion of the community, as would have interests the same with those of the community. [That is, the electorate.] This being the only resource for good government, those who say it is not yet attained stand in this dilemma; either they do not desire good government, which is the case with all those who derive advantage from

[24] *Ibid.*, p. 23.

bad; or they will be seen employing their utmost exertions to increase the quantity of knowledge in the body of the community.[25]

And, of course, the liberty of expression Mill champions has full value only when men are educated sufficiently to judge the contest between opposing views.

But, and this is a key point, however much Mill's political theories depend for their success on education, the education of the individual depends even more for its success on the political structure. The importance of education in a representative government is a commonplace, but the inseparability of the educational processes from the total structure of politics and society, though frequently recognized, is rarely as clearly stated as here by Mill.

To understand the overwhelming importance of this point for Mill one must continue to keep in mind the psychology set out in the *Analysis of the Phenomena of the Human Mind*. This is indeed easy enough for the reader of the essay on Education that Mill wrote for the *Britannica* (to which we now turn), for that essay not only summarizes many of the main explanations offered in the *Analysis* but employs the same vocabulary. The links between the *Analysis* and the doctrines set forth in Mill's other *Britannica* essays must be supplied by the reader; here they are given directly. "As the happiness, which is the end of education, depends upon the the actions of the individual, and as all the actions of man are produced by his feelings or thoughts, the business of education is, to make certain feelings or thoughts take place instead of others. The business of education, then, is to work upon the mental successions."[26] As this definition of education is explored in the essay, it becomes clear that education is not simply the ac-

[25] *Ibid.*, p. 29.

[26] *James Mill on Education*, p. 52.

quisition of knowledge. Knowledge of facts—of how things are—is a great and necessary aid to establishing beneficial as opposed to harmful trains. But much of education consists simply in the encouragement of the proper trains of association by repetition of certain ideas which, it is believed, are in the interest of utility to associate. Much of education consists in the *artificial* formation of associations. The reason for this is of central importance. Mill can say that "as the happiness of the individual is bound up with that of his species, that which affects the happiness of the one, must also, in general, affect that of the other."[27] This is true not only because a society in which all act in accordance with the principle of utility will produce a greater sum of happiness (in accordance with Bentham's principle that either to take all pleasure from one man and distribute it among others or to take all pleasure from many and give it to a few produces more total pain than pleasure) but also because of a more direct relationship: "It is interesting here to observe, by what a potent call we are summoned to Virtue. Of all that we enjoy, more is derived from those acts of other men, on which we bestow the name VIRTUE, than from any other cause. Our own virtue is the principal cause why other men reciprocate the acts of virtue toward us. With the idea of our own acts of virtue, there are naturally associated the ideas of all the immense advantages we derive from the virtuous acts of our Fellow-creatures." But it is nevertheless quite clear to Mill that the greatest happiness for a given individual, that is, the greatest happiness mixed with the least pain, is not always and necessarily to be achieved by actions that give the least pain and greatest pleasures to others. One's good actions are not always reciprocated. This is why the passage proceeds: "When this association is formed in due strength, *which it is the main business of a good education to effect*,

[27] *Ibid.*, p. 99.

the motive of virtue becomes paramount in the human breast."[28]

The overwhelming necessity of reinforcing purely selfish motives is implied throughout Mill's arguments and made explicit in the following long but extremely significant passage.

> The grand object of human desire is a command over the wills of other men. This may be attained, either by qualities and acts which excite their love and admiration, or by those which excite their terror. When the education is so wisely conducted as to make the train run habitually from the conception of the good end to the conception of the good means; and as often, too, as the good means are conceived, viz. the useful and beneficial qualities, to make the train run to the conception of the great reward, the command over the wills of men; an association is formed which impels the man through life to pursue the great object of desire, fitting himself to be, and by actually becoming, the instrument of the greatest possible benefit to his fellow men.
>
> But, unhappily, a command over the wills of men may be obtained by other means than by doing them good; and these, when a man can command them, are the shortest, the easiest, and the most effectual. These other means are all summed up in a command over the pains of other men. When a command over the wills of other men is pursued by the instrumentality of pain, it leads to all the several degrees of vexation, injustice, cruelty, oppression, and tyranny. It is, in truth, the grand source of all wickedness, of all the evil which man brings upon man. When the education is so deplorably bad as to allow an association to be formed in the mind of the child between the grand object of desire, the command over the wills of other men, and the fears and pains of other men, as the means; the foundation is laid of the bad character,—the bad son, the bad brother, the bad husband, the bad father, the bad

[28] James Mill, *Phenomena of the Human Mind*, II, 292.

neighbour, the bad magistrate, the bad citizen,—to sum up all in one word, the bad man.[29]

Mill is prevented from making a Shaftesburian identification of one's own interests with those of others by his belief in the insufficiency of the objects of pleasure on the one hand and on the other by his psychology, which makes action the result of trains of association commonly originating in desires. Knowledge will show us that some of our desires can best be achieved by fulfilling the desires of others, but it will also show that certain other desires can only, or most easily, or most fully, be obtained by giving or threatening (which is a form of giving) pain to others. Prudence, Fortitude, Justice, and Benevolence comprise Virtue, says Mill.[30] We have pleasurable associations with all four because of the pleasures they produce for us either directly or by their effect on other men. But nevertheless, "It requires the most perfect education to create those associations adequately, in other words, to give the motives such power within us, that, when counteracted by other motives, they may always prevail."[31] If we wish to maximize not the pleasures of any one individual but the happiness of the greatest number, trains of action that will produce more *total* pain than pleasure, however much pleasure they give to an *individual*, must be deflected by other trains of association introduced by two artificial means—by laws that annex a punishment, and therefore an association with pain, to certain actions, or by repetitions of two images together so that image A immediately calls up image B.

Locke had emphasized the necessity of counteracting Ideas allied by chance or custom rather than by nature through right education, which would set up the proper

[29] *James Mill on Education*, pp. 100–101.

[30] James Mill, *Phenomena of the Human Mind*, II, 288.

[31] *Ibid.*, II, 289.

habits or trains of association, but he had not recognized any necessity for setting up associations that do not have "a *natural* correspondence and connexion one with another."[32] Although Mill does not explicitly advocate the teaching of "unnatural" associations which will tip the balance toward benevolence, the whole direction of his argument implies its necessity. Now there are four "moral circumstances" which help to form the proper associations: Domestic Education (the sum of the child's experiences in the parental home); Technical Education (formal instruction); Social Education (the influence of "the principle of imitation" and "the power of the society over our happiness and misery"); and Political Education (the influence of the whole structure of government).

All reference to what he calls "Political Education" is crammed into the final pages of the essay, but, says Mill, "The Political Education is like the key-stone of the arch; the strength of the whole depends upon it. We have seen that the strength of the Domestic and the Technical Education depends almost entirely upon the Social. Now it is certain, that the nature of the Social depends upon the Political."[33] Moreover, the political machine determines the physical condition of men's lives, which in turn influences the whole educational process.

Let us turn then to the most significant sentence in the paragraphs quoted immediately above. "But, unhappily, a command over the wills of men may be obtained by other means than by doing them good; and these, when a man can command them, are the shortest, easiest, and the most effectual." What are the means of preventing this train from being the determining one? One is by a system of laws (a government, a political structure) that will prevent a man's being able to control others through "command over the pains of other men" and visit the man who

[32] Locke, *Essay Concerning the Human Understanding*, I, 529.

[33] *James Mill on Education*, pp. 117–18.

tries this method of achieving his desires with enough pain to discourage the effort. (That is, the structure of laws must be such that he associates more pain than pleasure with the improper mode of action, or, in other words, the improper train must be blocked at some point by the association of greater pain than pleasure with some idea in the train.) However, in those situations which law cannot directly influence, the proper train is to be the result of associations created through education. But education consists of the establishment of certain trains through our constant exposure to the proper associations; that is, these trains depend on domestic, technical, and social education, all of which will reflect the society's views of what is praiseworthy and blameworthy. The social sanction, however, is very much dependent on the total structure of life imposed by the political machine, that is, the government. Everything depends on obtaining that form of government which most encourages the greatest happiness of the greatest number. Such reasoning lies behind the assertion in Mill's review of Southey's *Book of the Church* that "of all the crimes which it is possible for a human being to commit against his fellow creatures, that of corrupting the springs of government is beyond all comparison the worst. . . . This strikes at the well-being of all the myriads of whom the great body of the community is composed, from generation to generation."[34] The utilitarian thus looks to the reform of government as the essential first step toward the increase of happiness and improvement of the condition of mankind. To call for direct moral reformation of individuals as the prerequisite to the reformation of society was, to Mill and his followers, necessarily absurd.

Now, of course, the aim of education is not merely to develop mechanical associations. An understanding of what it is good for man to do, that is, what associations *should* operate most powerfully on him, in itself strength-

[34] *Westminster Review*, III (1825), 191.

ens the proper associations. It is therefore good for all men to understand that the principle of utility is in all cases the guide to what men should do, and it is good for all men, insofar as possible, to be able to deduce the proper subordinate principles from the principle of utility.

Education then, in summary, serves utility in that it (1) imparts facts (creates associations in the mind corresponding to relations that exist outside it);[35] (2) inculcates associations that will engender those modes of actions that will give the greatest happiness;[36] (3) teaches and exemplifies the utilitarian principles. The combined effect will make the proper ideas predominate and thus control the associations. "When the grand sources of felicity are formed into the leading and governing ideas, each in its due and relative strength, Education has then performed its most perfect work; and thus the individual becomes, to the greatest degree, the source of utility to others, and of happiness to himself."[37] Since morality is action according to utility, all three modes of education also serve morality.

RELIGION. We have seen that questions of morality tend to be subsumed by Mill under other topics: psychology, government, education. (Bentham's *Principles of Morals and Legislation*, we recall, having presented utility

[35]"Numberless are the mischievous delusions to which a man is exposed by ignorance, against which knowledge presents the only preservative." *Works of Jeremy Bentham*, VIII, 12.

[36]Locke had given great importance to education for reasons essentially the same, although arrived at from a different direction. "Unnatural" or chance associations that have no correspondence with the world that produces our sensations are frequent and can be controlled only by an education that will insure the preponderance of "Natural" association. See the discussion of this point in Ernest Tuveson's *The Imagination as a Means of Grace*, pp. 33–36.

[37]James Mill, *Phenomena of the Human Mind*, II, 378.

as the principle man has imperfectly and generally unconsciously followed, and which he ought to follow as fully and as consciously as possible, has little more to say on morality; the great bulk of the volume treats legislation.) Religion, under which morality is subsumed by Coleridge, hardly figures into Mill's published writing. Mill, like Bentham, was circumspect in this regard, and he follows Bentham in including religion among the four sanctions (sources of influence) on man's action, implying that religious doctrines are one of the sources of pleasure and pain which, properly applied, will determine man to act in accordance with utility.[38]

But James Mill's skepticism and contempt for Church doctrines is occasionally clearly enough implied, as for instance in his defense of the Lancastrian schools in "Schools for All."[39] Here Mill accuses the churchmen who believe the Lancastrian schools dangerous to religion of thinking that ignorance is not dangerous to the church while knowledge is. The believer could interpret this as an attempt to reduce the anti-Lancastrian position to an absurdity—of course, he will feel, knowledge cannot be an enemy of the church, nor is the church an enemy to knowledge. However, utilitarian readers would recognize in Mill's accusation the guarded assertion that the church opposed education for the very good reason that it derived its power from the ignorance of the people. And, presumably, readers who, though regarding themselves as Christian, had a touch of the skeptical spirit, would at least be led to question the motives of the church in this matter.

There are similar stings in the phrasing of the following passages from the same article. "All those who believe in Christianity must therefore allow that Lancaster's schools

[38] Coleridge, of course, anathematized the fashionable mode of thought "where Religion is valued and patronized as a supplement of law, or an aid extraordinary of Police" (*Complete Works*, I, 294).

[39] See Chapter II, note 86.

are favourable to Christianity, as much as knowledge is favourable to it, and ignorance unfavourable." "Churchmen, therefore, if convinced of the utility of establishments, may be more at their ease. For, if they be useful, it is only necessary to make people see that they are useful, and their permanency is secure. . . ."[40] And in Mill's vigorous attacks on Southey's *The Book of the Church* and Ecclesiastical Establishments in the *Westminster Review*,[41] the selfish purposes of the ostentatiously devout and the sinister purposes of an established clergy are stated so uncompromisingly as to imply that both martyrdoms and church doctrines are less the result of devotion and revelation than the desire for admiration and power. "Not only is the Church of England essentially intolerant and persecuting, but she has always acted up to that character; and whatever instrument of mischief the spirit of the age permitted her to use against those who dissented from her, she has always eagerly employed."[42]

John Stuart Mill's summation of his father's religious views is well known: "He found it impossible to believe that a world so full of evil was the work of an Author combining infinite power with perfect goodness and rightness."[43] But this position James Mill never publicly avowed. As Leslie Stephen points out, "The Utilitarians contended themselves with sapping the fort instead of risking an open assault."[44] It was folly to risk massive opposition, and prosecution, by entering on the question of the existence of a Diety. (J. S. Mill reports his father felt that affirmations and denials of the existence of a Deity were equally absurd.) Once men could be got to see how opposed to utility were

[40] *James Mill on Education*, pp. 130, 153.

[41] *Westminster Review*, III (1825), 167–212, and V (1826), 504–48.

[42] *Westminster Review*, III (1825), 206.

[43] J. S. Mill, *Autobiography*, pp. 144–45.

[44] Stephen, *The English Utilitarians*, II, 338.

religious doctrines and to begin to think of the psychological sources of religious beliefs, the specific doctrines of Christianity would crumble.

However, an attack on Natural Religion, if properly managed, could undermine Christianity without directly attacking it. And that is what the one specific attack on religion published by the early utilitarians intends. The attack, which appeared as the *Analysis of the Influence of Religion on the Temporal Happiness of Mankind* under the pseudonym "Philip Beauchamp," was the result of George Grote's reworking of a manuscript of Bentham's. Locke had endeavored to show how the idea of God could arise out of sense impressions alone; Bentham would show what pernicious beliefs had necessarily become associated with the idea of God that had so arisen. As Leslie Stephen points out, "The book . . . represents the view of representative Utilitarians of the first and third generation, and clearly expressed the real opinions of the whole party."[45] It certainly represents James Mill's views. For instance, Mill's argument in his review of Southey's *Book of the Church* that it is in the interest of the priest "to perpetuate the reign of ignorance and darkness" and "prevent the diffusion of education among the people, and if that cannot be done, to get the management of it into his own hands, and to fix it as completely as possible upon frivolous objects" and "to prevent the freedom of the press, if possible, altogether" is precisely parallel to that in the final portion of the *Analysis*.[46] Certain passages sound indeed considerably more like Mill than Bentham, the result perhaps of Grote's part in the composition, and one of the most fascinating aspects of *The Influence of Natural Religion* is the way arguments used by Mill in the discussion of psychology, government, and jurisprudence are turned to account here.

[45] *Ibid.*, II, 339–400.

[46] See, *Westminster Review*, III (1825), 212.

Though the definitions given of "religion" and "natural religion" in the first chapter call no particular attention to themselves, the entire essay turns on them. "By the term *religion* is meant the belief in the existence of an almighty Being, by whom pain and pleasures will be dispensed to mankind, during an infinite and future state of existence."[47] The emphasis here, as in the whole work, is less on "the existence of an Almighty Being" than on the pains and pleasures of the "infinite and future state of existence." "And religion is called natural, when there exists no written and acknowledged declaration, from which an acquaintance with the will and attributes of this almighty Being may be gathered."[48] The emphasis in this definition is less on the distinction between natural and revealed religion than on the implications, developed fully in the work, that only by means of a "written and acknowledged declaration" could "the will and attributes of the almighty Being" be determined.

Man's experience is that pain is a more frequent and vivid experience than pleasure. Therefore, *The Influence of Natural Religion* argues, the unknowability of the Deity of natural religion will necessarily lead to the association of pain rather than pleasure with the unknown almighty power. "Pain is a far stronger, more pungent, and more distinct sensation than pleasure. . . . Pain, therefore, is far more likely to obtrude itself upon the conceptions, where there exists no positive evidence to circumscribe their range, than pleasure." Moreover, "pain alone, and want or uneasiness, which is a species of pain, are the standing provisions of nature. . . . Want and pain, therefore, are natural; satisfaction and pleasure, artificial and invented: and the former will on this ground also be more likely to present itself as the characteristic of an unknown state,

[47] "Beauchamp," *Analysis of the Influence of Natural Religion on the Temporal Happiness of Mankind*, p. 3.

[48] *Ibid.*, p. 3.

than the latter."[49] The case is little better if we regard the Deity as at least partly known through his creation. To the extent that the world provides evidence of the characteristics of a supreme power, he must be regarded as incomprehensibly distributing good and evil—we are no more able to predict and explain his actions than those of a madman, but here we are confronted with a madman of unlimited power.

Is there a model to be found in human experience that will illuminate the attributes of this all-powerful Being? The nearest analogy Beauchamp finds is that of the absolute despot. This identification immediately imports all the conclusions drawn about the inevitable tendencies of the reign of an absolute sovereign presented by James Mill in the essay on Government. A despot wishes absolute obedience and can tolerate no happiness in others except that which he grants as proof of his power. "It thus plainly appears that the despot can never derive any pleasure from the genuine well being of the community, though he may at times gratify himself by exalting individuals to sudden pre-eminence over the rest."[50] The praise man accords the Deity is as hollow as that given an absolute sovereign. It would be useless, and to the last degree dangerous, to blame such a sovereign; one resorts to praise in the hope that this will bring a repetition of whatever small favors he grants. Moreover, the Deity is a tyrant with unlimited powers of espionage. "It would be madness, therefore, to hazard an unfavourable judgement of his proceedings, while constantly under his supervision."[51] The attribution of the qualities of a merciful or just judge to the Deity is absurd flattery. For, as Mill had pointed out in the essay on Jurisprudence, a judge will be beneficent and just only so long as his power is revocable.

[49] *Ibid.*, pp. 46–47.

[50] *Ibid.*, p. 30.

[51] *Ibid.*, p. 27.

Finally, the whole system under which the Deity is supposed to render judgment is the worst that could be designed. The laws under which he operates can never be known. As Bentham and Mill both argue elsewhere, a severe but delayed and uncertain punishment is less effective as a deterrent than a milder but immediate and certain punishment. The more delayed and uncertain, the less effective even the harshest penalties. Divine punishment for evil in this life is delayed until after death, and may be averted by atonement—under these circumstances, hell's hottest fires are not terrifying enough to outweigh temptation. On the other hand, the fear of the Deity's punishment, ineffective in preventing evil in the presence of strong desire, is perfectly capable of inflicting painful apprehensions after the evil deed is done. Moreover, such apprehension is strongest toward the end of life, when it is too late to prevent the greater number of evils. Such an arrangement is the most profitless a government can impose—it inflicts pain without being a deterrent to wrong actions.

Why are not all those who believe in a Deity then more miserable than they seem to be? Because for most men, for most of their lives, the real influence of religion comes not from fear of the day of judgment but through an illegitimate alliance of the religious sanction and the social sanction. Except in times of stress, and toward the end of life, it is public opinion rather than the Deity most men fear, and only acts that are forbidden by public opinion as well as religion will they avoid. The menace of religion here is in its constant tendency to mislead public opinion into approving acts that are not in conformity with utility. Religion "thus draws off a portion of the popular favour, from its legitimate task of encouraging acts conducive to human felicity: She cheats the public into the offer of a reward for conduct always useless, sometimes injurious. . . ."[52] For in-

[52] *Ibid.*, p. 86.

stance, "You wish to give proof of your attachment to the Deity, in the eyes and for the conviction of your fellow-men? There is but one species of testimony which will satisfy their minds. You must impose upon yourself pain for his sake; and in order to silence all suspicion as to the nature of the motive, the pain must be such as not to present the remotest prospect of any independent reward.[53] I have already attempted to shew," Beauchamp reminds us, "that this condition effectually excludes, and renders improper for the purpose, all suffering endured for the benefit of mankind."[54]

The result is that "the science of morality has been enveloped in a cloud of perplexity and confusion. . . . The practices on which the same epithets of approbation is [*sic*] bestowed, appear so incurably opposite, that it has been found impossible to reduce them to one common principle, or to discover any constituent quality which universally attracts either praise or blame."[55] In other words, religion has obscured the identity of utility and morality.

I have given only a selection of examples from the "catalogue of the various modes in which Natural Religion produces temporal mischief," which makes up Part II of the *Influence of Natural Religion*. Other important mischiefs are "creating of factitious antipathies" between different sects and "disqualifying the intellectual faculties for purposes useful in this life," that is, divorcing belief from experience. Such divorce, anathema to empiricists, is, says

[53] Cf. Mill's review of Southey's *Book of the Church*: "The motives are no mystery at this time of day, which lay the Indian Yogee on a bed of spikes, which made, but a few years ago, the convulsionaries in Paris submit to the pains of the cross, which supported Servetius, as well as Cranmer, at the stake. When credit is to be gained by suffering, when was there a want of parties to suffer?" (*Westminster Review*, III [1825], 170).

[54] "Beauchamp," *Influence of Natural Religion*, p. 68. It excludes "suffering endured for the benefit of mankind" because such suffering is unlikely to give rise to esteem.

[55] *Ibid.*, p. 87.

"Beauchamp," the source of madness and all lesser intellectual weaknesses.

The final "mischief" discussed is that of "creating a particular class of person incurably opposed to the interests of humanity." That class is of course the priesthood, those who claim to represent, interpret, and directly serve the Deity. The members of the priesthood, like all other men, will be animated by self-interest, a thriving self-interest like that of any aristocracy unchecked by "securities." It will be in their interest to make God as terrible as possible, to impede all progress that threatens them, to propagate "extra-experimental" beliefs (i.e., beliefs not grounded in experience). Therefore, "all those whose influence rests on an imputed connexion with the Divine Being, cannot fail to be animated by an interest invariably opposed to all human happiness . . . the inevitable aim of such persons must be to extend and render irremediable, those evils which natural religion would originate without them, viz. ignorance, extra-experimental belief, appalling conceptions of the Deity, intense dread of his visitations, and a perversion of the terms of praise and censure in his behalf."[56]

Here, in the final section, the grounds for discrediting *revealed* (as opposed to *natural*) religion are clearly implied. For the priests will necessarily devote themselves to "promulgating and explaining the will of their incomprehensible master," that is, although "Beauchamp" does not quite explicitly say so, to fabricating revelation. The effect of Natural Religion, particularly as aggravated by the priesthood, is therefore almost totally pernicious. "Thus the nature of the religious sanction, though very ill adapted for the purpose of actually terminating the practices it forbids, is yet calculated in the most precise manner to exalt and enrich the officer busied in enforcing it."[57]

[56] *Ibid.*, p. 218.

[57] *Ibid.*, pp. 129, 132.

THE POETIC IMAGINATION. Mill collides with Coleridge no less directly in the realm of aesthetic theory—though since the phenomena usually discussed under the heading of aesthetics are for Mill clear cases of the ordinary operation of association, it is perhaps misleading to imply that he has a separate theory of aesthetics. What he has to say on the subject is to be found in his discussions of the Imagination, the Sublime, and the Beautiful.

Imagination is simply another name for the process of association. "I am said to have an imagination when I have a train of ideas; and when I am said to imagine, I have the same thing; nor is there any train of ideas, to which the term imagination may not be applied."[58] Why, then, asks Mill, are the trains of a poet generally called "imagination" while those of, say, lawyers or merchants are not? The difference is not in the laws of association that link the ideas but in the kind of ideas. The ideas that make up the poet's train "are ideas of all that is most lovely and striking in the visible appearance of nature, and all that is most interesting in the actions and affections of human beings."[59] This difference in the kind of ideas does however give an additional quality to the train. The pleasure of almost all other trains lies in the anticipated end; the poet's train, being made up of pleasure-giving ideas, is pleasurable throughout. Indeed, Mill points out, those other trains that are pleasurable in themselves, for instance reveries, are likely to be called imaginations. A major difficulty in Mill's explanation, as Alexander Gerard and Meyer Abrams have pointed out, is that all ideas are related by association to an infinite number of others—how does the mind of the poet

[58] James Mill, *Phenomena of the Human Mind*, I, 239.

[59] *Ibid.*, I, 242.

impose sufficient control to give form to the associative trains? This is of course a form of the major problem the associationists constantly faced: how can a mind governed by association exert active power?[60]

It is interesting to note that wholly different as his view of imagination is, the definition of poetry here implied by Mill is close enough to Coleridge's own.

> The end of the metaphysical, and the end of the mathematical inquirer, is the discovery of truth: their trains are directed to that object; and are, or are not, a source of pleasure, as that end is or is not attained. But the case is perfectly different with the poet. His train is its own end. It is all delightful, or the purpose is frustrate.[61] (Mill)

> A poem is that species of composition, which is opposed to works of science, by proposing for its *immediate* object pleasure, not truth; and from all other species (having *this* object in common with it) it is discriminated by proposing to itself such delight from the *whole* as is compatible with a distinct gratification from each component *part*.[62] (Coleridge)

But of course Mill would never agree to Coleridge's definition of the poet as one who "brings the whole soul of man into activity, with the subordination of its faculties to one another, according to their relative worth and dignity."[63]

One may push the inquiry a step back and ask what is the source of the "lovely" ideas that make up the poet's train. Part of the answer will be found in Volume II under the sub-section, "The Objects called Sublime and Beautiful, and their contraries, contemplated as Causes of our Pleasures and Pains." Mill disposes of the mystery sur-

[60] See Abrams, *The Mirror and the Lamp*, p. 164.

[61] James Mill, *Phenomena of the Human Mind*, I, 242–43.

[62] Coleridge, *Biographia Literaria*, in *Complete Works*, III, 371.

[63] *Ibid.*, III, 374.

rounding the Beautiful and the Sublime as magisterially as that surrounding the Imagination. The Beautiful and the Sublime are really two members of the same species, that species of sensations which are accompanied by trains of pleasurable ideas. Drawing heavily on the 1790 essay by Archibald Alison, *Essay on the Nature and Principles of Taste* (which in turn is indebted to Hartley), Mill argues that sounds, colors, and forms are indifferent in themselves, and only by association with other ideas call up those feelings we call the beautiful or sublime. The noise of the cataract is sublime only by association with the power of falling water. The trains of association that add the pleasure we call beauty to certain sounds and sights are, like poetic trains, pleasurable in themselves. Thus, presumably, music, painting, and sculpture give pleasure through the provision of sensations that give rise to trains pleasurable in themselves. And, if I interpret Mill correctly, the pleasurable train that is the result of the poet's imagination will be constituted largely of ideas like that, for instance, of a waterfall, itself the cause of a pleasurable train.

As WE HAVE SEEN, one of Coleridge's major problems was finding a way to communicate the Ideas of the Reason, language being conformable only to the Understanding. Another was the immense difficulty of constructing a total system in which the organic relationship of all knowledge in all areas would be manifest. Mill faced neither sort of problem. "The power of Language essentially consists," he wrote, "in two things; first, in our having marks of our SENSATIONS, and IDEAS: and, secondly, in so arranging them, that they may correctly denote a TRAIN of those mental states or feelings."[64] How language does this

[64] James Mill, *Phenomena of the Human Mind*, I, 134.

is the subject of the central third of the first volume of the *Analysis*—to summarize it here would be unprofitable. But it is clear that inasmuch as language consists merely of the means of "marking" (referring to) sensations, ideas, and the order of association of those sensations and ideas, there can be nothing in the mind that language is unable to treat. Or, to put it another way, there is nothing that Mill would wish to say to which language could be inadequate.[65] Second, sensations, ideas, and associations provide all the foundation necessary for Mill to explain everything that passes in the human mind. Choose what area of human thought you will, ask the meaning of whatever you please, Mill can explain it on the basis of his three counters. And although, as I've tried to show, all phenomena turn out to be interrelated for the empiricists if pursued far enough, it is not necessary to consider much more than its relationship to the association mechanism and the principle of utility to explain any particular given phenomenon.

But, although Mill's philosophy avoids the problems that pressed so hard on Coleridge, it has its own characteristic weaknesses. A great problem in the Millian scheme of things is that passivity of the mind already noticed. One of the difficulties to which this leads is in explaining the *origin* of the trains of association which cause us to act for the greatest happiness of the greatest number, when that goal is in opposition with our own great happiness. That such trains can be artificially created Mill demonstrates; but the reason men approve those trains and strive to inculcate them is not apparent. We are back to the question

[65] Language can, of course, be refined so as to be more accurate. One third of the *Chrestomathia* is given over to Appendix IV, the "Essay on Nomenclature and Classification," which attempts to give the proper names to each branch of knowledge, and a considerable portion of the rest of the work deals in one way or another with this question. Similarly, Bentham's essay on Ontology is as much concerned with the names of various areas of human knowledge as with their classification, that is, relations to one another—and properly so on Bentham's view, since the two are really aspects of the same activity of mind.

already pointed out as resulting from the mechanical nature of the will as Mill sees it. Why do men will the creation of trains of association that are beneficial to the greatest happiness of the greatest number if will is simply the name of the train leading from a personal desire to act? The mutually supporting relationships between Government, Jurisprudence, Freedom of the Press, and Education developed by Mill create an impressive, even an aesthetically pleasing, intellectual circuitry. But, what is the source of the "ought" which transforms the desire to increase my balance of pleasure into a desire to increase the happiness of all? What we are looking at is of course a case of the very common fallacy of converting the descriptive (each man desires a maximum of pleasure) to the normative (each man ought to be given the maximum amount of pleasure possible). Few of the opponents of utilitarianism were content to direct their attack at this merely logical difficulty however. Seeing no way to explain how benevolence and unselfishness could ever have gotten into the Millian system, they overlooked the fact that, however illogically, it *was* there, having been smuggled in from the beginning. The obvious conclusion, to those opposed to utilitarianism, was that the system and its proponents were inhumanly cruel and selfish. Thus Coleridge: "Let us beware of that proud philosophy, which affects to inculcate philanthropy while it denounces every home-born feeling by which it is produced and nurtured."[66]

An even larger problem must not be passed over. It is passing strange that empiricism could be so confident, inasmuch as its whole system rested on the Lockian analysis which denied that one could ever know the essence of those objects "out there" which were the cause of sensations and which admitted that the mind imposed "secondary qualities" not actually inherent in whatever was "out there." Technically, of course, Locke's system was a form of

[66] Coleridge, *The Friend*, in *Complete Works*, II, 305.

idealism; it had already led to the more extreme idealism of Berkeley and the skepticism of Hume by the time Bentham began to write. Though Locke assumed a working correspondence between sensations, their external causes, and the resultant ideas, he opened the door to the acceptance of wide variations in the quality of human awareness, the result of each individual's reception of different sensations, and the formation of unique personal associations. However, in both Locke and Hume the emphasis on sense data as the source of all knowledge overshadows the idealist ramifications of their positions; Bentham and James Mill were content to ignore the idealist implications of Locke's position. Only with the publication of J. S. Mill's *Logic*, which set out the methods for avoiding subjective errors in physical and social sciences (though it did not touch upon the similar problems in the aesthetic sphere) would the empiricist/utilitarian system meet this challenge.

The specific form of empiricism that took the name "utilitarianism" appealed to its disciples because it led so directly to practical programs, seemed so clear and unambiguous in both its fundamental assumptions and the manner in which its characteristic arguments could be deduced from those assumptions, and appeared to harbor so little mystery, ambiguity, or personal crochet. Bentham might be personally eccentric, but James Mill, George Grote, John Bowring, Francis Place, John and Charles Austin, or David Ricardo, despite differences in interests and emphases, seemed in many ways interchangeable spokesmen for his utilitarianism.

IV

Metaphysical Predispositions in J. S. Mill and Matthew Arnold

T

O SAY either that all empiricists or all transcendentalists excluded the least tincture of the opposing system from their own thought or that no empiricist or no transcendentalist saw value in or tried to arrive at an accommodation with the other system is manifestly untrue. What is striking, however, is the enormous difficulty of reaching such an accommodation and the tendency of thinkers to maintain their apparently inherent alignments. One example is John Stuart Mill, who, though frequently regarded as having been wooed away from the central utilitarian line by the influence of Wordsworth's poetry and Coleridge's thought, will be found rarely inconsistent with the core of beliefs with which he grew up. Another is Matthew Arnold, who, I believe, never freed himself from the influences of the Coleridgean/Christian thought transmitted by his father and reinforced by Newman. He retained much more of a transcendental habit of thought than he would admit or than has been generally acknowledged.

J. S. MILL'S *Autobiography*, the well-known essays on Bentham and Coleridge, and the essay on poetry all seem to provide evidence of the importance of Coleridge's influence, especially between 1826, the year of Mill's mental crisis, and 1843, the year of the publication of the *Logic*. There has been an increasing tendency not only to emphasize a Coleridgean admixture in Mill's thought but to discuss it as though systems of thought were totally miscible, as though blends of, say one-third Coleridge to two-thirds Bentham, or one-quarter each of Wordsworth, Coleridge, Bentham, and Comte, plus a pinch of Carlyle, were attainable by some intellectual alchemy. That J. S. Mill's mind came to represent some such mixture is most often assumed by those who wish to emphasize the difference between a humane and sensitive Mill and a coldly mechanical earlier generation of utilitarians. But Mill's mind was not, I think, any more than that of other major thinkers, a sophisticated mixing apparatus; rather, to use the metaphor he himself suggests, it was a constantly rewoven web.

Mill began his intellectual life with as firm an inheritance of basic principles as any young man ever had, and despite the fashion of viewing him as one whose whole life was a process of discovering the worthlessness of his intellectual inheritance, ordinary care in distinguishing the results of chains of deduction, always liable to errors and incompleteness, from basic postulates shows Mill never to have repudiated his intellectual patrimony. This can perhaps best be shown by examining some of the better-known instances of Mill's apparent divergence from Benthamism. It will be found, I think, that as much as he recognized weaknesses in the utilitarian system and as much as he was attracted to thinkers outside of it, Mill never repudiated Bentham's root principles—those that I have indicated as held unquestionably by his father as well—and in only one of the five instances I wish to examine did he take a position inconsistent with them.

One may begin by briefly looking first at two instances often cited as evidence of Mill's abandonment of the utilitarian motives of thought—instances that are not, however, generally regarded as reflecting any assimilation of transcendentalism. One is his divergence, to which he specifically calls attention, from the system of political economy adopted by the utilitarian school, a divergence he describes as in its "general tone" a product of Harriet Taylor's influence. This "tone" consisted chiefly in making the distinction between "the laws of the Production of Wealth, which are the real laws of nature, dependent on the properties of objects, and the modes of its Distribution, which, subject to certain conditions, depend on human will."[1] Mill is understating his divergence from the whole previous line of economic thought which his father had summed up in *Elements of Political Economy*, for the consequence of presuming the modes of distribution immutable had been the production of a great many of the injustices that were (properly enough) charged to the economic precepts of the utilitarians.[2] Carlyle had been quite correct when he began *Past and Present* with a vision of the riches of England lying under an enchantment that forbade their wise or humane distribution, and cried in the chapter entitled "Gospel of Mammonism": "'Impossible': of a certain two-legged animal with feathers it is said, if you draw a distinct chalk-circle round him he sits imprisoned, as if girt with the iron

[1] J. S. Mill, *Autobiography*, p. 160.

[2] This was the really important error, not the blind espousal of laissez-faire doctrine commonly attributed to them. See J. E. Cairnes, *The Character and Logical Method of Political Economy*, and Lionel C. Robbins, *The Theory of Economic Policy in English Classical Political Economy*, for the numerous departures from laissez-faire in both Adam Smith and his utilitarian disciples.

ring of Fate. . . ."[3] That "chalk-circle," that enchantment, was of course the belief in the immutability of the modes of distribution. Having once denied this immutability, the door was at least opened for the modifications of classical laissez-faire rigidity which appeared in the revised editions of J. S. Mill's *Political Economy*. Such an overturning of the received doctrine of the Benthamites, though spectacularly far-reaching in its effects, did not however depend on a similarly radical overturning of philosophical principles basic to utilitarianism. It denied neither the metaphysical principle of empiricism, nor the prime empirical generalization of man's being governed by pleasure and pain, nor the faith in logical analysis. The economic system adopted by the utilitarians was not a direct deduction from Bentham's principle of utility, though it was compatible with their other basic assumptions since it depended on generalizations from experience and the deduction of consequences. Mill simply perceived that some of the generalizations were in fact fallacious.

Indeed, in the argument of such chapters as the last in Book Four, "On the Probable Futurity of the Labouring Classes," Mill's centrally utilitarian principles are not only unambiguously expressed but developed by contrast with both conservative political positions and with conclusions derived ultimately from transcendental premises. Specifically, he denies "the theory of dependence and protection" which supposes it the duty of the higher classes to think for the poor, "and to take the responsibility of their lot, as the commander and officers of an army take that of the soldiers composing it. . . . Their morality and religion should be provided for them by their superiors, who should see them properly taught it, and should do all that is necessary to ensure their being, in return for their labour and attachment, properly fed, clothed, housed, spiritually edified, and innocently amused." The fact is, says Mill—and

[3]Carlyle, *Complete Works*, XII, 146.

one hears the voice of his father distinctly—"All privileged and powerful classes, as such, have used their power in the interest of their own selfishness"; therefore it is well that "the poor have come out of leading-strings, and cannot any longer be governed or treated like children. To their own qualities must now be commended the care of their destiny."[4]

Similarly, Mill's major modification in the theory of government set forth by his father and godfather is, however influential his presentations of it have been, essentially a correction of their line of reasoning, not a rejection of the principles from which that line of reasoning is suspended. The same argument that drove Bentham and James Mill to defend men against the tyranny of a minority led Mill to defend them against the tyranny of a majority. James Mill's essays on Government and Freedom of the Press and his son's "On Liberty" equally assume a total empiricism and the principle of utility. The son simply sees that his father's logic had been faulty to the extent that it led him to regard democracy as the government of each by each or all by all; it also meant the government of each man by all men.

Mill's empiricism is the basis of his belief that truth is a product of the collision of opinions and that therefore provision must be made for making such collision not only possible but profitable. His belief that there is no other standard of moral judgment than utility, that society should be structured for no other end than the greatest happiness of the greatest number, led him to emphasize the necessity of allowing men to find happiness as far as possible in their own way. Both themes are sounded in the

[4]J. S. Mill, *Principles of Political Economy*, pp. 753–54, 755, 757. To those interested in the more technical aspects of Mill's economic theory may be recommended Samuel Hollander's "Benthamism, J. S. Mill, and the Neo-Classical Change," which argues that Mill kept much more of the Ricardian doctrines than is generally assumed, in *James and John Stuart Mill: Papers of the Centenary Conference*, ed. J. M. Robson and M. Laine.

essay on Bentham, argued from first principles in "On Liberty," and made to determine forms of government in *Considerations on Representative Government.* Bentham's basic postulates will be found intact at the basis of all three. Just as James Mill found errors in both emphasis and logic in Bentham's arguments, his son found similar errors in both men's thought, and in that of others of the utilitarian party of the previous generation.

More significant are three instances often cited as examples of J. S. Mill's accommodation with or adoption of views identified with transcendental metaphysics. One may look first at the instance of actual apostasy: Mill's well-known introduction of qualitative distinctions into the evaluation of pleasures as formulated in the series of essays in *Fraser's Magazine* which were republished under the title *Utilitarianism* (1863). Bentham had said that "to a person considered *by himself*, the value of a pleasure or pain considered *by itself*, will be greater or less" according to four circumstances: intensity, duration, certainty or uncertainty, and propinquity or remoteness, and in relation to other pleasures or pains, its fecundity (chance of being followed by sensations of the same kind) and its purity (chance of not being followed by sensations of the opposite kind).[5] Now all of these properties are, strictly speaking, capable of being described and calculated quantitatively, and necessarily so within Bentham's system, since the sole standard of value in judging experience is the amount ("lot" is Bentham's word) of pleasure or pain produced. To judge the quality of a pleasure would obviously require the imposition of a standard of value other than and superior to the only one Bentham recognizes. But the charge that the principle of utility justified low, mean, or degrading pleasures had obviously troubled Mill long before he published these essays defending utilitarianism; he had tried to add an additional dimension to Bentham's system of

[5] *The Works of Jeremy Bentham*, I, 16.

evaluating pleasures and pains in his essay on Bentham twenty years earlier. There he found it a defect that Bentham never recognized "the desire of perfection" or "the pursuit of any other ideal and for its own sake." But though Mill was trying in the essays on Bentham and Coleridge to say as much as possible for Coleridge while pointing out Bentham's deficiencies, even here whenever it was clear to Mill that to follow Coleridge he must reject the basic assumptions of Bentham, he drew back. The qualitative evaluation of pleasure that Mill introduces in the later *Utilitarianism* is at once more modest and more precise than the earlier attempt to get beyond what Mill saw as Bentham's defects; what Mill vaguely but grandly referred to as "the desire for spiritual perfection" in the earlier essay now becomes "nobler feelings" and "higher feelings." But the fact is that neither formulation will serve.

Ringing as is the statement that "it is . . . better to be Socrates dissatisfied than a fool satisfied," it has long been clear that Mill was introducing a palpable inconsistency. It is simply not true that it is "compatible with the principle of utility to recognize the fact, that some *kinds* of pleasure are more desirable than others." Alexander Bain argued that the proper way of meeting the objection would have been "to have resolved all the so-called nobler or higher pleasures into the one single circumstance on including, with the agent's pleasure, the pleasure of others."[6] Another possibility would have been to give much greater emphasis to the importance of the characteristics "fecundity" and "purity"—that is to identify the higher pleasures with those which lead to other pleasures, or repetition of the same pleasure, and not eventually to pain. Bentham himself had argued that one of the values of "intellectual instruction" was to teach men to avoid pleasures that were ultimately not satisfying: "it is necessary to render men duly sensible of the value, and to engage them in the steady pursuit of

[6] Bain, *John Stuart Mill*, p. 117.

those perennial springs of enjoyment which are the more productive the more copiously they are drawn upon, in preference to those which, in proportion as they are drawn upon to excess, yield in the shape of ennui, at the least, if not in still more afflicting shapes, pain and grief instead of the expected pleasure."[7] In any case, Mill's method of attempting to "humanize" Bentham's calculus led to confusion, and Mill must have come to recognize this, for he never again tried to press his modification, nor rest any other portion of his system on it.

The two other instances most often pointed out as examples of Mill's radical divergence from the strict interpretation of the principle of utility are in the areas of aesthetics (specifically poetry) and religion. The rigor of Mill's education, his mental crisis, and the role of Wordsworth's poetry in rescuing him from that crisis are perhaps the best-known facts of Mill's life. The entire sequence is so pat an apology for poetry that it is no wonder that it has been eagerly seized by champions of the power of poetry and the imagination, but a careful reading of the chapter on the crisis in the *Autobiography* and of the subsequent essays on poetry should lead those who make the highest claims for poetry to restrain their jubilation over Mill's conversion. Wordsworth's poems did indeed offer Mill the "culture of the feelings" he had desired; but nowhere does he suggest that they offered any kind of imaginative truth or made possible any grasp of reality not available to the ordinary, logical intellect. Poetry, he finds, is useful as a means of refreshing one's capacity for feeling, particularly where this has been paralyzed by the habit of analysis. It thus has utility: it offers pleasure from a fresh source, one not dependent on the analytical intellect. Moreover, it would appear to reinforce the beneficial associations which, having been inculcated by education in order to produce the "desires and aversions" necessary for the promotion of the

[7] *Works of Jeremy Bentham*, VIII, 9–19.

greatest happiness of the greatest number, are unfortunately to some extent "artificial and casual."[8] It has, thus, a sort of secondary utility in increasing the balance of happiness over pain.

That the values Mill assigns poetry are unexceptionably utilitarian becomes clearer when we turn to the two essays on poetry of 1833, reprinted as "Thoughts on Poetry and its Varieties" in Volume I of *Dissertations and Discussions* (1859). He begins with a bow toward Coleridge and Wordsworth in acknowledging that "the word 'poetry' imports something quite peculiar in its nature, something which may exist in prose as well as in verse," but when, after "attempting to clear up the conception" mankind attaches to poetry by gradually distinguishing it from all other things—following the Socratic method he admires—we arrive at the final definition, we find that poetry is "man's thought tinged by his feelings."[9] This borrowed definition is sharpened by a distinction between poetry and eloquence, poetry being "feeling, confessing itself to itself in moments of solitude, and embodying itself in symbols which are the nearest possible representations of the feeling in the exact shape in which it exists in the poet's mind."[10] But attention to the aptness of the resulting distinction between eloquence as "heard" and poetry as "overheard" should not lead us to overlook the main portion of the definition—"man's thought tinged by his feelings." As Mill states earlier in the essay, in his view, "every truth which a human being can enunciate, every thought, even every outward impression, which can enter into his consciousness, may become poetry when shown through any impassioned medium, when invested with the colouring of joy, or grief, or pity, or affection, or admiration, or reverence, or awe, or even hatred or terror: and, unless so col-

[8] See J. S. Mill's *Autobiography*, p. 89.

[9] J. S. Mill, *Dissertations and Discussions*, I, 63, 64, 70.

[10] *Ibid.*, I, 71.

oured, nothing, be it as interesting as it may, is poetry."[11] The important thing to note is that it is presumed that the truth can be enunciated, the thought entertained before it is transformed into poetry; that is, poetry appears to play no part in helping one to win one's way to the truth or thought, or even to clarify it.[12]

The limits of Mill's definition of poetry can be illustrated by comparison with the poetic theory of a man like Shelley who regards poetry as creative and prophetic in the highest sense. For Shelley, "the functions of the poetical faculty are twofold; by one it creates new materials of knowledge, and power and pleasure; by the other it engenders in the mind a desire to reproduce and arrange them according to a certain rhythm and order which may be called the beautiful and good."[13] The first function which Shelley assigns to the imagination, that of creating new materials of knowledge, power, and pleasure, the result of his distinction between the reason and imagination giving to the latter the ability to grasp "those forms which are common to universal nature and existence itself" so that the poet "participates in the eternal, the infinite, and the one,"[14] Mill could not for a moment accept. (Neither could he have accepted Coleridge's more circumscribed and tentative attempt in the *Biographia Literaria* to give powers of transcendence to the imagination.)

The second portion of Shelley's statement Mill could indeed endorse; in fact, it is the view he himself adopts.

[11] *Ibid.*, I, 70.

[12] J. S. Mill does not here directly maintain his father's associational theory of aesthetics, but "thought tinged with feeling" is perfectly compatible with James Mill's account of poetry as trains of pleasure in themselves. Mill's notes to his father's *Analysis of the Phenomena of the Human Mind* in the edition of 1878 indicate that, with minor exceptions, he endorsed his father's theory of the origin of the Sublime and Beautiful.

[13] *Complete Works of Shelley*, VII, 134.

[14] *Ibid.*, VII, 112.

Shelley argues the direct, practical moral power of poetry in several ways, but certainly a central argument is that the good man is the one able to "imagine intensely and comprehensively; he must put himself in the place of another and of many others; the pains and pleasures of his species must become his own."[15] Mill implies the same function and value of the imagination in a passage in the essay on Bentham; Imagination is "that which enables us, by a voluntary effort, to conceive the present as if it were absent, the imaginary as if it were real, and to clothe it in the feelings which, if it were indeed real, it would bring along with it. . . . [It] is the power by which one human being enters into the mind and circumstances of another."[16] Mill did not of course have to go to Shelley for this argument—he would have come across it, for instance, in his reading of Adam Smith, who stated that the power of the imagination causes us to sympathize with others by allowing us to have a vivid conception of the sensations of others.

Mill's definition of poetry as "man's thought tinged by his feelings" leads directly into and justifies the first assertion of the second portion of Mill's essay. To write poetry is not the privilege of a few who are born poets; all persons who pursue the proper means and who acquire sufficient intellectual culture may write what will be "unquestionable poetry."[17] Mill, as is well known, then makes a distinc-

[15] *Ibid.*, VII, 118. Shelley's phrasing at times directly recalls Addison in the "Pleasures of the Imagination" essays: Poetry "awakens and enlarges the mind itself by rendering it the receptacle of a thousand unapprehended combinations of thought" (*Complete Works of Shelley*, VII, 117). Shelley interprets this enlargement, however, now as cognitive, now as purely in the realm of feeling and sympathy.

[16] J. S. Mill, *Dissertations and Discussions*, I, 354. Mill did not have to step far outside his direct heritage to arrive at this defense of poetry; Adam Smith had stated the power of the imagination to cause us to emphathize with others by allowing us to have a vivid conception of the sensations of others.

[17] Cf. Shelley: "Poetry is not like reasoning, a power to be exerted accord-

tion between the poets of nature whose "emotions are the links of association by which their ideas . . . are connected together" and the poets of culture who are able to invest their thoughts in poetry. In the first, says Mill, "feeling waits upon thought"; in the other, "thought [waits] upon feeling."[18] But though he values the "poets of nature" highly, it turns out that to attain the highest rank, the poet of nature must cultivate philosophical reason. "Because at one time the mind may be so given up to a state of feeling, that the succession of its ideas is determined by the present enjoyment or suffering which pervades it, this is no reason but that in the calm retirement of study, when under no peculiar excitement either of the outward or of the inward sense, it may form any combinations, or pursue any train of ideas, which are most conducive to the purposes of philosophic inquiry; and may, while in that state, form deliberate convictions, from which no excitement will afterwards make it swerve."[19] The philosopher-poet is clearly superior to the "mere poet," whether the latter be a poet by nature or cultivation; all of which supports the thrust of the first part of the essay: poetry is not a form of thinking, not a form of seeking the truth, but a nevertheless useful tinging of thought with feeling. Mill might value poetry much more highly than Bentham, but the reasons he values it would hardly have disconcerted Bentham. As a source of pleasure, poetry may be no better than pushpin, but both pleasures are permissible, and those who find particular pleasure in poetry would, one supposes, be perfectly welcome to it, so long as Mill's injunction that it not be allowed to confuse strictly intellectual processes be obeyed. Moreover, Bentham smiled benignly on whatever

---

ing to the determination of the will. A man cannot say, 'I will compose poetry'" (*Complete Works of Shelley*, VII, 135).

[18] J. S. Mill, *Dissertations and Discussions*, I, 83.

[19] *Ibid.*, I, 92.

aided the process of establishing and maintaining the proper mental associations, and insofar as it could be shown to do this, poetry could find a place in the utilitarian system.

Mill's final divergence, the most shocking to the orthodox disciples of the Benthamic succession, was his argument, in the posthumously published essay "Theism," that the probability of a Creator can be asserted, and that, if his power is assumed to be limited, the Creator can be regarded as benevolent in his intentions. Now a good bit has been written about the extent to which this essay reverses the conclusions of the two others which, although written before "Theism," were published posthumously along with it. Close reading of the three will show that the contrast is not so great as it may seem. Twice in the conduct of the argument of "Theism," Mill refers to the central argument of his "Essay on Nature"[20] in support or extension of certain important points. It would seem that he continued to regard the earlier essay as sound, believed it compatible with "Theism," and intended either to publish it or incorporate it more fully into the later essay.[21] And indeed, in "Theism," Mill is simply affirming and developing a position already advanced in the "Essay on Nature." Mill's argument in the "Essay on Nature" that Nature cannot be regarded as a model of the good or the just leads to the point that the only explanation for the obvious evils of the world possible to those who believe in a good and benevolent Creator is the Creator's imperfect power. "The only admissible moral theory of Creation is that the Principle of Good *cannot* at once and altogether subdue the powers of evil . . . could not place mankind in a world free from the necessity of an incessant struggle with maleficient powers . . . but could and did make them capable of carrying on

[20] *Three Essays on Religion*, ed. Helen Taylor, pp. 187, 194.

[21] According to Helen Taylor, Mill had intended to publish "Nature" in 1873 (see the Introduction to *Three Essays on Religion*, pp. viii–ix).

the fight with vigour and with progressively increasing success."[22]

Similarly, "Theism" incorporates the argument of the other earlier essay on religion, "The Utility of Religion." In that essay, after dismissing the larger claims of orthodox religion, and most particularly its claim to be the ground of morality, Mill nevertheless concludes that "the value . . . of religion to the individual, both in the past and present, as a source of personal satisfaction and of elevated feelings, is not to be disputed."[23] As in the "Essay on Nature" he again sets forth the belief in a benevolent Creator of limited powers as the "one only form of belief in the supernatural" which "stands wholly clear both of intellectual contradictions and moral obliquity."[24] However, he continues to reject this belief for himself, this time on the specific grounds that it is "too shadowy and insubstantial . . . to admit to its being a permanent substitute for the religion of humanity," but he is willing to state that "the two may be held in conjunction."[25]

Between the composition of the essay on "The Utility of Religion" and "Theism," Mill lost his optimism about the possibilities of inculcating—that is of forming man's mental associations fully enough to make possible—the "Religion of Humanity." Indeed, he had suggested in "The Utility of Religion" that religion, like poetry, could serve powerfully to reinforce the utilitarian associations, and Mill came increasingly to see that the Comtian Religion of Humanity was not only too authoritarian but too weak in its appeal to the imagination. In his essay on Coleridge, Mill had argued that a major error of the eighteenth-century philosophers had been the assumption that the moral fruits

[22] *Three Essays on Religion*, p. 39.

[23] *Ibid.*, p. 104.

[24] *Ibid.*, p. 116.

[25] *Ibid.*, p. 117.

of religious belief could "subsist unimpaired . . . when the whole system of opinions and observances with which they were habitually intertwined was violently torn away,"[26] and he came to recognize the same error in the advocates of a secular religion. But as his hopes for an altogether secular religion dimmed, his recognition of the beneficent effect of what he had already proclaimed the only rational and moral form of religious hope increased in importance until it came to occupy the place it does in "Theism."

In "Theism," after examining in Part I the usual "evidence" offered for a Creator, Mill concludes that the argument from marks of design affords a probability, though no more than a probability, of the creation of the world by intelligence. One may be surprised to find Mill in the company of Paley, but reflection suggests that a secular utilitarian entering the area of religious thought will likely end within hailing distance of Paley's theological utilitarianism. Of course Paley throws into the calculation of the value of both morality and faith a possible eternity in the fires of Hell, while Mill includes in the calculation a mere Hope in a benevolent Deity and the pleasure of imagining that one lives in a world at least partly under the governance of Divine Benevolence.[27] In Part II, he follows the course already marked out in "Nature" as the only logical one compatible with any belief in a Creator, finding that though there is some evidence of such a Creator having desired the happiness of his creatures, He cannot both have desired their perfect happiness and have possessed omnipotence. Part III rejects all arguments about the immortality of the soul—no inferences about the matter can be drawn from anything we know. Part IV denies the authority of Revelation. The result to this point is that "the whole do-

[26] J. S. Mill, *Dissertations and Discussions*, I, 414.

[27] For further exploration of the relationship between Mill's thought and Paley's, see chapter XII of *An Examination of Sir William Hamilton's Philosophy*, in *Collected Works of John Stuart Mill*, IX, espec. p. 192.

main of the supernatural is thus removed from the region of Belief into that of simple Hope." The question remaining for Part V, then, is "whether the indulgence of hope, in a region of imagination merely, in which there is no prospect that any probable grounds of expectation will ever be obtained, is irrational, and ought to be discouraged as a departure from the rational principle of regulating our feelings as well as opinions strictly by evidence."[28] Actually, Mill's question is of the utility of indulging such a hope, and the argument supporting his answer that such hope does have utility is the same he offered in "The Utility of Religion."

When finally Mill brought together his analyses of various questions connected with belief in a deity, positions that he had already recognized as ones that could be held without dishonoring the intellect or upsetting the delicate calculations of utility were found not only compatible but mutually illuminating. The feeling that one is "a fellow-labourer with the Highest, a fellow-combatant in the great strife,"[29] as it is phrased in "The Utility of Religion," is presented as not only reconcilable with but a valuable reinforcement of the Religion of Humanity. Mill's final comment on the hope that there exists a benevolent though not omnipotent creator is "to the other inducements for cultivating a religious devotion to the welfare of our fellow-creatures as an obligatory limit to every selfish aim, and an end for the direct promotion of which no sacrifice can be too great, it superadds the feeling that in making this the rule of our life, we may be co-operating with the unseen Being to whom we owe all that is enjoyable in life."[30] Thus, the arguments of "Nature" and "The Utility of Religion" come together in "Theism."

It is no wonder that those of generally Benthamite per-

[28] J. S. Mill, *Three Essays on Religion*, p. 244.

[29] *Ibid.*, p. 117.

[30] *Ibid.*, p. 256.

suasion who had gone on to give allegiance to Positivism felt betrayed, but there is nothing traitorous or even inconsistent in Mill's altered stance. In fact, as in the case of the essay on poetry, the conclusions of "Theism" not only remain within the boundaries of those possible on the initial Benthamite premises but find part of their force in offering a way to reinforce the system of association on which those of the Benthamite party so heavily relied. Karl W. Britton has recently summarized the conclusions at which Mill arrives in a way that makes clear that the Hope in the existence of a benevolent God, which Mill authorizes, is a kind of superadded and inessential pleasure. "Since in every case the evidence is indecisive, we cannot go wrong in suspending judgment—although to hope is profitable." But, "such a view is tenable only if it is clear that the kind of life we are to live now in no way depends upon whether there is a God or not, a last judgment, another life."[31]

There is indeed a vast difference in tone and direction of argument between Bentham and Grote's *Influence of Natural Religion* and Mill's "Theism." The difference, however, is largely one of intention. Bentham, finding the beliefs and practices recommended by religion to be very heavily in opposition to the principle of utility, set out to develop that contrast in such a way as to show the absurdity of religious belief and the perniciousness of its influence. Bentham and Grote's purpose is polemic. Accordingly, their greatest emphasis is on the evil results of the belief in a future state in which an omnipotent Deity will distribute rewards and punishments. One notes that though they do not explain why belief in an "almighty Being" is necessarily coupled to a belief in a future state, they never consider the influence of a belief in such a Being which is not united with a belief in the future state. Bentham and Grote convincingly trace the sources of the

[31] Britton, "John Stuart Mill on Christianity," in *James and John Stuart Mill: Papers of the Centenary Conference*, p. 34.

usual attitudes toward a Deity and the meretricious effect of such beliefs on human happiness. The younger Mill is interested in the validity of the evidence for the existence of a Deity, a Creator, and in the possible utility of belief in such a Creator, apart from all the doctrines that are normal accretions. His aim is not to demonstrate the source and influence of the usual doctrines but to establish to what conclusions a thoughtful, honest man, trained in the Benthamite tradition of scrupulous analysis, will come. Belief in a future state is not one of these conclusions—immortality can be neither affirmed nor denied—and in any case, there is no reason to expect that a future state of existence would be much different from the present. There is no warrant for belief that one must dwell either in golden streets or everlasting fire. Once that concomitant of religious belief is dismissed, many of the evils that Bentham found intertwined with such belief disappear. There is of course one other essential difference—Mill's analysis leads him, as emphasized above, to insist that if there is a benevolent Creator, his power must be limited. Bentham was concerned to attack orthodox religion, one of the tenets of which is, of course, the omnipotence of the Deity. "Beauchamp" does, however, go out of his way in a note to attack precisely the view to which J. S. Mill arrived. "Plato tells us that the Deity is perfectly and systematically well intentioned, but that he was prevented from realizing these designs, by the inherent badness and intractable qualities of matter."[32] This he finds ridiculous—why not argue that the Deity was wholly malevolent but prevented from making things as bad as he wished by the inherent goodness of matter? However, on Bentham's own principle that super-experimental possibilities must nevertheless be judged by analogy with experience, this argument fails. Our experience is of human creators working against the limits imposed by recalcitrant material. The note is essentially a de-

[32]"Beauchamp," *Influence of Natural Religion*, p. 19.

bater's point—the pseudonymous and cunningly contrived argument of the *Influence of Natural Religion* is less rigorous and complete in analysis than Bentham's usual writings.

In the *Autobiography*, Mill describes his constant concern that his system of thought remain consistent, speaking of constantly "weaving anew" the fabric of his thought. "When I had taken in any new idea, I could not rest till I had adjusted its relation to my old opinions, and ascertained exactly how far its effect ought to extend in modifying or superseding them."[33] Mill undoubtedly never completed his reweaving, but the uncertainty and relative brevity of life are such that a man who is constantly rethinking and adjusting can hardly be expected at the moment of death to leave a totally comprehensive web of thought just completed on the loom. Nevertheless, Mill came closer to doing so than most men, and he who will work his way through *An Examination of Sir William Hamilton's Philosophy* (1865)—where Mill enters most deeply into metaphysical problems—or his extensive annotations to the 1869 edition of his father's *Analysis of the Phenomena of the Human Mind*, will find his empiricism unimpaired. The fact is that, stale as the debate with the now-forgotten thought of Hamilton may be, the *Examination* is fascinating in its revelation of the combined tenacity and dubiousness of Mill's empiricism. Oppose Hamilton he must—neither Reid nor Kant will mix with utilitarian empiricism—and the combination of the two in Hamilton must be challenged. But now that he is forced to enter the metaphysical realm directly, we find him driven to treat the question of the relation between the mind and external objects which had plagued all descendants of Locke by resolving matter into "Permanent Possibilities of sensation" and mind into "Permanent Possibilities of feeling." Mill then must admit that the question of how a mind described

[33] J. S. Mill, *Autobiography*, p. 101.

as a series of feelings can be aware of itself as having those feelings and aware of a past and future can only be answered as the "final inexplicability."[34] The arguments of Chapters 11 and 12 of the *Examination* are perhaps the weakest passages in Mill.

But Mill neither here nor elsewhere abandons a strict empiricism, nor did he ever discard the basic Benthamite principles and methods which form the warp and frame of his thought. Indeed, not only is J. S. Mill surprisingly consistent, but for all his criticism of Bentham, he hewed closer to the Benthamic lines of argument than his father. Like Bentham, he accepts the associationist theory without erecting it into the major principle of thought, and, like Bentham, he is able to see the world as a vast arena of competition and pursuit of personal ends without coming to think of human endeavor as the result of a struggle between insatiable human desire and cosmic niggardliness.[35]

But the differences in emphasis between the three major spokesmen for English utilitarianism are much less important than their essential agreement. Bentham's system was extended, interpreted, and filled in by James Mill, and the work of both extended, interpreted, and reinforced by John Stuart Mill with a consistency almost unparalleled in the history of relationships between master and disciples. The result is a carefully articulated body of thought the completeness of which, both in its foundation and its ramifications, added enormously to its impressiveness.

Coleridge had argued against the utilitarian position on the ground that though a man "should begin by calculating the consequences with regard to others, yet by the mere habit of never contemplating an action in its proportions and immediate relations to his moral being, it is

[34] J. S. Mill, *Sir William Hamilton's Philosophy*, in *Collected Works*, IX, 194.

[35] Bentham cheerfully points out that if man were not, in the first instance, self-regarding, he would soon cease to exist.

scarcely possible but that he must end in selfishness."[36] By espousing prudential calculation over immutable moral principle, argued Coleridge, man warps himself into selfishness. Bentham and J. S. Mill both began at the other end of the argument and attempted to turn a seemingly damning postulate about human nature into a hopeful foundation. Since all men are selfish, they said, and since all calculate consequences, it is possible to train them to regard larger consequences, calculate more accurately, and see ultimately that they cannot calculate their own happiness without considering that of the whole society. The two arguments meet head on, and though J. S. Mill was perhaps more aware of the insights of the "German-Coleridgean" point of view than any other of his philosophical party, he was never able to reconcile the two.

ONE DOES NOT ordinarily think of Matthew Arnold as a transcendentalist, and he himself both denied an interest in metaphysics of any sort and devoted years of his life to trying to disassociate the supernatural *Aberglaube* from what he regarded as the experientially supportable moral center of religion. But there is no doubt that his father was strongly influenced by Coleridge—Basil Willey speaks of Thomas Arnold's having translated the "Ideas" from *The Constitution of Church and State* into his own program of action—and few have doubted the power of the Headmaster of Rugby to transmit his beliefs to those around him.[37] Matthew Arnold at least inherited both an anti-empiricist and anti-mystical bent; the result was a lifelong endeavor to remodel an essentially transcendental way of thought so as to deny the sufficiency of empiricism

[36] Coleridge, *Complete Works*, II, 140.

[37] Willey, *Nineteenth Century Studies*, p. 53.

without affirming the existence of a *noumenal* or transcendent realm.

A number of critics have seen that much of the difficulty Arnold experienced in working out his own belief was a result of the residual attraction of an essentially transcendental mode of thought.[38] Moreover, a transcendental bias was indeed clear enough to some of the contemporary empiricists with whom he broke lances. Frederic Harrison's witty attack on Arnold's thought in "Culture, A Dialogue" several times reminds us of Arnold's Platonic and "transcendental" affinities while at the same time satirizing the affectation of metaphysical innocence. Harrison makes his Arminius ask of Arnold's "great doctrines": "Are they, as one may say, *a priori* or *a posteriori*, metaphysical or positive, experimental or intuitional?" The reply: "My dear Arminius . . . so also ask the Sadducees and the publicans. What, again, I say, has culture to do with all these finalities, rigidities, inadequacies, and immaturities? Where be their quiddits, and their quillits, now? Do you ask of culture what are its principles and ideas? The *best* principles, the *best* ideas, the *best* knowledge: the perfect! the ideal! the complete!"[39] Fitzjames Stephen's *Saturday Review* article accuses Arnold of transcendentalism; Arnold's answer in "My Countrymen" is a denial of an interest in metaphysics, not a repudiation of the assumptions Stephen attributes to him.[40] Actually, though he could not finally accept either the specific forms transcendentalism took in Coleridge or Carlyle nor the general premises on which a transcendentalist structure could be raised, on the majority of

[38] See William Robbins's *The Ethical Idealism of Matthew Arnold*, p. 113: "He should have recognized more explicitly his leaning toward idealism, permanence, and unity as against materialism, flux, and multiplicity, a leaning apparent in his early desire for 'an Idea of the world, in order not to be prevailed over by the world's multitudinousness.'"

[39] Harrison, *The Choice of Books*, p. 109. This appeared originally in the *Fortnightly Review* (Nov. 1867).

[40] Stephens, "Mr. Arnold and His Countrymen," *Saturday Review*, XVIII (3 December 1864) 684; Arnold, *Complete Prose Works*, V, 3*ff.*

issues he will be found taking the side to which such premises naturally lead.

William Robbins's *The Ethical Idealism of Matthew Arnold* presents a carefully documented interpretation of Arnold as an "ethical idealist"—one who interprets the nature of God on the basis of man's moral experience and holds that moral truths are verifiable in man's experience. William Madden's *Matthew Arnold: A Study of the Aesthetic Temperament in Victorian England* equally carefully documents an interpretation of Arnold as one who came to look upon the creative, disinterested aesthetic response as the highest form of ethical life. Both approaches helpfully illuminate Arnold's thought and have roughly equal validity. There is no real quarrel between them; each is simply emphasizing one aspect of Arnold's total thought in which, in transcendental fashion (though with certain qualifications), the good, the true, and the beautiful become identical.

Arnold never states his major premises and never attempts to present his major conclusions as part of a total system. Where one should begin in attempting to trace out the general tendencies of that system is therefore rather a matter of choice, but the preoccupation with conduct is as good a place as any. No one has ever denied that Arnold gave enormous importance to conduct; the fact is, however, that too much effort has been devoted to asking whether conduct is really three fourths of life and whether Arnold himself really thought it was. More important questions are (1) what *is* proper conduct for Arnold, and (2) why is conduct so important; specifically, *what happens* if we conduct ourselves *im*properly?

The answer to the first is not easy, once one comes to think about it. Robbins cites as the two important Christian principles at the center of Arnold's ethical thought "the brotherhood of man" and "chastity, or pureness."[41] The first is unexceptionable, inclusive, and notoriously hard to

[41] W. Robbins, *The Ethical Idealism of Matthew Arnold*, p. 132.

translate into a principle bearing on specific problems of politics, economics, or education. The second, Robbins amplifies into the belief that inward pureness is the necessary ground of morality. In any case, though Arnold will indicate defects in the Judeo-Christian tradition, he is clearly leaning heavily on the orthodox moral teachings of that tradition. As William Madden points out, his morality has, at least as its base, a great concern with overcoming the specifically animal instincts that the Judeo-Christian tradition is so much concerned with eradicating. Arnold could hardly have relied on his readers to interpret his use of the term "conduct" correctly had he not been looking to a shared religious tradition. He does, however, in many places indicate that right conduct is not simply a matter of following rules. There is not only a lower animal self to subdue, but a higher, truer self to which to rise. There is a kind of self that one should be. Presumably, the Hellenic element—informed, disinterested thought—as well as the Judaic element—obedience to prohibitions—is necessary to reach this goal. Therefore, other elements of culture must be added to Christianity, but what specifically constitutes the best that has been known and thought can be shown only by citing examples. How one knows whether a particular act violates the brotherhood of man, or one's own purity, or the best that is known and thought remains unclear.

Why should one conduct oneself in accordance with the moral principles—whatever they are? One answer is that obedience to moral law brings joy and happiness. The proof? Try it and see, says Arnold. Obedience to moral law, to conscience, to one's best self will bring joy; disobedience will bring sorrow. Thus does Arnold dispose of metaphysics, of theology; experience is to be the test. But Arnold is not really willing to ground morality on experience. He must have seen that it is very difficult to keep the proposition that moral action leads to happiness from converting itself into the proposition that happiness is the guarantee that our action is moral. (The utilitarians were in fact happy to accept both propositions.) If Arnold were to accept the latter formulation, the first problem we are considering would be solved—conduct would be those actions that give joy and happiness. But the Carlylean sundering of duty and happiness dominates his thought. For Arnold, happiness cannot be the ultimate principle but the result of action in accordance with a higher principle. (Here and in Arnold's sense of the self-evidence and attractiveness of the cultural best, we are reminded of Henry More's "boniform" faculty by which "we relish or savour what is absolutely best and rejoice in it alone.") That higher principle is the "not ourselves" which makes for righteousness. Morality does not simply find certain rules in orthodox religion, it is religion; that is, "morality touched by emotion" is religion.[42]

The importance of "emotion" in this formula is enormous: it is the most effective motive force behind the moral rules. That something more than a knowledge of right conduct is needed Arnold recognizes as fully as the utilitarians recognize the need for something more than the ability to calculate abstractly which of two or more possible acts would produce the greatest happiness for the greatest number. The right system of association is the necessary key, say the utilitarians. Added emotion is the key, says Arnold. The addition of the right emotion quickens morality and increases its power over our actions.

The difficulty of obeying the moral law is presented in another way in Arnold's doctrine of the two selves. Robbins, who emphasizes the importance of this doctrine for Arnold, cites the following passage as "the clearest statement of this central doctrine":

> It will be generally admitted . . . that all experience as to conduct brings us at last to the fact of two selves, or instincts, or forces,—name them how we will, and however we may sup-

[42] Arnold, *Complete Prose Works*, VI, 176.

> pose them to have arisen,—contending for the mastery in man: one, a movement of first impulse and more involuntary, leading us to gratify any inclination that may solicit us, and called generally a movement of man's ordinary or passing self, of sense, appetite, desire; the other, a movement of reflection and more voluntary, leading us to submit inclination to some rule, and called generally a movement of man's higher or enduring self, of reason, spirit, will.[43]

What is expressed here as the higher self is of course the best self, the buried self, the true self which reappears throughout Arnold's poetry and prose.[44] Presumably, both morality and religion address themselves to this higher self, but the difficulty of penetrating through the superficial self and its constant distractions to the true self is great indeed; morality needs to draw all the power of the emotions that transform it into religion if it is to reach so deeply.

Arnold meets the obvious challenge of differentiating between instances of morality and religion by comparing moral and religious aphorisms—a procedure strongly reminiscent of Coleridge.

> "Hold off from sensuality," says Cicero; "for, if you have given yourself up to it, you will find yourself unable to think of anything else." That is morality. "Blessed are the pure in heart," says Jesus Christ; "for they shall see God." That is religion. "We all want to live honestly, but cannot," says the Greek maxim-maker. That is morality. "O wretched man that I am, who shall deliver me from the body of this death!" says St. Paul. That is religion.[45]

The easy retort is obvious. The difference, the skeptic is tempted to say, is that one sentence refers to ordinary human experience, the other to specifically religious ideas:

[43] *Ibid.*, VIII, 154.

[44] See W. Robbins's discussion, *Ethical Idealism*, p. 165.

[45] Arnold, *Complete Prose Works*, VI, 177*ff*.

God, eternal life, etc. Religion has reference to God, morality to man—Arnold has indeed brought forth a mouse. Arnold's own answer would be, of course, that the reference to God is simply a sign that the emotion has attached itself to an otherwise merely moral maxim. Or, in other words, when we couch our moral feeling in words that suggest more than logical language can, we are exhibiting, through poetry, the extra dimension of emotion that converts morality to religion. Poetry, then, becomes the sign of essential difference. St. Paul's "O wretched man that I am, who shall deliver me from the body of this death!" is religion, says Arnold. Why? The answer, though Arnold does not himself offer it, is that "death" is here used metaphorically to call forth ideas of powers and sanctions and rewards beyond those that can be known and manipulated in man's experience. It is not literal death from which St. Paul wishes to be delivered, but a life so wretched that it has the qualities man's imagination associates with actual, physical death. An even better example is the following. Arnold tells us that we may observe a third stage between these two stages, which shows us the transition from one to the other.

> "If thou givest thy soul the desires that please her, she will make thee a laughing stock to thine enemies;"—that is morality. "He that resisteth pleasures crowneth his life;"—that is morality with the tone heightened, passing, or trying to pass, into religion. "Flesh and blood cannot inherit the kingdom of God;"—there the passage is made, and we have religion.[46]

In the first example, nothing evokes a sense of powers beyond man's ken. In the second, the key word is "crowned": for the ordinary man to be kinglike, for him to receive a reward for which the word "crowned" is appropriate, suggests powers and sanctions beyond human experience. (This is reinforced by the associations between "crowned"

[46] *Ibid.*, VI, 178.

and all the terms that have been used in a similar poetic fashion so consistently that they automatically call up extra-experiential powers: "King of kings," "Lord's anointed," "crown of thorns.") In the third, the Christian's response to the kingdom of God is so immediate that he is unlikely to recall that "Kingdom" is here used metaphorically for an idea that we really can express in no other way than through such figures of speech.

The point is that religion would seem to be expressible only through poetry, which suggests more than human power, goodness, and reward. The emotion that lights up morality into religion would then seem to be the emotion evoked by the sense of "the eternal not ourselves." Arnold's "catechism" in "A Comment on Christmas"[47] is usually read as an effort to translate Christian doctrine into empirical and moral terms—it is at least as accurate to recognize that Arnold is translating empirically based morality into terms that add the proper emotions to it.

Now there are many empirical elements in Arnold's thought, some conscious, some apparently not. His assurance that the importance of conduct is to be discovered in experience is the most obvious example of a conscious appeal to empiricism. A very interesting parallel with one of the major, if not logically essential, doctrines of the empiricists, which Arnold probably never recognized, exists between the empiricist's associational prescription for assuring right conduct even when it would seem to be against a

[47] "Therefore, when we are asked: What really is Christmas, and what does it celebrate? we answer: The birthday of Jesus. But what, then, is the miracle of the Incarnation? A homage to the virtue of pureness, and the manifestation of this virtue in Jesus. What is Lent, and the miracle of the temptation? A homage to the virtue of self-control and to the manifestation of this virtue in Jesus. What does Easter celebrate? Jesus victorious over death by dying. By dying how? Dying to re-live. To re-live in Paradise, in another world? No, in this. But if in this, what is the kingdom of God? The ideal society of the future. Then what is immortality? To live in the eternal order, which never dies. What is salvation by Jesus Christ? The attainment of this immortality. Through what means? Through faith in Jesus, and appropriation of his method, secret, and temper." Arnold, *Complete Prose Works*, X, 234.

man's interests and Arnold's prescription for strengthening the moral impulse so that distractions, including tempting pleasures, could be overcome. Here is Arnold's argument:

> So what is meant by the application of emotion to morality has now, it is hoped, been made clear. The next question will probably be: But how does one get the application made? Why, how does one get to feel much about any matter whatever? By dwelling upon it, by staying our thoughts upon it, by having it perpetually in our mind. The very words *mind, memory, remain*, come, probably, all from the same root, from the notion of staying, attending. Possibly even the word *man* comes from the same; so entirely does the idea of humanity, of intelligence, of looking before and after, of raising oneself out of the flux of things, rest upon the idea of steadying oneself, concentrating oneself, making order in the chaos of one's impressions, by attending to one impression rather than another.[48]

There are, in one way, no great differences between that and Mill's argument that the mind must be made to follow the right trains, entertain the proper ideas, make the right associations habitually. The key difference, however, is that Mill presumes that the right associations must be stamped on the mind from without; Arnold seems to assume that one attends to the right impression by the right exercise of the will.

Despite these concessions to empiricism, there remains a strong transcendental bias in Arnold's thought. When he speaks of "those moral conclusions which all races of men, one may say, seem to have reached," there is nothing in the context to indicate that those conclusions were not reached by calculations based on the direct experience each man has through his senses. But Arnold's constant concern for the buried but true self within and the not-ourself without, both of which are guides to a righ-

[48] *Ibid.*, VI, 178–79.

teousness that brings happiness but is not defined by it, are clearly transcendental. The "not-ourselves" that makes for righteousness is also "the stream of tendency by which all things seek to fulfill the law of their being";[49] the buried, true self is that which should and would be fulfilled. Arnold quotes one of the Cambridge Platonists: "And so Henry More was led to say, that 'there was something about us that knew better, often, what we would be at than ourselves.'"[50] The two are in harmony—the ground of that harmony is totally beyond experience. The idea of a buried self alone is essentially incomprehensible to the empiricist. What could James Mill possibly have made of "the unregarded river of our life," which pursued "with indiscernible flow its way," which is the subject of Arnold's "The Buried Life"?

The doctrine of the inward self is intimately connected with Arnold's conception of the reasonableness, method, secret, and temper of Jesus.[51] To acquire these is to know one's buried self, to reform the individual from within. Arnold's impatience with mechanism, with tinkering with the structure of government, arises out of his conviction, shared with transcendentalists in general, that the improvement of mankind depends on the reform of the individual. And of course the belief that the purely intellectual recognition of the need for moral laws is not enough, that to it must be added a sense that human action has meaning beyond all calculation of consequences, is squarely in the transcendental tradition.

Poetry is the means by which we express the morality touched with emotion that is religion. But equally "we may

[49] *Ibid.*, VI, 189.

[50] *Ibid.*, VI, 181.

[51] "Sweet reasonableness" is a key term in *Saint Paul and Protestantism* (1870); "method" and "secret" join "sweet reasonableness" in *Literature and Dogma* (1873); "method," "secret," and "temper" are the central words in *God and the Bible* (1875).

call art and science touched with emotion *religion*, if we will."[52] From this I draw the inference that the expression of the results of art and science, when touched by emotion, requires poetry, a conclusion which throws a certain amount of light on the formula, poetry is the criticism of life. Presumably, then, if the emotion that transforms art and science into religion is the same as that which similarly transforms morality, what poetry adds is the extra-experiential dimension. One great function of poetry then is the expression of such dimensions, and that this is the highest function of poetry for Arnold becomes a very strong suspicion if we remember how many of his "touchstone" passages imply the existence of a super-experiential realm. The very intimate relationship, if not identity, between poetry (the highest form of the beautiful), moral conduct (the good), and the streams of tendency that make for righteousness and are reflected in our best selves (the highest truth) is thus forged.

The link can be seen from other points of view. Arnold argues that poetry should bring joy, righteousness bring joy, experience of our best self bring joy. Or one can note how easily Arnold's definitions of the "kingdom of God" as "the ideal society of the future" and "immortality" as "to live in the eternal order, which never dies" are convertible into the disinterested contemplation that is the aesthetic experience.[53] Or, finally, "to see things in their beauty is to see things in their truth, and Keats knew it"[54] because the beauty, at least of poetry, represents the addition of the emotions associated with the not-ourselves on the one hand and the correlative buried self on the other.

But finally, Arnold avoids claiming that man has received any divine revelation that explicitly defines conduct (how would he receive such from the not-ourselves?).

[52] Arnold, *Complete Prose Works*, VI, 177.

[53] Cf. William Madden, *Matthew Arnold*, p. 165.

[54] Arnold, "John Keats," in *Complete Prose Works*, IX, 213.

What he can do is try to discern the direction in which the power not ourselves that makes for righteousness is indeed tending, an attempt not unlike that which Carlyle imposes on man. This can be accomplished partly by striving to penetrate to one's own best self but also by profiting from the race's collective best self—that is, by looking to culture.[55] (The first method Carlyle could understand, but not the second, unless we translate culture as well as history into the lengthened shadows of great men.)

Of course the relationship between culture and conduct may be demonstrated by a less circuitous route. But, as I indicated in beginning this analysis, one can choose any number of points of entry into the Arnoldian system of thought. If one begins by trying to understand "culture," "criticism," "poetry," or the "method," "secret," and the "temper" of Jesus, instead of "conduct," one's emphases will be different, but the total system of interrelationships will be found, I think, pretty much the same. Despite the fact that Arnold refuses to affirm transcendental premises, or, as Robbins points out, to admit that his Eternal Force is created by an act of faith,[56] his orientation toward that mode of thought creates for him the same problems faced in communication by all who do not make logic and sense experience their base. But Arnold, unlike Coleridge and Carlyle, is not anxious lest his readers fail to grasp the total system. Though he develops an interlocking structure as he goes along, he strives to present "criticism," "culture," "conduct," etc., as comprehensive each in itself. Suspicious of metaphysics, Arnold never explicitly advances first principles nor a total scheme that would lay him open to the charge of attempting to be the metaphysician of his iron age. However, his habit of quoting himself, and especially

[55] This, I take it, is what Robbins means when he says that "what Arnold does is to substitute for the philosophical sanction of logical necessity the humanistic sanction of cumulative human experience" (*Ethical Idealism*, p. 102).

[56] W. Robbins, *Ethical Idealism*, p. 79.

of opening essays with quotations from earlier essays, allows him to suggest his own conviction of his consistency. On the other hand, the careful collection of significant quotations from others which he entered in his notebooks and judiciously used as cultural "touchstones" in his essays allows him, whenever his argument requires a firm anchor, to draw on authoritatively phrased thoughts of others instead of abstract first principles.

The relation between Arnold's position and that of a more thorough-going transcendentalism appears clearly in a comparison of Arnold's use of the opposition between culture and "machinery" and Coleridge's use of that between cultivation and civilization. In the second section of the *Treatise on Method*, Coleridge contrasts those who looked up "to that Spirit of Truth, which, after all, we find to be at the head of wisdom" and whose "Ideas were plain and distinct" with those who pursued the opposite method and "determined to shape their convictions and deduce their knowledge from *without*, by exclusive observation of outward things, as the only realities."[57] The latter, says Coleridge, "became rapidly *civilized*" and were able to build cities and manipulate the external world for their pleasure. "They became great masters of the agreeable, which fraternized readily with cruelty and rapacity; these being, indeed, but alternate moods of the same sensual selfishness." "Thus," he continues, "both before and after the Flood, the vicious of Mankind receded from all cultivation, as they hurried towards civilization." Coleridge's "civilization" is of course Arnold's "machinery" (and Carlyle's "Mammonism"); "cultivation" is the pursuit of the good, true, and beautiful. Coleridge, working hard to unite science and philosophy, Bacon and Plato, sees science as the discovery in the mind (and not *originally* in the external world), of Ideas, and thus dissipates the sense of mystery, of ineffability, surrounding attainment to the realm of Ideas, but the tran-

[57] *S. T. Coleridge's Treatise on Method*, pp. 47–48.

scendentalist phrasing breaks in at times: "for there is a gradation of Ideas, as of ranks in a well-ordered State, or of commands in a well-regulated army; and thus above all partial forms, there is one universal form of GOOD and FAIR, the καλοκάγαθον of the Platonic Philosophy."[58] Arnold, unable to find meaning in words like "Idea" or in concepts like that of an Absolute, finds a surrogate in culture; it is to provide the model against which to measure the products of "machinery."

In summary, then, "culture" is Arnold's great substitute for the belief in a transcendent world, a belief which faded as the century went on. When he refers to himself as a transcendentalist—as he does, for instance, in the Preface to *Essays in Criticism*—he is, for all the playfulness of the passage, as accurate as ironic.

Whereas Mill tried to accommodate elements that he felt were missing from utilitarianism without violating its empiricist epistemology and associationist psychology, Arnold seemingly drew together those principles which appeared good to him without regard to their ultimate metaphysical compatibility. It might be said that of the high Victorian prophets, Arnold was most successful in accomplishing that blending of Coleridge and Bentham, of empiricism and transcendentalism, which John Stuart Mill desiderated. From the point of view of everyday discursive thought, Arnold's total structure appears more balanced than either the Coleridgean or Benthamite. However, the "not ourselves that makes for righteousness" and "best self" are terribly vulnerable to rigorous analysis, as indeed is his very concept of culture. At the same time one admiringly recognizes the quiet urbanity with which Arnold would have dipped all such objections into his universal solvent, whether called culture, criticism, sweet reasonableness, or sweetness and light.

[58] *Ibid.*, p. 9.

V

Freedom and Responsibility

N

NEVER FAR from the center of Victorian ethical or political debate was the question of the proper limits of individual freedom and the corollary question of defining responsibility. Obvious examples for comparison are the positions taken on freedom of the press by Coleridge and James Mill, on the total relationship between liberty and culture by J. S. Mill and Arnold, and on the power and authority of political rulers by J. S. Mill and Carlyle.

COLERIDGE found an examination of the "duty of the communication of truth and the conditions under which it may be safely communicated" an appropriate topic to include in the section titled "General Introduction" in the 1818 edition of *The Friend.* Nine essays are devoted to the topic, of which the first two set out the conditions under which a man may conscientiously refrain from conveying the whole truth, the next three apply those conditions to the questions a conscientious individual would consider before publishing what he believes true, and the last four consider the law of libel and the limitations the state may enforce on the press. James Mill's very different analysis of the last of these questions, the limitations on public expression of beliefs, is to be found in the article "Freedom of the Press" contributed to the supplement to the fifth edition of the *Encyclopaedia Britannica.*

Coleridge finds that England is justified in not requiring that a book be licensed prior to printing because this would be both "impracticable and inefficient" but that the question of defining that against which action should be taken after publication is extremely difficult because "in the case of libel, the degree makes the kind, the circumstances constitute the criminality" so that "from the very nature of a libel it is impossible so to define it, but that the most meritorious work will be found included in the description."[1] His major conclusion is that in regard to allegations against the state, enlightened juries must consider the intention of the author and its connection with overt acts, remembering that the possibility of mischief in charges against the state is balanced by the improbability that these will actually lead to mischief. The major conclusion to which James Mill comes is that all censures of the government should, without regard to their truth, be permitted so long as they do not serve as exhortations "to obstruct the operation of the Government in detail" (that is, at a particular place and time).

The extent of the differences between these conclusions is, at first reading, somewhat obscured by a variety of points made along the way, and even when the major points are detached and juxtaposed, the significance of the differences is not clear until one compares the conclusions with the metaphysical assumptions of the two men. These differing metaphysical assumptions lead Mill and Cole-

[1] Coleridge, *Complete Works*, II, 76, 79.

ridge to address themselves to rather different questions. How, asks Coleridge, is the individual to determine whether he can conscientiously publish all that he knows to be truth, and how is the individual juryman conscientiously to determine the degree of good or mischief which the publication of that truth, or untruth, caused? Coleridge builds his series of essays from the problems posed for the individual conscience and leaves the judgment of the most difficult question—the culpability of the man who libels the government—to the enlightenment of the conscience of the jury. "The understanding and conscience of the Jury are the Judges, *in toto*: the law a blank *congé d'elire*. The law is the clay, and those the Potter's wheel."[2] Mill, finding no innate principles in the individual mind to which he can appeal either for a conscientious judgment or the determination of whether a published statement is true or false, builds from the question of the proper social structure that will enable whatever degree of truth man can attain to best survive. He thus prescribes the principles of the laws, not the principles by which the judge and jury are to evaluate the individual act. He could never have agreed with Coleridge that the jury are "to consider the law as a blank power for the punishment of the offender, not as a light by which they are to determine and discriminate the offence."

Although he admits that the law cannot regard intention only, Coleridge dwells heavily on the judgment of intention, presuming that the morality of a man's purpose can be judged against unquestioned moral principles. Mill sets up his principles solely on the question of general consequences, asking which principles will produce the greatest preponderance of pleasure over pain. Coleridge's praise for the advances of England and his distaste for the heretical, deistical, and anti-Christian as expressed in the course of his argument are based on unquestioned values; he never considers the difficulty of establishing the truth

[2] *Ibid.*, II, 89.

or falsity of what is published. Mill bases a great part of his argument on the value of difference of opinion in an uncertain world; truth is a product of trial by battle, and, therefore, challenges to received truth ought never to be prohibited. The choices are thus perfectly consistent with the principles of each side. The disagreement on the most crucial issue—the judgments concerning charges against the government—is similarly a function of the metaphysical principles of each. If there is a model and if the truth can be infallibly known, the question of separating true from false charges is not the central problem, and we must punish the makers of false, and even in some cases true, charges against the government by judging intentions and consequences. If there is no model, and truth is not easily separable from error, the state can prevent itself from falling into the perpetuation of error and injustice only by framing laws that allow almost all censure.

The results of the two positions are ultimately paradoxical. Coleridge might seem to be less rigid and authoritarian in leaving judgment to the consciences of the jury, but in fact by weighing both true and false charges by the intention of their authors and by the individual results, he is much more severely limiting freedom of publication than Mill, and by allowing the jury to determine by their consciences (a faculty not here defined but which is ultimately based, as *Aids to Reflection* makes clear, on intuition and revelation), he is erecting a much more fragile bulwark against arbitrary condemnation of minority opinion than does Mill.[3] The transcendentalist position thus moves, as we would expect, toward restriction of freedom and the view that certain truths are known so completely that they ought not to be further questioned, while the empiricist

[3] In the immediate situation, Coleridge's desire to give more power to the jury would have served as a curb on a dictatorial government (see John Colmer's *Coleridge: Critic of Society*, pp. 96–97), but one cannot build safely on such historical accidents.

position necessarily demands the greatest possible freedom and right of calling all things into question.

The difference is nicely illustrated by the positions taken by Mill and Coleridge on religious freedom, addressed in the closing paragraphs of each argument. Mill finds that man must have the power of choosing his own religious position because "it is well known with what ease religious opinions can be made to embrace everything upon which the unlimited power of rulers, and the utmost degradation of the people, depend." "But if the people here, too, must choose opinions for themselves, discussion must have its course. . . ."[4] Coleridge, asking whether there should be "the right of punishing by law the authors of heretical or deistical writings," concludes that tolerance is advisable. But his very mode of asking the question reveals certain assumptions: he does not inquire of the rights of the heretic or deist to publish but of the rights of the orthodox to punish. He does not ask about the rights of religious belief in general but cites two classes of belief apparently so odious that whether the orthodox have the right to punish them is hardly questionable. And he concludes his discussion of the freedom of utterance and toleration to be extended in religious matters with an attack on those who question the truth of Christianity.

> In one of those poisonous journals, which deal out profaneness, hate, fury, and sedition through the land, I read the following paragraph. "The Brahmin believes that every man will be saved in his own persuasion, and that all religions are equally pleasing to the God of all. The Christian confines salvation to the believer in his own Vedas and the Shasters. Which is the more humane and philosophic creed of the two?" Let question answer question. Self-complacent scoffer! Whom meanest thou by God? The God of truth?—and can He be

[4] James Mill, *Essays on Government, Jurisprudence, Liberty of the Press and Law of Nations*, p. 34.

pleased with falsehood, and the debasement or utter suspension of the reason which he gave to man that he might receive from him the sacrifice of truth?[5]

The forms as well as the content of the two discussions reflect the basic opposition. Mill begins his article on "Freedom of the Press" by carefully defining the matter to be considered as the violation of rights by the press. The meaning and maintenance of rights, he points out, is to be found stated in his articles on Government and Jurisprudence. He thus is able to build his argument on previously developed positions which ultimately rest on Bentham's basic assumptions. The end of the sciences of Government and Jurisprudence is the establishment and protection of rights. "All rights of course are objects of human desire."[6] The objects of human desire are the sources of human happiness. And the greatest happiness of the greatest number is the goal. Behind the formula "the greatest happiness of the greatest number" lies the empirical principle—all things, including ultimate goals, must be deduced from experience.[7]

Mill's entire discussion of freedom of the press proceeds by implicit and explicit reference to the principles of government and jurisprudence he has established as necessary for the greatest happiness of the greatest number. The advantage of such an interlocking structure is that the writer who subscribes to it can economically develop a limited subject by simply indicating its relation to the rest of the structure. The carefully focused treatment Mill gives to the question of liberty of the press is partially the result of his writing an encyclopedia article; however, Coleridge,

[5] Coleridge, *Complete Works*, II, 94–95.

[6] James Mill, "Jurisprudence," in *Essays*, p. 5.

[7] Bentham's satire on all forms of intuition in support of the basic principle that "Nature has placed mankind under the government of two sovereign masters, *pain* and *pleasure*" at the beginning of *An Introduction to the Principles of Morals and Legislation* is a classic statement of his anti-transcendental faith.

whose discussion of liberty of the press is extremely diffuse, was operating within the similarly limiting demands of the periodical essay form.[8] The fact is that Coleridge cannot determine a starting point for his system and so cannot depend on a system of mutually supporting principles. Each principle must be buttressed and propped as he sets it out. Often enough in fact we see Coleridge erecting a temporary scaffolding around a position against the day he can return and make it self-sufficient. The problem, as we have seen, is not Coleridge's alone—it is the problem of the transcendentalist. One might think the model existing beyond experience that the transcendentalist affirms would provide him with a total system which he could then clearly elucidate. But the transcendental model, by definition, transcends not only the experience but the ordinary categories of thought and processes of logic. Even if one feels for a moment that he has been granted a comprehensive vision, it must prove almost incommunicable. The "General Introduction" to *The Friend* would seem the very place to set down one's basic principles—especially in the third version of that work (1837), by which point the series of essays could be seen as a whole—but Coleridge was evidently unable to do this.

His habit of binding up the loose edges of the argument as he goes along leads Coleridge into the practice of developing a particular idea beyond what was relevant at a given stage of an argument. Thus, the reader of the nine essays in *The Friend* on the communication of truth is treated to digressions on the proper reading matter in the family, the perniciousness of the French Encyclopedists, the greater readiness of man to submit to torture than to think, the follies and beliefs of contemporary fanaticism, the oppressions of Charlemagne and Bonaparte, and similar tangential matters. At one point Coleridge writes: "My

[8]The same contrast in clarity of organization and development exists between James Mill's essay on Education and Coleridge's *Treatise on Method.*

feelings have led me on, and in my illustration I had almost lost from my view the subject to be illustrated."[9] Form itself is not independent of metaphysics.

THAT *Culture and Anarchy* was in some sense an answer to *On Liberty* was pointed out by Lionel Trilling in 1939; since then, a considerable body of commentary on the relationship between Arnold and J. S. Mill has grown up. The fruits of this commentary, together with his own extensive original analysis, are to be found in Edward Alexander's *Matthew Arnold and John Stuart Mill.* Professor Alexander has patiently set forth the areas of agreement between the two men, equally patiently isolated their oppositions, and traced a variety of influences operating on each (the most notable being their respective fathers). He finds the key to the differences that partially mask their similarities in their different responses to the historical process. The book is a perceptive and valuable one, but I should like to supplement it by taking one step further back to the sources of Mill's and Arnold's characteristic arguments. If we look back to the basic assumptions of Arnold and Mill and allow their metaphysical assumptions to throw light on the whole of the arguments of *Culture and Anarchy* and *On Liberty*, we find ourselves looking on at the contest between Mill's empiricism, however enlightened, and Arnold's transcendentalism, however attenuated.

I have attempted to show that, for all his attempt to ameliorate the strictness and somewhat inhuman rigor of the Benthamite system, no more than his father did Mill ever question the basic assumption that there is no source of truth other than the interpretation of experience. For all

[9] Coleridge, *Complete Works*, II, 53.

of Mill's strictures on Bentham and praise of Coleridge, Bentham's premise that man's knowledge comes only from experience is never questioned, while Coleridge's transcendentalism is specifically denied. Even "Utilitarianism," in which the attempt to insist that pleasure may be judged qualitatively as well as quantitatively significantly undercuts Bentham's system, opens with a denial of the *a priori* systems of ethics which assume a nonexperiential sanction. There is no model, no set of revealed laws, no transcendent realm to which man can turn for guidance.

On Liberty, published four years earlier than the essay on "Utilitarianism," deviates from the straight utilitarian road even less; it is essentially a reorganization of leading ideas to be found in James Mill's essays on "Government," "Liberty of the Press," and "Jurisprudence." James Mill, we recall, had arrived at his conclusions by a formal critique of the alternative forms that government, given its end—the greatest happiness of the greatest number—might take. He considers in turn government by pure democracy, by aristocracy, by monarchy, and by a mixture of the three, and finds that government by a representative body provides the only answer. His son, in the opening pages of *On Liberty*, covers the same ground, though here the development of the representative system is historically traced, not formally analyzed (the difference is partly a result of the interpretation of history J. S. Mill derived from the St. Simonians and others).[10]

James Mill goes on to consider the general rules which will insure that representatives represent the interest of the whole people. *On Liberty* proceeds to argue for the general rules that will prevent the majority from tyrannizing a minority, either through their representatives or through direct social pressure. In so doing, it takes the next historical step. Recognizing that "the 'self-govern-

[10] See Mill's *Autobiography*, pp. 105–7. J. S. Mill's approach will generally be found more historical and less formal than his father's.

ment' spoken of is not the government of each by himself, but of each by all the rest,"[11] the son points out the necessity of guarding against the possible tyranny of the majority which the father had overlooked. But he does so primarily by expanding arguments taken from James Mill's "Jurisprudence" and "Liberty of the Press." In the first, James Mill argues that "rights" are created by the individual society and have no existence prior to their creation by society. In the second, he considers what rights the Press—and ultimately all men—should be given by society to say what they think true. *On Liberty* considers what rights should be given to all men to say what they think true and then discusses the right of men to act in accordance with what they believe, developing in regard to the latter question views that were present by implication in James Mill's "Government." J. S. Mill's recognition that if society "issues wrong mandates instead of right, or any mandates at all in things with which it ought not to meddle, it practices a social tyranny more formidable than many kinds of political oppression" grows out of his father's discussion of the "misdirection of the favourable and unfavourable sentiments of mankind" in Section II of "Freedom of the Press."[12] Both father and son are assuming an end—the creation of a society that will make possible the greatest happiness of the greatest number—and are deducing the rules that such a society must observe. Both arrive at their rules by way of the empiricist assumption that the only way truth makes itself known is in emergence from the dust of the jousting-place, showing itself the victor in open contest. Thus the lists may never be closed.

Edward Alexander is clearly correct in pointing out that Mill at times seemed to accept the view that there is finally a body of truth which all men should accept. Mill seems to recognize a growing body of accepted truths even

[11] J. S. Mill, *On Liberty*, p. 6.

[12] *Ibid.*, p. 7, and James Mill, "Freedom of the Press," in *Essays*, p. 11.

in *On Liberty*: "As mankind improve, the number of doctrines which are no longer disputed or doubted will be constantly on the increase: and the well-being of mankind may almost be measured by the number and gravity of the truths which have reached the point of being uncontested."[13] But though Mill believes unanimity will increase, he can invoke no absolute, even as a goal. And though he feels it a duty to argue for what he believes true, he writes as a competitor, confident of the value of his intellectual wares, not as a prophet to whose vision all should immediately bow. Mill is not simply urging that men have open minds but that there is no possibility of comparing any belief, however widely and strongly held, against a transcendent absolute (and Mill would equally deny the authority of the cultural norms that Arnold substituted for the transcendent).

For Arnold, culture is capable of pronouncing authoritatively on many a question. That is why, for all his urbanity, a note of impatience with fools comes into Arnold's voice much more often than into Mill's, and that is why Arnold's use of phrases like "free play of the mind" is somewhat misleading. The mind is to play freely, that is, without prejudice, but if it does so, it will come to certain foreseeable conclusions. It will come to the conclusion that religious establishments are valuable, that the "feudal habits of succession" of the barbarians have endured "out of their due time and place," that there is something indelicate about marriage with one's deceased wife's sister, that economic laws do not in themselves lead the poor to act in conformity with them, and that one is not free to do as one likes in Hyde Park. Mill's dictum that "the only freedom which deserves the name, is that of pursuing our own good in our own way, so long as we do not attempt to deprive others of theirs, or impede their efforts to obtain it,"[14] which necessarily follows from his premises, must equally be re-

[13] J. S. Mill, *On Liberty*, p. 53.

[14] *Ibid.*, pp. 16–17.

jected by Arnold, who finds "an Englishman's right to do what he likes" absurd in all those matters in which culture can clearly pronounce what he should do.

The debate over the value of at least certain kinds of what Arnold would dismiss as mere "machinery" is illuminated by going back to basic premises. If culture can provide a guide as sure as a transcendent model, there is no need for the machinery of the law or of principles of free discussion which so occupied the Mills. "And because machinery is the one concern of our actual politics, and an inward working, and not machinery, is what we most want, we keep advising our ardent young Liberal friends to think less of machinery, to stand more aloof from the arena of politics at present, and rather to try and promote, with us, an inward working."[15] Culture condemns machinery, systems, disciples, and schools not only as imperfect but as obstacles to perfection. But if, as Mill believes, there is no set of peremptory standards to be found in culture or anywhere else, these mechanisms become of immense importance. Early in the second section of *On Liberty*, Mill reminds the reader that Marcus Aurelius, "placed at the summit of all the previous attainments of humanity, with an open, unfettered intellect," failed to see the value of Christianity. The great Roman misjudged its consequences. For all their concern for calculating consequences, for calculating balances of pleasure and pain, Bentham's followers knew well that any particular individual in a particular situation might well err disastrously in his calculations. That is the reason for laws and rules, for machinery, which, conscientiously followed, will minimize the possibility of miscalculation. The "mechanical" invocation of the principles of liberty for which Mill contends would have preserved Marcus Aurelius from an action which Mill finds "one of the most tragical facts in all history."[16]

[15] Arnold, *Complete Prose Works*, V, 254.

[16] The difficulty of evaluating pleasures and pains is as clear to the utili-

Thus, as much as Arnold and Mill both emphasize the importance of new ideas, continued growth, and those eras in which, in Arnold's phrasing, the currents of new and fresh ideas flow most strongly, as much as both emphasize the need to preserve balance between opposing positions (Arnold's prescription of Hellenism for a Hebraistic age, Mill's of individualism in a time of growing uniformity), as much as they feel the necessity of re-evaluating custom and general opinion, and impatient as they both are with assumptions about the all-sufficiency of Christianity, their different premises cause them to answer (and ask) basic questions quite differently. A succinct summation of the differences is found in the implications of two quite similar statements: Mill's "He who knows only his own side of the case, knows little of that," and Arnold's "No man, who knows nothing else, knows even his Bible."[17] Mill naturally thinks of opposed sides, the clash of which reveals truth, while Arnold thinks of a total system of culture, the grasping of which is necessary for the interpretation of any portion of man's experience, however important.

That Arnold is disturbed by the root-position of the Benthamite empiricists more than their practical proposals is made explicit in Chapter III of *Culture and Anarchy* where, after setting forth his argument for "a sound centre of authority" he remarks that

> not only do we get no suggestions of right reason, and no rebukes of our ordinary self, from our governors, but a kind of philosophical theory is widely spread among us to the effect that there is no such thing at all as a best self and a right reason having claim to paramount authority, or, at any rate, no

tarians as that of calculating consequences or determining truth. How does one judge of another's happiness, asks Coleridge. "*Your* mode of happiness would make *me* miserable" (*Table Talk*, in *Complete Works*, VI, 370). Just so, say the utilitarians, but the principle of liberty allows each man to pursue what *he* judges to be happiness.

[17] J. S. Mill, *On Liberty*, p. 45; Arnold, *Culture and Anarchy*, in *Complete Prose Works*, V, 184.

> such thing ascertainable and capable of being made use of; and that there is nothing but an infinite number of ideas and works of our ordinary selves, and suggestions of our natural taste for the bathos, pretty nearly equal in value, which are doomed either to an irreconcilable conflict, or else to a perpetual give and take.[18]

This is a summary of Mill's basic assumptions as seen by the other side, and it is these assumptions that disquiet Arnold. If this were not so, he could reasonably have been expected to concentrate his attack on the "Applications" of Mill's doctrines as set forth in the final chapter of *On Liberty*. This is clearly the weakest part of Mill's treatise: that "both the cheapness and the good quality of commodities are most effectually provided for by leaving the producer and sellers perfectly free," "that it is unnecessary to dwell" on the problems of dealing with "offenses against decency," that Mill "will not venture to decide" about certain vexed questions pertaining to those who solicit others to "self-regarding" but nevertheless almost certainly damaging activities are positions which invite attack, as does Mill's shuffling on the questions of the taxing of liquor, the regulation of marriage, and the restriction of the government's power to undertake programs for the benefit of the people which the people themselves might be able to carry out. Arnold passes over these likely targets to devote his major effort to setting up an alternative to what he regards as a pernicious basic assumption.

But if Mill finds himself in difficulties in regard to the application of his arguments to particular problems, Arnold's weaknesses are equally apparent. As an alternative to either "irreconcilable conflict" or "perpetual give and take," Arnold offers "right reason," one's "best self," "the best light," and "the best which has been thought and said in the world," all of them the products of culture. But how is one to be sure that one has grasped the best self, light,

[18] Arnold, *Complete Prose Works*, V, 155–56.

thought, or saying? That which is intended as a surrogate for a transcendent model inevitably appears inadequate precisely because it lacks any transcendent guarantee. Even if a man devotes himself to acquiring balance and culture, how can he be sure he has achieved them? "Socrates has drunk his hemlock and is dead; but in his own breast does not every man carry about with him a possible Socrates?" asks Arnold;[19] but how is a man to know that the inner voice he hears represents that "disinterested play of consciousness" of which Socrates was an example rather than the siren voice of self-interested sophistry? Reason and the will of God ought to prevail, but how can we be sure that what we think ought to prevail is indeed reason and the will of God? Arnold's "best self" seems to be certain that "to be reared a member of a national Church is in itself a lesson of moderation," that it can be settled "what is indeed beautiful, graceful, and becoming" in dress so that the "raw person" can be got to like that, and that his father was right in his Roman prescription for dealing with rioters, but how can one be certain that it is something less than the "best self" in another which argues against these beliefs? One can be certain in these matters only if culture speaks with a voice that is both unmistakable and of more authority than those voices that argue from empirical grounds.

The basic assumptions of Arnold and Mill are reflected in the forms in which their arguments are cast as well as in their content. Mill defines his subject, traces the history of the problem, states his thesis, and outlines his approach in the first chapter. The grounds for defending liberty of thought and discussion are given in Chapter II; the necessary extension of freedom of thought to freedom of actions by individuals in all cases in which it is undertaken "at their own risk and peril" is argued in Chapter III; the resulting question of locating the boundaries between the

[19] *Ibid.*, V, 228.

sovereignty of the individual and of society is taken up in Chapter IV; and the applications of the doctrines thus derived make up Chapter V. The argument, its stages summarized at strategic points, advances step by step, demanding assent by the appeal to logic and consistency. Mill rarely uses the first person pronoun and rarely states a point aphoristically; he tries to project little more than an atmosphere of reasonableness.

In *Culture and Anarchy*, if we except the Introduction and the Preface (which quickly wander away from the "foremost design" given in the opening sentence), both of which were added later, we have six chapters that move generally from a definition of culture through a series of attempts to show that culture is the only bulwark against individual eccentricity, aberration, error, and provinciality, to the application of the sweetness and light of culture to contemporary issues. But though Arnold's treatment is roughly parallel to *On Liberty*, Arnold gives not so much the impression of a logical thinker setting forth the grounds and consequences of an important principle as a virtuoso doing variations on a theme. To this extent he might be said to be engaging in an exercise in imitative form—the free play of the mind about a question; the "stream of fresh and free knowledge" which is to "float" the subject is suggested in the very form of the argument. But Arnold's choice of forms was not a wholly free one. To attempt to reduce culture to a set of formulas, as Mill does the principles of liberty, would be folly. Like a vision of the transcendent, it defies formulation. But if culture cannot be anatomized in itself, perhaps it can be shown in action, as embodied by Arnold himself. Arnold thus projects an urbane, witty, charming personality. Irony, good humor, and a proper modesty flavor the style throughout. "I" and "we" abound, for "I" and "we" are not merely Arnold, but ultimately culture. A series of turns and new starts in the argument, often marked by self-quotation or quotations from Bishop Wilson which serve as texts for annotation, take the place of Mill's lineal, logical development, each stage of which proceeds out of the previous one. Paradoxically, though it is Arnold who insists that the critic, culture's commentator, stay above the fray, Mill is much more careful to eschew embroilment in actual issues. Arnold, the true knight of culture, attacks real, living dragons, especially when he discusses "Our Liberal Practitioners"—this provides much of the color and interest of his writing. Mill, the disciple of utility, on the other hand, takes it upon himself to read out to us the *general* laws that produce the greatest happiness of the greatest number.

Although Mill does not directly discuss contemporary issues in *On Liberty*, it is of course possible to look beyond that work for his position on certain issues treated by Arnold in *Culture and Anarchy*. The most illuminating opposition is perhaps to be found in their reactions to the Hyde Park disturbances which occurred in 1866, seven years after the publication of *On Liberty* and just prior to the composition of *Culture and Anarchy*. Arnold refers to the matter repeatedly in *Culture and Anarchy*; Mill's position, which turns out to be what one would expect from the author of *On Liberty*, is expressed in his *Autobiography*, his speeches in parliament, and his actions at the time.

Arnold's position is made clear in a central passage in the chapter "Doing as One Likes": "this and that body of men, all over the country, are beginning to assert and put in practice an Englishman's right to do what he likes; his right to march where he likes, meet where he likes, enter where he likes, hoot as he likes, threaten as he likes, smash as he likes. All this, I say, tends to anarchy. . . ."[20] Arnold sees no need to argue in detail what rights an Englishman may or may not be presumed to have, but he is sure that where an Englishman marches, meets, and enters and how, where, and whether he hoots, threatens, and

[20] *Ibid.*, V, 119.

smashes can be prescribed, and that the limits will fall far short of such "outbreaks of rowdyism" as occurred in Hyde Park. There must be a standard; culture will prescribe it; our best selves will certify it.[21] Behind Arnold's desire to prevent Hyde Park's becoming a "bear-garden" is, of course, his belief that open conflict is not the way to solve problems; it does not encourage that free play of the mind that will "float" the issue, presumably floating it, with the aid of the winds of right reason, in the direction of its one proper solution.

On the other hand, the right of conflict, the necessity of conflict, is here, as elsewhere, overriding in Mill's mind. "Right reason," "culture," and "best selves" are as illusory as transcendental visions; conflict must serve as the winnower of truth. "I maintain," said Mill in his speech to the Parliament on 24 July 1866, "that if the people have not that right [of meeting in Hyde Park] now, they ought to have it." Moreover, open discussion, which causes men to think about an issue, is the least dangerous way of effecting change: "It has been the anxious wish of all those who understand their age, and are lovers of their country, that the necessary changes in the institutions of the country should be effected with the least possible, and if possible without any, alienation and ill blood between the hitherto governing classes and the mass of the people. Her Majesty's present advisers seem resolved, so far as it depends upon them, that this anxious desire should be frustrated."[22] Mill subsequently had a part in defeating a Tory attempt to pass a bill to prevent public meetings in parks.

Mill's position throughout the debates over the Hyde

[21] Arnold's response to situations of social stress in which disorder occurs or is imminent is, as John Gross has pointed out in *The Rise and Fall of the Man of Letters*, to counsel repression; chapter VI of Patrick J. McCarthy's *Matthew Arnold and the Three Classes* examines at length Arnold's support for the coercive measures advocated by his brother-in-law, W. E. Forster, during the Irish unrest of the 1880s.

[22] *Hansard's Parliamentary Debates*, Third Series, CLXXXIV, 1410.

Park incident was entirely consistent not merely with the espousal of as much liberty as possible but with the whole structure of arguments by which the necessity of this liberty was deduced from the inherent and insurmountable uncertainty of man's knowledge of truth. When it seemed that the Reform League, prepared to use violent means if necessary, would again attempt a meeting in the Park, Mill, as he recounts in the *Autobiography*, was primarily responsible for dissuading them from openly challenging the government with force. "I told them that a proceeding which would certainly produce a collision with the military, could only be justifiable on two conditions: if the position of affairs had become such that a revolution was desirable, and if they thought themselves able to accomplish one."[23] That argument was not forged especially to meet the particular occasion but was taken from the utilitarian armory, specifically from James Mill's "Liberty of the Press." It is the argument that the government must allow any censure, any exhortation, any mode of censure or exhortation short of direct interference with "the operations of Government in detail." It cannot allow that, or it will cease to be able to perform the functions of government at all. But to forbid a general call for resistance against the government, James Mill argued, is ultimately an attempt to forbid all censure of the government, for any censure could be so interpreted as to seem a call for general resistance. Moreover, to forbid even so drastic an exhortation as a call to take arms against the government must fail to accomplish anything useful. "The people cannot take arms against the government without the certainty of being immediately crushed, unless there has already been created a general consent. If this consent exists in such perfection as to want nothing to begin action but an exhortation, nothing can prevent the exhortation; and forbidding it is useless."[24]

[23] J. S. Mill, *Autobiography*, p. 186.

[24] James Mill, "Liberty of the Press," in *Essays*, p. 15.

James Mill was writing about published exhortations, not mass meetings, but his son's use of his arguments, here reversed to guide the actions of the censuring people rather than the censured government, is obvious. The people should have the right to assemble in Hyde Park, but to take that right by force is in effect to obstruct the operations of the government in detail. Since government has every right to oppose and punish this obstruction, to challenge the government in this way is folly unless one intends to go on to overthrow the government, an intention that is also folly unless one can be sure of the support of the nation. Thus counsels utility.

A FINAL well-known controversy over rights and freedoms equally exemplifies the way in which the logic of basic metaphysical assumptions operated so as neatly to divide empiricists and transcendentalists. In November 1865, the first news of a Negro uprising in Jamaica reached England. As details came in, and it became clear that the uprising had been immediately suppressed, fear for the safety of the white population gave way to concern over the brutality with which the rebellion had been put down. That, in reaction to the deaths of some twenty-two Englishmen, all but two of whom were killed in the single open encounter between whites and blacks, almost 450 Jamaican blacks were executed, and hundreds were flogged, seemed, on the face of it, to represent indefensible harshness.[25] By December, a "Jamaica Committee" headed by Charles Buxton and numbering Thomas Hughes, John Bright, Francis Newman, and John Stuart Mill among its

[25] The fullest and most damning summation of atrocities is that delivered in the House of Commons on 31 July 1866, by Charles Buxton. See *Hansard's Parliamentary Debates*, Third Series, CLXXXIV, 1763–1785.

members had been formed to see that those responsible for flagrant injustice or cruelty were punished.

Popular clamor forced a reluctant Colonial Office to appoint a Commission of Inquiry, which finally reported in April 1866. The report, while not going so far as wished by those who most strongly condemned the actions of the Governor of Jamaica, Edward Eyre, and the British military forces under his command, showed clearly that serious injustices and even atrocities had been committed. The grounds for continuing to demand punishment appeared to be these: that Eyre had allowed the military authorities to extend the operation of martial law well beyond what was necessary, that he had countenanced a long succession of summary court-martial proceedings in which Jamaican men and women were sentenced to flogging or death (or both) on wholly inadequate evidence, that he had failed to punish officers who had not only exceeded their authority but acted in a bloodthirsty manner, and that he had personally had George William Gordon, the Jamaican he regarded as most responsible for stirring up the populace, transported from Kingston, where Gordon had given himself up and where civil courts were functioning, to Morant Bay where he could be tried by court-martial and summarily hanged.[26] After the report of the Commission of Inquiry, the Jamaica Committee split on the question of the severity of the action that should be taken; Buxton argued that dismissal and public condemnation were sufficient, but others, led by Mill, demanded the prosecution of Eyre for murder. Mill carried the day and was elected in July to replace Buxton as chairman. In August, immediately after Eyre's return to England, his defenders began to organize the Eyre Defense Committee, the first meeting of which was chaired by Thomas Carlyle.

A good many eminent Victorians felt obliged to take

[26] For a twentieth-century defense of Eyre, see Geoffrey Dutton's *The Hero as Murderer: The Life of Edward John Eyre.*

sides. Most of the important literary figures who did so joined with Carlyle: Ruskin, Tennyson, Dickens, J. Froude, and Kingsley (the last vacillatingly) supported Eyre. Most of the important men of science, on the other hand, joined in the prosecution: Darwin, Huxley, Spencer, and Lyell, for instance, came in with Mill, as did men of letters with a more or less positivistic cast of mind like Frederic Harrison and Leslie Stephen. It has been remarked as surprising that the men of letters defended Eyre, while the presumably colder and more logical philosophical radicals and scientists felt that the harshness with which the Jamaican natives had been treated deserved prosecution. A complex web of personal loyalties and antipathies, of earlier allegiances and commitments, lies behind this polarization; much of it has been analyzed by Bernard Semmel, and Carlyle's role has more recently been reassessed by Gillian Workman.[27] But the mass of detail that can be brought to bear ought not to obscure, as it does not invalidate, the larger explanation. The split, here again, lies precisely between the empiricist and transcendental orientations.

Despite the fact that he is writing as a partisan, T. H. Huxley accurately described the point at issue:

> In point of fact, men take sides on this question, not so much by looking at the mere facts of the case, but rather as their deepest political convictions lead them. And the great use of the prosecution, and one of my reasons for joining it, is that it will help a great many people to find out what their profoundest political beliefs are.
>
> The hero-worshippers who believe that the world is to be governed by its great men, who are to lead the little ones, justly if they can; but if not, unjustly drive or kick them the right way, will sympathize with Mr. Eyre.
>
> The other sect (to which I belong) who look upon hero-worship as no better than any other idolatry, and upon the

[27] Semmel, *The Governor Eyre Controversy*; Workman, "Thomas Carlyle and the Governor Eyre Controversy," *Victorian Studies*, XVIII (Sept. 1974), 77–102.

attitude of mind of the hero-worshipper as essentially immoral; who think it is better for a man to go wrong in freedom than to go right in chains; who look upon the observance of inflexible justice as between man and man as of far greater importance than even the preservation of social order, will believe that Mr. Eyre has committed one of the greatest crimes of which a person in authority can be guilty, and will strain every nerve to obtain a declaration that their belief is in accordance with the law of England.[28]

It is important to recognize that Huxley's use of the word "hero-worshippers" to designate his opponents is more than a rhetorical dig at Carlyle; it uses Carlyle's prescription of the worship of heroes to sum up the end toward which one form of transcendental belief seems to lead. "Any road, this simple Entepfuhl road, will lead you to the end of the world," discovers Professor Teufelsdröckh, but it is also true that the road which Carlyle has so clearly set out on by the time he writes *Sartor Resartus* leads, at least in one of its main branches, to the doctrine of the hero.

It seems, therefore, appropriate at this point to untangle some of the Carlylean web. The great purpose of *Sartor*, of course, is to unveil the vast panorama, the transcendent, infinite, eternal world that everyday experience hides from us. Chapter IX of the second book, "The Everlasting Yea," supports like a great central pier and is in turn braced by the rest of the book. No portion of Victorian prose is better known, but perhaps it will be helpful to remind ourselves, by glancing at central statements there, how fully congruent are Carlyle's thought and the central transcendental tradition.

"How paint to the sensual eye . . . what passes in the Holy-of-Holies of Man's Soul; in what words, known to these profane times, speak even afar-off of the unspeakable."

[28] Quoted by Semmel, *The Governor Eyre Controversy*, p. 123.

"It is only with Renunciation . . . that life, properly speaking, can be said to begin."

"The first preliminary moral act, Annihilation of Self . . . had been happily accomplished; and my mind's eyes were now unsealed, and its hands ungyved."

" . . . what is Nature? Ha, why do I not name thee GOD? Art not thou the 'Living Garment of God'?"

"The Universe is not dead or demoniacal. . . ."

"Love not Pleasure; love God."

"Our Life is compassed round with Necessity; yet is the meaning of life itself no other than Freedom, than Voluntary Force."

One notices, and this is a point to which we must return later in a different context, that each of these principles is presented in *Sartor* as a discovery. The order in which I give them above, which is not the order in which they appear in "The Everlasting Yea," represents a kind of progression, but one is not the logical precursor of the next. Implied in each is the existence of an extraphenomenal world; once that world is dimly apprehended, the way is open for the reader to begin to grasp the entire set. Taken all together, they offer the familiar transcendental tenets and may be translated into lay language thus:

The most profound and important knowledge does not come directly through the senses, nor can it be adequately revealed in language primarily intended to describe sense experience. Knowledge begins in an act of will, in an internal moral reform, which looks to something beyond the desires which arise in the senses. The first great insight which follows is that behind the phenomena experienced by the senses lies the Creator's plan. The phenomena of ordinary experience both conceal and disclose the visible structure behind them; which they do is partly dependent on the beholder. The universe is therefore filled with meaning; it is man's duty to discover that meaning and act in accordance with it; it is not his duty to seek pleasure. The phenomenal world is governed by

> cause and effect and one lives in this world to the extent one pursues one's pleasure; but by the exertion of the will which denies the self, searches for the meaning behind phenomena, and is obedient to the transcendental imperatives it thus discovers, freedom is obtained.

As he puts it in *Latter-Day Pamphlets*, "The free man is he who is *loyal* to the Laws of this Universe; who in his heart sees and knows, across all contradictions, that injustice *cannot* befall him here; that except by sloth and cowardly falsity evil is not possible here."[29]

As early as "Signs of the Times," Carlyle was insisting that all reform begins with obedience to such supra-phenomenal imperatives; the essay closes with "to reform a world, to reform a nation, no wise man will undertake, and all but foolish men know, that the only solid, though a far slower reformation, is what each begins and perfects on *himself*."[30] "Signs of the Times" is throughout a warning against "the Mechanical Age" in which "not only the external and physical alone is now managed by machinery, but the internal and spiritual also."[31] Man looks to "mere political arrangement" so that "the Philosopher of this age is not a Socrates, a Plato, a Hooker, or Taylor, who inculcates on men the necessity and infinite worth of moral goodness, the great truth that our happiness depends on the mind which is within us . . . but a Smith, a De Lolme, a Bentham, who chiefly inculcates the reverse of this—that our happiness depends entirely on external circumstances."[32] The protest against "machinery" and the cry for individual reformation is, as we have seen, a mark of the transcendentalist. However, "Signs of the Times" is early in the series of Carlyle's diagnoses of the condition of England, and

[29] Carlyle, "Parliaments," in *Complete Works*, XII, 321.

[30] Carlyle, "Signs of the Times," in *Complete Works*, XIII, 487.

[31] *Ibid.*, XIII, 466.

[32] *Ibid.*, XIII, 472.

by the time he writes *Sartor*, he recognizes the impossibility of self-reformation. The whole protest against the machinery of government which makes up so much of *Latter-Day Pamphlets* is the result of the extension of this position. The average man is not only unable to see the transcendental vision but also to recognize the leader who will give him proper guidance. "I have always understood," writes Carlyle in the pamphlet on "Parliaments," "that true worth, in any department, was difficult to recognize; that the worthiest, if he appealed to universal suffrage, would have but a poor chance."[33] Moreover, assuming that the proper leader has been chosen, ordinary mankind is unable to assess the probity or correctness of that leader's decisions. The function of parliamentary discussion and the press, for Carlyle, as the same pamphlet makes clear, is simply to keep the leader or governor informed, not to provide checks. "By all manner of means let the Governor inform himself. . . . To which end, Parliaments, Free Presses, and such like are excellent; they keep the Governor fully aware of what the People, wisely or foolishly, think."[34] The leader, following "heavenly lodestars," has need of a knowledge of the people's temper, not to discern his goal, not to keep him honest, but simply to choose with prudence the path by which he follows those lodestars.

Carlyle again and again offers through Teufelsdröckh, the unraveling of whose thought is the great strategic device of *Sartor Resartus*, a sense of transcendent reality, but to pierce the veil of sense oneself, and to read lessons directly from it, is given to very few. So rarely is the unmediated vision granted that the most Carlyle seems to hope for in *Sartor* is that his readers will grasp the notion that all the generalizations, deductions, and categorizations by which they have attempted to order sense experience are impermanent pieces of clothing, cut and sewn by conjec-

[33] Carlyle, "Parliaments," in *Complete Works*, XII, 313.

[34] *Ibid.*, XII, 312.

ture and thrown over (rather than fitted to) certain transcendental forms to make them visible. The fable of the Emperor's Clothes is reversed: without clothes we should be unable to see the Emperor at all.[35] But although we all may believe in a transcendental world, our knowledge of it, like that knowledge of God's will given the tribes of Israel, must come through the inspired prophetic few. As readers of Carlyle know well, the doctrine and definition of the great man which will be developed in *Heroes and Hero-Worship* and *Past and Present* is set forth clearly enough in *Sartor*:

> Great Men are the inspired (speaking and acting) Texts of that divine BOOK OF REVELATIONS, whereof a Chapter is completed from epoch to epoch, and by some named HISTORY; to which inspired Texts your numerous talented men, and your innumerable untalented men, are the better or worse exegetic Commentaries, and wagonload of too-stupid, heretical or orthodox, weekly Sermons. For my study the inspired Texts themselves![36]

It matters not whether the seer is recognized as prophet, poet, priest, man of letters, or king, so long as he is recog-

[35] Many a whole-hearted empiricist of course employed the fable the other way and would argue that what one came to see through was Carlyle's rhetoric and that Carlyle, stripped of his rhetoric, had nothing to offer but his naked ego. Frederic Harrison writes, "He was a wonderful literary artist. . . . Thinker, prophet, or judge he was not. It was the long mistake of his life to imagine himself thinker, prophet, and judge; to mistake literary mastery for philosophic power." And, "Hence Carlyle, rejecting at once all theologies, all philosophies, all syntheses alike . . . was forced into a creed that at last got stereotyped into the simple words, 'I believe in Thomas Carlyle; which faith, unless a man keep, without doubt he shall perish everlastingly.'" (Review of Froude's *Life of Carlyle*, in *The Choice of Books*, pp. 191, 196). Morley similarly sums up the orthodox empiricist's view: as much as one might admire Carlyle's insights and denunciations of evil, "the writer who in these days has done more than anybody else to fire men's hearts with a feeling for right and an eager desire for social activity, has with deliberate contempt thrust away from him the only instrument by which we can make sure what right is, and that our social action is wise and effective" (*Critical Miscellanies*, I, 148–49).

[36] Carlyle, *Complete Works*, I, 16–17.

nized. That is the message of *Heroes and Hero-Worship*: the true belief is "that there is a *Greatest* man; that *he* is discoverable; that, once discovered, we ought to treat him with an obedience which knows no bounds!"[37] The great man is the text which translates the transcendent sanction into terrestrial imperatives. (One remembers that Coleridge used Sir Alexander Ball as a concluding summary example of the message of *The Friend* in a way not much different from Carlyle's use of the hero.)

By *Past and Present*, the difficulties of seeing beyond sense experience are pressing more insistently on Carlyle, at the same time the necessity of doing so becomes more urgent.

> How true, for example, is that other old Fable of the Sphinx, who sat by the wayside, propounding her riddle to the passengers, which if they could not answer she destroyed them! Such a Sphinx is this Life of ours, to all men and societies of men. . . . Answer her riddle, it is well with thee. Answer it not, pass on regarding it not, it will answer itself; the solution for thee is a thing of teeth and claws.[38]

There is one answer only to the riddle asked at any particular point of history; the riddle is only to be answered by reading "the inner sphere of Fact" rather than "the outer sphere and spheres of Semblance"; and this only the great man is able to do. However, it is at this point that a certain deflection occurs in Carlyle's thought. The monks had wisely elected Abbot Samson, but until the Abbot Samsons of nineteenth-century England can be discovered, man may at least order his efforts by certain principles grounded in even an imperfect glimpse of the transcendent. The answers to certain riddles can be known. How does one know and understand oneself? By work.[39] Toward what does one

[37] *Ibid.*, I, 239.

[38] *Ibid.*, XII, 8.

[39] Carlyle's doctrine of work, though closely integrated into his system of thought, is of course not a result of his transcendentalism but an addition to it.

work? Order. Thus in the third portion of *Past and Present* these answers blend into the rule by which to gauge the worthiness of a man's actions: is he working toward order? The descent from heralding the great man who will guide to backing the lesser man who blunderingly but staunchly tries to pursue the right direction is striking. But, after all, Abbot Samson himself is in truth only a profitable worker in the vineyard, not a great seer. The great men in *Heroes and Hero-Worship*, one remembers, were found by Carlyle to have had finally only imperfect vision. At a time when one finds no heroes to follow, might not one as well lower the standard, and if not wholly follow at least support the efforts of those who struggle toward order, and thus give even to Plugson of Undershot his due? Thus viewed, the descent from great men to men who seem to work for order appears quantitative only; it is, of course, qualitative, and it involves an actual reversal. For if the great man alone is capable of transcending the errors into which sense experience necessarily leads us, only he can judge which man is in the right path. Moreover, if we once get the idea of the pursuit of order fixed as the mark of the great man, the danger is that we will confuse the man who seems to be successfully creating what we recognize as order with the great man who, if once recognized as the true prophet, would tell us what kind of order we should pursue. The problem is to be certain that "your numerous talented men" are following the true "inspired Texts." As Carlyle's frustration at the failure of the nineteenth century to find the necessary great men grew, he became the more intolerant, the more sure of the need for authority, the more likely to support any who exercised their authority in support of order. Thus, Carlyle's support of Governor Eyre.

Governor Eyre stood for order; although he was not a great man, not fully a "hero," he was, to Carlyle's eyes, fit for the Jamaicans to obey. The metaphor in which Carlyle summed up his conception of Eyre's position in his letter to the Eyre Defense Committee is revealing: "his late services in Jamaica were of great, perhaps incalculable value, as certainly they were of perilous and appalling difficulty,—something like the case of 'fire,' suddenly reported, 'in the ship's powder-room' in mid ocean. . . ."[40] The same metaphor (which had already done service in the *Latter-Day Pamphlets*)[41] appears in J. A. Froude's report of Carlyle's views. "It was, Carlyle said to me, as if a ship had been on fire; the captain, by immediate and bold exertion, had put the fire out, and had been called to account for having flung a bucket or two of water into the hold beyond what was necessary. He had damaged some of the cargo, perhaps, but he had saved the ship."[42]

Returning to Huxley's letter, then, we can see the extent to which the reduction of the issue to the "hero-worshippers" and those who "look upon hero-worship as no better than any other idolatry" implies the ultimate issues. When Huxley wrote that hero-worshippers believe that great men "are to lead the little ones, justly if they can; but if not, unjustly drive or kick them the right way" he may well have had in mind passages like the following from *Past and Present*: "Every stupid, every cowardly and foolish man is but a less palpable madman: his true liberty were that a wiser man, that any and every wiser man, could, by brass collars, or in whatever milder or sharper way, lay hold of him when he was going wrong, and order and compel him to go a little righter."[43] The question of the difficulty of finding the right path is ignored. Huxley assumes there are just and unjust ways of treating men and that justice is defined by "the law of England," the rules governing the relationship between "man and man" which have been adopted by England. He might not endorse all the rules desired by Bentham and the Mills, but he would

[40] Quoted in Hamilton Hume's *The Life of Edward John Eyre*, p. 289.

[41] Carlyle, "The Present Time," in *Complete Works*, II, 274–75.

[42] Froude, *Thomas Carlyle: A History of His Life in London 1834–1881*, II, 51–52.

[43] Carlyle, *Complete Works*, XII, 205.

accept the principle on which they insist that there must be such rules defined by law. (He rejects Carlyle's view that, as Morley unkindly phrases it, "The multitude stands between Destiny on the one side, and the Hero on the other; a sport to the first, and as potter's clay to the second."[44]) Carlyle sets forth his quite different, unblushingly transcendental view of justice in the second chapter of *Past and Present*:

> What is justice? that, on the whole, is the question of the Sphinx to us. The law of Fact is, that Justice must and will be done. The sooner the better; for the Time grows stringent, frightfully pressing! "What is Justice?" ask many, to whom cruel Fact alone will be able to prove responsive. . . . The clothed embodied Justice that sits in Westminster Hall, with penalties, parchments, tipstaves, is very visible. But the *un*embodied Justice, whereof that other is either an emblem, or else is a fearful indescribability, is not so visible! For the unembodied Justice is of Heaven; a Spirit, and Divinity of Heaven,—*in*visible to all but the noble and pure of soul. The impure ignoble gaze with eyes, and she is not there.[45]

John Stuart Mill's speech in parliament following Buxton's condemnation of Eyre is built on the argument of the necessity of proceeding by law. Had Eyre and the military not suspended civil law, they would not have been responsible for the results of the judicial processes, however misguided those might later have appeared. But once they chose to suspend it and act under martial law, they became totally responsible for the results of their actions. Having so chosen, and having erred in their subsequent actions, they must be tried in the manner prescribed by law—only thus can the degree of their culpability and the appropriate punishment be determined. Rights established by law have been violated; punishment sufficient to overbalance

[44] Morley, *Critical Miscellanies*, I, 186.

[45] Carlyle, *Complete Works*, XII, 15.

the desire to violate such rights must be assigned. The grounds of Mill's position here are evidently the same as we have examined in *On Liberty*. Convinced that truth is difficult to establish and all men are prone to error, Mill demands rules and laws that will minimize the jeopardy in which any man might be put by the errors of another, and he insists that these rules remain always in force; Carlyle, convinced of most men's proneness to error but convinced also that there are truths that only certain men can read, demands that the man who is pursuing that order presumably grounded in the structure of the world be regarded as the embodier of the law and the creator of the rules.

One should note here that the need for rules and laws insisted on by the utilitarians is increased by their tendency to emphasize the selfishness of human nature. While Bentham's tendency to translate the pursuit of pleasure and avoidance of pain directly into the pursuit of objects of desire is not, strictly speaking, a result of his empiricist metaphysics, he believed his analysis of the selfishness of human motives empirically certain. That all men not only wish unlimited fulfillment of all their desires but will attempt to attain such fulfillment where possible, is the basis of the argument against monarchy and oligarchy in James Mill's "Government," in which the following passage, an interesting comment on an earlier episode similar to that in Jamaica in 1866, occurs:

> An English Gentleman may be taken as a favourable specimen of civilization, of knowledge, of humanity. . . . In the West Indies, before that vigilant attention of the English nation, which now, for thirty years, has imposed so great a check upon the masters of slaves, there was not a perfect absence of all check upon the dread propensities of power. But yet it is true, that these propensities led English Gentlemen, not only to deprive their slaves of property, and to make property of their fellow-creatures, but to treat them with a degree of cru-

> elty, the very description of which froze the blood of their countrymen, who were placed in less unfavourable circumstances. The motives of this deplorable conduct are exactly those which we have described above, as arising out of the universal desire to render the actions of other men exactly conformable to our will.[46]

Most of the other arguments that were employed in the controversy over Eyre can be related to one or the other of these basic sets of assumptions. For instance, to Carlyle and others it was self-evident that the Jamaican natives were not only so much less civilized that they must necessarily be much further from harmony with the structure of the world than their English rulers but that the rules of a more advanced culture did not apply to them. Mill had gone so far in *On Liberty* as to admit that "Liberty, as a principle, has no application to any state of things anterior to the time when mankind have become capable of being improved by free and equal discussion."[47] That a ruler over a less-developed culture is not answerable to the strictest interpretation of the laws of his country which establish his rulership never occurred to him. And where possible by any exertion to avoid it, to deprive a human being of his life without providing for a trial at which the truth of the charges against him might emerge out of the clash of conflicting argument was unthinkable. Even clearer are the grounds of his abhorrence at the execution of Gordon. All that had ever been shown was that Gordon had spoken in a manner to inspire general revolution; it was never proved that he had been responsible for the particular obstruction of the operation of the government which began the Jamaican struggle. He was thus wholly within the rights the Mills had argued for as essential to all liberty.

[46] James Mill, "Government," in *Essays*, p. 12.

[47] J. S. Mill, *On Liberty*, p. 14.

The Omnipresent Debate

Not all the better-known writers of the nineteenth century formulated their premises as clearly as Coleridge, the Mills, Carlyle, Matthew Arnold, and Huxley. But in trying to comprehend the relationships between the major beliefs of such writers and between their positions on such subjects as freedom and responsibility, an approach by way of metaphysical traditions proves quite as important as analyses of biographical episodes, historical setting, or psychological quirks. That belief in the possibility of individual transcendence of the ordinary interpretation of experience leads to opposition to individualism and democracy, while belief in the similarity of minds and their collective educability leads to the espousal of both individualism and democracy is a paradox which illuminates much in the nineteenth century.

VI

Meanings and Uses of History

THE NINETEENTH CENTURY has been credited with the discovery of history; one can at least give it credit for wide exploration of the uses of history, uses which can be both spectacular and puzzling.[1] A heightened consciousness of historical processes, what William Morris called "the gift of the historical sense which may be said to be a special gift of the nineteenth century,"[2] is to be found among the most diverse thinkers. This is most strongly reflected in the widespread reassessment of the middle ages and the variety of attempts to set out a law governing the progress of each nation or culture. Interest in the middle ages was growing throughout the latter part of the eighteenth century, as Kenneth Clark has solidly

[1] The eighteenth century was, of course, in its own way fascinated by history. As Ernest Tuveson puts it, "A typical preoccupation of the Enlightenment was the construction of 'conjectural' or 'philosophic' histories of mankind" (*Millenium and Utopia*, p. 153).

[2] "The Revival of Architecture," in *Collected Works of William Morris*, XXII, 321. For a more extended statement of the change in man's view of history, see "Architecture and History," in *Collected Works*, XXII, 296–98.

demonstrated.[3] Discussion of Gothic architecture begins to become important in the *Gentleman's Magazine* from 1780 on, Clark points out, and battles over the restoration of Gothic Churches are being bitterly waged by 1800.[4] The Gothic revival was fed by literary romanticism, archaeology, and the drawing of economic contrasts by writers like Cobbett. The interpretation of history as a regular progress was also becoming familiar enough by 1800. R. G. Collingwood traces the idea of an ordered series of historical stages to Rousseau, Herder, and post-Kantian German idealism.[5] "According to this conception, past stages in history led necessarily to the present; a given form of civilization can exist only when the time is ripe for it, and has its value just because those are the conditions of its existing."[6] That history represents a progression from stage to stage, each preparatory to the next, thus came to be held by many besides Saint-Simonians and Comtists—for instance, Dr. Thomas Arnold, Comte's contemporary, held the view in his own way:

> New states, like individuals, go through certain stages in a certain order, and are subject at different stages of their course to certain peculiar disorders. But they differ from individuals in this, that though the order of the periods is regular, their duration is not so; and their features are more liable to be mistaken, as they can only be distinguished by their characteristic phenomena. . . .
>
> We may also learn a more sensible division of history than that which is commonly adopted of ancient and modern. We shall see that there is in fact an ancient and a modern period in the history of every people; the ancient differing, and the

[3] Clark, *The Gothic Revival*. See especially the first four chapters.

[4] *Ibid.*, pp. 71–78.

[5] See Collingwood, *The Idea of History*, Part III.

[6] *Ibid.*, p. 87.

> modern in many essential points agreeing with that in which we now live. Thus the largest portion of that history which we commonly call ancient is practically modern, as it describes society in a state analogous to that in which it now is; while, on the other hand, much of what is called modern history is practically ancient, as it relates to a state of things which has passed away.[7]

Nevertheless, there was a wide range of opinion about the importance and meaning of history as a guide. Superficially, it would seem that the empiricists would look eagerly to history, finding it an inexhaustible source of empirical evidence. As R. G. Collingwood put it, "If all knowledge is based on experience, it is an historical product; truth, as Bacon had already reasserted, is the daughter of time." And we should expect equally that the transcendentalists would tend to discount history, like all other phenomena, as obscuring the invisible structure of the world: "The conception of innate ideas is an anti-historical conception," says Collingwood.[8] In some cases indeed, nineteenth-century writers do follow these patterns. However, there were counter-tendencies in both metaphysical camps. Many an empiricist, regarding both physical phenomena and human nature as unchanging, preferred to analyze present rather than past instances. Why look at possibly erroneous reports from the past when the raw material for empirical observation is all around one? And, on the other hand, many a transcendentalist seems to have felt that though a correct reading of history depended on one's bringing to it a vision whose source lay outside the study of history, the noumenal realm symbolized itself more clearly in a sweeping pattern of events extending through time than in immediate experience. Besides, his-

[7] *The Miscellaneous Works of Thomas Arnold*, p. 306.

[8] Collingwood, *Idea of History*, p. 72.

torical incidents could always be used for vivifying illustrations if not as conclusive guides.[9] There is, therefore, no clear-cut correspondence between a writer's metaphysical views and the importance he assigns to history. Nevertheless, the *use* made of history by those who find it significant *is* determined by their metaphysics.

One empiricist who finds little of value in history is Bentham. It is true that "historical chronology" and "history" appear in the list of courses planned for inclusion in his Chrestomathic school, but he says almost nothing about the study of history in the *Chrestomathia*, and, more significantly, omits it from his "encyclopaedic Table . . . Exhibiting the first lines of a Tabular Diagram of the principal and most extensive branches of Art and Science, framed in the exhaustively-bifurcate mode." Bentham occasionally finds it worthwhile to study at least the folly of our ancestors because in Leslie Stephen's paraphrase, "though their opinions were of little value, their practice is worth attending to; but chiefly because it shows the bad consequences of their opinions." However, neither a theory of history nor the citation of history bulk large in Bentham's thought.[10]

Neither, despite his *History of British India*, was James Mill much concerned with history as a guide to human endeavor or to the understanding of the world. R. G. Collingwood argues that Lockian empiricism was prevented from developing a true philosophy of history by its assumption of an unchanging human nature, which thus

[9]Collingwood indeed points out that strictly mathematical, theological, and scientific modes all are inapplicable to history: mathematics abstracts from time and space, theology is directed to "a single finite object," and science depends on verification through present observation and experiment (*Idea of History*, p. 5). As history came to be regarded as more important, historical knowledge had to be accommodated within theories of knowledge that focused primarily on explaining one or more of these three.

[10]Stephen, *The English Utilitarians*, I, 296–97; see also *The Works of Jeremy Bentham*, II, 401.

smuggled in a "substantialist" belief that only the unchanging can be known.[11] The elder Mill's thought clearly betrays such an orientation; it explains why he wrote about government in such a way that, in Macaulay's famous comment, "but for two or three passing allusions, it would not appear that the author was aware that any governments actually existed among men."[12] That no theory of history is necessary for the translation of documentary evidence into historical narrative would seem to have been James Mill's unquestioning view. The following passages from the introduction to Mill's own *History of British India* state this view with a fascinating starkness.

> In regard to evidence, the business of criticism visibly is, to bring to light the value of each article, to discriminate what is true from what is false, to combine partial statements, in order to form a complete account, to compare varying, and balance contradictory statements, in order to form a correct one.
>
> If, then, we may assume it as an acknowledged fact, that an account of India, complete in all its parts, at any one moment, still more through a series of ages, could never be derived from the personal observations of any one individual, but must be collected from the testimony of a great number of individuals, of any one of whom the powers of perception could extend but a little way, it follows, as a necessary consequence, that the man best qualified for dealing with evidence, is the man best qualified for writing the history of India.[13]

The final instrument for surveying and ordering the materials of history, the instrument that comprehends all

[11] Collingwood, *Idea of History*, pp. 76–85.

[12] *The Complete Writings of Thomas Babington Macaulay*, Cambridge edition, I, 384.

[13] James Mill, *The History of British India*, I, xvii, xxii. Mill is of course here anticipating the objection that he had never been in India, but there is no reason to doubt his honest subscription to the arguments here quoted.

others, turns out to be a grasp of the presumably immutable laws of the mind.

> To qualify a man for this great duty, hardly any kind or degree of knowledge is not demanded; hardly any amount of knowledge, which it is within the competence of one man to acquire, will be regarded as enough. It is plain, for example, that he needs the most profound knowledge of the laws of human nature, which is the end, as well as instrument, of every thing. It is plain, that he requires the most perfect comprehension of the principles of human society; or the course, into which the laws of human nature impel the human being, in his gregarious state, or when formed into a complex body along with others of his kind. The historian requires a clear comprehension of the practical play of the machinery of government; for, in like manner as the general laws of motion are counteracted and modified by friction, the power of which may yet be accurately ascertained and provided for, so it is necessary for the historian correctly to appreciate the counteraction which the more general laws of human nature may receive from individual or specific varieties, and that allowance for it with which his anticipations and conclusions ought to be formed.[14]

If Bentham and James Mill are empiricists who show little interest in the meaning of history, Coleridge serves as an outstanding example of the transcendentalist's depreciation of the value of history. The plan evolved for the *Encyclopaedia Metropolitana*, we note, creates four great divisions: (1) The Pure Sciences, (2) The Mixed and Applied Sciences, (3) The Biographical and Historical, and (4) The Miscellaneous and Lexicographical. The first two, taken together, comprise the "Philosophical" portion of the work, and it is this that receives Coleridge's greatest interest. He does say that "assuredly the great use of History is to acquaint us with the Nature of Man."[15] But the discovery of

[14] *Ibid.*, I, xxvii.

[15] *S. T. Coleridge's Treatise on Method*, p. 65.

"evils and imperfections" of mankind revealed by the study of history serves mainly to lead us "back to the importance of intellectual Method as their ground and sovereign remedy." Moreover, the "Biographical department" is "to teach the same truths by example, that have been evolved in the former divisions, and stimulate to the exertions that have developed them."[16] That is, the use of biography is simply to illustrate conclusions already arrived at through philosophical Method. It is true that in the *Statesman's Manual* Coleridge states that cures for the ills of the day must be sought "in the collation of the present with the past, in the habit of thoughtfully assimilating the events of our own age to those of the time before us";[17] but in *The Friend* appears the warning that "human experience, like the stern lights of a ship at sea, illumines only the path which we have passed over," and in the same work, Coleridge assures us that "an honest man . . . possesses a clearer light than that of history."[18] Our surest guide is a set of principles discovered through the exercise of philosophical Method, not in history, although examples from history have an illustrative value of which Coleridge makes considerable use. The only histories that seemed of direct value to Coleridge were those found in the Bible, where they are "the living educts of the imagination" rather than the products of "an unenlivened generalizing understanding."[19]

WHERE COLERIDGE searched the mind for evidence of the transcendent, Thomas Carlyle looked to his-

[16] *Ibid.*, p. 76.

[17] Coleridge, *Complete Works*, I, 424–25.

[18] *Ibid.*, II, 166 and 45.

[19] *Ibid.*, I, 436.

tory. There is a grandeur in Carlyle's rhetorically offered vision of history. Each man for him is "a living link in that Tissue of History, which inweaves all Being: watch well, or it will be past thee and seen no more." "Is not God's Universe a Symbol of the Godlike; is not Immensity a Temple; is not Man's History, and Men's History, a perpetual Evangel?" "Generation after generation takes to itself the Form of a Body; and forth issuing from Cimmerean Night, on Heaven's mission APPEARS. What Force and Fire is in each he expends. . . . Earth's mountains are levelled, and her seas filled up, in our passage. . . . On the hardest adamant some footprint of us is stamped in; the last Rear of the host will read traces of the earliest Van." "If now an existing generation of men stand so woven together, not less indissolubly does generation with generation. Hast thou ever meditated on that word, Tradition: how we inherit not Life only, but all the garniture and form of Life. . . ."[20] "Consider History with the beginnings of it stretching dimly into the remote Time: emerging darkly out of the mysterious Eternity: the ends of it enveloping *us* at this hour, whereof we at this hour, both as actors and relators, form part! In shape we might mathematically name it *Hyperbolic-Asymptotic*; ever of *infinite* breadth around us: soon shrinking within narrow limits: ever narrowing more and more into the infinite depth behind us. In essence and significance it has been called the true Epic Poem, and universal Divine Scripture, *whose* 'plenary inspiration' no man, out of Bedlam or in it, shall bring in question."[21]

To a man with such a vision of history there is no conflict between such statements as "history recommends itself as the most profitable of all studies" and a contempt for Dry-as-Dust the historian, digging his "mountains of dead ashes, wreck and burnt bones" from the past.[22] History is

[20] Carlyle, *Sartor Resartus*, in *Complete Works*, I, 17, 192, 201–2, and 186.

[21] Carlyle, "On History Again," in *Complete Works*, XV, 82.

[22] *Ibid.*, XV, 74; XII, 48.

indeed, as Carlyle explicitly sets the matter forth in an essay of 1830, "Philosophy teaching by Experience." But historical records preserve more of the trivial than the significant, and we can never fully comprehend anything in the past. "For though the whole meaning lies far beyond our ken; yet in that complex Manuscript, covered over with formless inextricably entangled unknown characters,—nay which is a *Palimpsest*, and had once prophetic writing, still dimly legible there,—some letters, some words, may be deciphered; and if no complete Philosophy, here and there an intelligible precept, available in practice, be gathered. . . ."[23]

Carlyle's *use* of history, we find, is precisely that suggested in this passage. He uses historical events, in the main, as illustrative; an event which suggests an "intelligible precept, available in practice" is offered in a way that insists on its complexity, fragmentary character, and ultimate mystery as much as on its intelligibility. The great example is of course *Past and Present*: the story of Abbot Sampson's election does not pretend to explain *how* the right nineteenth-century English leader may be found and elected. It nevertheless assures us that such men have been found and put in charge. It does not tell us precisely what measures should be taken in 1843 but shows us that certain effective measures have been applied in desperate situations in the past and underlines the principles which seem to Carlyle to underlie those measures. *Heroes and Hero-Worship* uses Odin, Mahomet, Dante, Shakespeare, Luther, Knox, Cromwell, Napoleon, and other historical figures as illustrative of principles, not as explanations of facts. This principle we find here, says Carlyle, but never does he imply that the cause or meaning of the event is exhausted in the principle. *Sartor* even may be read in this way—we grasp what meaning we can from the fragments of Teufelsdröckh's life possessed by the Editor; the Teufels-

[23] Carlyle, "On History," in *Complete Works*, XIV, 66.

dröckh thus created is a transmogrification of what Carlyle feels he can grasp from his own life, but the book never definitely explains either Teufelsdröckh or Carlyle. Detailed as are the actual historical narratives of *The French Revolution* and the *History of Frederick II*, the detail does more to vivify and stress the complexity of the man or period treated than to imply a definitive explanation. The sense of mystery, of forces underneath the surface, which Carlyle so often evokes becomes simple honesty rather than picturesque mystification: Carlyle is thus reminding us that he is offering the little which is decipherable from a blotted and mutilated page of history, offering fragments to shore against our present.

Past and Present is of especial significance in understanding Carlyle and history because of the importance for Carlyle of the period of English history from which the story of Abbot Samson comes. Unable to point directly to the eternal model he pursues, or to offer through ordinary language and logic a way of validating that vision, the transcendentalist is in sore need of some means of representing, however inadequately, what man's life ought to be like. The two likeliest solutions are the creation of an imagined Utopia in the future or the burnishing of a seemingly more golden age from the past. Carlyle chooses, in *Past and Present* and elsewhere, to look back. There had been, presumably, a time when power lay in the hands of the wisest, the overwhelming importance of transcendental norms had been acknowledged, and the order behind appearance had been reflected by an ordered hierarchy on earth.

Carlyle was of course swimming with the tide; interest in and praise for the quality of life in the middle ages had been swelling since the end of the eighteenth century. Coleridge had briefly contrasted feudal loyalties with nineteenth-century utilitarian theory in his 1817 *Lay Sermon Addressed to the Higher and Middle Classes*.[24] Cobbett's

[24] Coleridge, *Complete Works*, VI, 212. Cf. Carlyle, *Past and Present*, in *Complete Works*, XII, 260–64, and Ruskin, *The Works of John Ruskin*, X, 194–95.

iconoclastic *History of the Protestant Reformation* had appeared in 1824; *Sartor Resartus* and Keble's sermon on "National Apostasy," which initiated the Oxford Movement with all its devotion to the drama of the history of ecclesiastical controversy, share the year 1833; *Sartor* and *Past and Present* bracket Pugin's *Contrasts*, first published in 1836. And, as Margaret Grennan is at pains to establish in her very readable survey of the nineteenth-century enthusiasm for the middle ages in the introductory chapter to *William Morris, Medievalist and Revolutionary*, it proved possible, by emphasizing different features, to use medieval analogues to support a wide variety of remedies for the contemporary disorders of English culture. Carlyle picked those features we have already seen appeal to the transcendentally oriented.

In this regard, the transcendentalist is likely to be somewhat at one with the primitivist. Carlyle was hardly a primitivist in the popular sense—the period at which Abbot Sampson flourished was not all that primitive—but one finds a tincture of both chronological and cultural primitivism in his outlook. In the introductory chapter to *Primitivism and Related Ideas in Antiquity*, A. O. Lovejoy and George Boas explain the appeal of cultural primitivism—of the preference for a less civilized, and especially, less commercial and industrial society—as arising either out of approval of the simpler, less demanding and more self-expressive earlier culture or of admiration for the renunciation and self-discipline which, regarded from a different perspective, the same more primitive society will likely seem to exhibit. Carlyle seems to have felt both appeals—the culture of the earlier period was one whose hierarchical structure made life better for both Cedric and Gurth. Knowing their station gave them security, while imposing responsibilities and inculcating self-denial.[25] Moreover, as the authors of the study point out, primitivism, which must

[25] See Lovejoy and Boas, *Primitivism and Related Ideas in Antiquity*, pp. 9–10.

explain man's decline, generally opposes a belief in the "natural goodness of man."[26] Man must be led and taught. And, finally, Carlyle's injunction to decrease his denominator has the authentic Primitivist ring.

But Carlyle's attitude toward history can be reduced to no simple formula. Real complexity and difficulty become apparent when one asks the direction and meaning of historical change for Carlyle. Four major image clusters are used to represent change: the horloge of time, the Phoenix, the manufacture of cosmos out of chaos, and the wearing out and replacing of the clothes with which man strives to give visibility to the invisible or spiritual structure of the world. Each offers a different emphasis, though all four may be harmonized.

1) "Our clock strikes when there is a change from hour to hour; but no hammer in the Horloge of Time peals through the universe when there is a change from Era to Era."[27] This image appears in the 1830 essay "On History," and Carlyle quotes from this in the 1832 essay, "Death of Goethe."[28] Each time it is used to call attention both to the succession of "historical Transactions" which introduce new Eras and to the likelihood that at the time of occurrence the importance of such "historical Transactions" will be overlooked—and never perhaps correctly identified.

2) That history is a distinct succession of eras or periods appears even more strongly in the Phoenix metaphor, which is central to Chapter V of the third book of *Sartor*. The Editor sums up Teufelsdröckh's fragments on this head: "Thus is Teufelsdröckh content that old sick Society should be deliberately burnt (alas, with quite other fuel than spicewood); in the faith that she is a Phoenix; and

[26] *Ibid.*, pp. 17–18.

[27] Carlyle, *Complete Works*, XIV, 64.

[28] *Ibid.*, XV, 10; and see XVI, 384.

that a new heaven-born young one will rise out of her ashes!"[29] In context, the emphasis would seem to be on the convulsiveness of the burning, which will produce the new society and its difference from the old. And we recall that again and again throughout his works, apparent evils are seen by Carlyle, even as he is denouncing them, as the hopeful kindling of the conflagration that will burn the old and create the new—the French revolution, the reform bills, the new poor-laws, etc. However, Carlyle is at pains to remind us that change is accomplished continuously and often silently. "In that Fire-whirlwind, Creation and Destruction proceed together; ever as the ashes of the Old are blown about, do organic filaments of the New mysteriously spin themselves: and amid the rushing and the waving of the Whirlwind-Element come tones of a melodious Death-song, which end not but in tones of a more melodious Birth-song."[30]

3) "Be no longer a Chaos, but a World, or even Worldkin. Produce! Produce! Were it but the pitifullest infinitesimal fraction of a Product, produce it, in God's name!" This portion of the climax of "The Everlasting Yea" defines what work is: it is to be the manufacturing of a world, a cosmos, out of chaos. The opponent is chaos; the distinguishing characteristic of the world-to-be is order.

4) What is order, and how is it achieved? By making the invisible visible, by shaping the finite and transient as closely as possible to the eternal and infinite. We are led to the central doctrine of *Sartor*: that language, convention, and thought are all symbols with which one tries to clothe an invisible, infinite, eternal structure that already exists unseen and is to be recreated in the world of action and perception. "Art not thou too perhaps by this time made aware that all Symbols are properly Clothes; that all Forms

[29] Carlyle, *Sartor Resartus*, in *Complete Works*, I, 180.

[30] *Ibid.*, I, 185.

whereby Spirit manifests itself to sense, whether outwardly or in the imagination, are Clothes. . . ."[31] But symbols, like all other clothes, wear out, become too dull and threadbare to perform their function, and must be replaced. "In every new era . . . such Solution [of the problem of evil] comes out in different terms; and even the Solution of the last era has become obsolete, and is found unserviceable. For it is man's nature to change his Dialect from century to century; he cannot help it though he would."[32] The new clothes, however, will fit a little more exactly the invisible forms they make manifest. The "Descriptive-Historical" portion of Teufelsdröckh's volume, we are told, discussed the "origin and successive Improvement" of Clothes. Or again, "Society . . . is not dead: that Carcass, which you call dead Society, is but her mortal coil which she has shuffled off, to assume a nobler; she herself, through perpetual metamorphoses, in fairer and fairer development, has to live till Time also merge in Eternity."[33] Or, as he puts it in "Characteristics," "Thus in all Poetry, Worship, Art, Society, as one form passes into another, nothing is lost . . . under the mortal body lies a *soul* which is immortal; which anew incarnates itself in fairer revelation; and the Present is the living sum-total of the whole Past."[34] And, most hopeful of all: "The progress of man towards higher and nobler developments of whatever is highest and noblest in him, lies not only prophesied to Faith, but now written to the eye of Observation, so that he who runs may read."[35]

The implications of these metaphors are not wholly incompatible, yet one feels that the necessity of "retexturing" worn-out clothes is more emphasized than their successive

[31] *Ibid.*, I, 204.

[32] *Ibid.*, I, 144.

[33] *Ibid.*, I, 179.

[34] Carlyle, *Complete Works*, XIV, 379; and see I, 344.

[35] *Ibid.*, XIV, 377–78.

improvement, that the clear contrast between eras is more emphasized than the continuous combination of destruction and creation, that the duty of working against chaos is more emphasized than the possibility of gradually achieving order. Peter Allan Dale (*The Victorian Critic and the Idea of History*) believes that "like most of his contemporaries, Carlyle accepted the prevailing myth of progress" but goes on to say that Carlyle's "pessimism grew blacker, and his rage against the rotten fabric of society more bitter as he went on in his career without receiving any clear sign that the spiritual state of man was, in fact, getting better rather than worse."[36] The fact seems to be that while plenty of passages can be hunted out to show that Carlyle believed in progress,[37] on balance he is more impressed by the ever-renewed necessity to do battle than by man's victories.

A believer in progress would seem almost necessarily drawn to the painting of a future Utopia rather than the virtues of a former era. If, as Carlyle maintains, that which is good survives, there can hardly be any point in calling on mankind to reinstate old virtues. Nevertheless we are asked to look not forward but back to "the clear-beaming eyesight of Abbot Samson . . . [which] penetrates gradually to all nooks, and of the chaos makes a *kosmos* or ordered world!"[38] Carlyle's later pessimism is thus not so much an about-face as the relinquishment of an optimism for which his system of thought provided no adequate ground. Many a transcendentalist has pointed encouragingly toward and struggled for permanent improvement, but there seems something in the nature of the transcendentalist premise

[36] Dale, *The Victorian Critic and the Idea of History*, pp. 53–54.

[37] For instance, from "Characteristics": "Nay, if we look well to it, what is all Derangement, and necessity of great Change, in itself such an evil, but the product simply of *increased resources* which the old *methods* can no longer administer; of new wealth which the old coffers will no longer contain?" (Carlyle, *Complete Works*, XIV, 380).

[38] Carlyle, *Complete Works*, XII, 90.

which ultimately is uncomfortable with the idea that man as a whole is approaching, even asymptotically, the transcendental ideal; the belief that only a few in each age approach that ideal and attain that vision which allows them to see through clothes-symbols seems more congenial. After all, we must remember, time itself, in which historical change takes place, is an illusion. "But deepest of all illusory Appearances, for hiding Wonder, as for many other ends, are your two grand fundamental world-enveloping Appearances, SPACE and TIME. These, as spun and woven for us from before Birth itself, to clothe our celestial ME for dwelling here, and yet to blind it,—lie all-embracing, as the universal canvas, or warp and woof, whereby all minor Illusions, in this Phantasm Existence, weave and paint themselves."[39]

We find a similar tension in Ruskin. Probably the most significant of Ruskin's statements on history is the following from *Fors Clavigera*: "Wherever the Christian Church, or any section of it, has indeed resolved to live a Christian life, and keep God's laws in God's name,—there, instantly, manifest approval of Heaven is given by accession of *worldly* prosperity and victory. . . . This is the Temporal lesson of all history, and with that there is another Spiritual lesson,—namely, that in the ages of faith, conditions of prophecy and seer-ship exist, among the faithful nations, in painting and scripture, which are also immortal and divine."[40] History records the reward of virtue and the punishment of sin; art records man's understanding of God. I argue in a later essay that Ruskin's transcendentalism consists of a single principle: that God created man's faculties to be in harmony with the manifestation of Himself which is nature—true knowledge of the natural world, ardent appreciation of the beauty of that world, and obedience to right moral principle all result from the achievement of

[39] *Ibid.*, I, 197.

[40] Ruskin, *Complete Works*, XXIX, 337–38 (italics in original).

harmony with nature which is the worship of God. The Platonic interrelationship between a transcendental realm of Ideas and corresponding ideas implanted in man's mind here appears in its religious form. That man was created in God's image means, says Ruskin in Volume V of *Modern Painters*, "that the soul of man is still a mirror, wherein may be seen, darkly, the image of the mind of God."[41] This whole relationship between God, art, and man is nowhere in Ruskin better summed up than in the 1888 Epilogue to that volume:

> and now, in writing beneath the cloudless peace of the snows of Chamouni, what must be the really final words of the book which their beauty inspired and their strength guided, I am able, with yet happier and calmer heart than ever heretofore, to enforce its simplest assurance of Faith, that the knowledge of what is beautiful leads on, and is the first step, to the knowledge of the things which are lovely and of good report; and that the laws, the life, and the joy of beauty in the material world of God, are as eternal and sacred parts of His creation as, in the world of spirits, virtue; and in the world of angels, praise.[42]

The true, the good, and the beautiful are here bound together in the right transcendental manner. However, Ruskin's belief floats free from any larger transcendental framework of corollaries, deductions, or metaphysical proofs, because Ruskin is drawing directly on an established religious tradition, seasoned by Platonism, which he never anatomizes, even during the period he questioned it. As John Rosenberg's study of Ruskin insists, significant as is Ruskin's 1858 rejection of Evangelicalism, and tortured as were the years after about 1860, "One element of Ruskin's attitude toward nature remains constant: God is felt not only as the author of creation but as an actual power in

[41] *Ibid.*, VII, 260.

[42] *Ibid.*, VII, 464.

it." Or again, as developed in Robert Hewison's helpful analysis in *John Ruskin: The Argument of the Eye*, Ruskin was taught to read the world according to the Evangelical system of typology: "the Evangelicals believed that both the Bible and the external world were expressions of the same Divine Being: there was no doubt that the external world continued in its existence expressing the will of God; and similarly the historical figures of the Bible performed their own worldly functions as well as foreshadowing the coming of Christ."[43] Though Ruskin may have abandoned his Evangelicalism in his "unconversion" of 1858, the typological mode of thought remained. It is not surprising then that his almost constant view of history is that of the Old Testament—men and nations who are faithful are rewarded, those who go whoring after strange Gods are punished, perhaps destroyed.

Ultimately, for all his reforming zeal, Ruskin does not seem to expect steady progress toward perfection. Society constantly changes, but the direction of change will be now toward, now away from, harmony with God. "Change *must* come; but it is ours to determine whether change of growth, or change of death."[44] There are victories for individual men and individual societies, but their effect is not lasting. The Lord's battle is a never-ceasing one. Venice had grown toward and then away from morality, a fact of especial significance to nineteenth-century England, for, according to the opening sentences of *The Stones of Venice*, "Since first the dominion of men was asserted over the ocean, three thrones, of mark beyond all others, have been set upon its sands: the thrones of Tyre, Venice, and England." "The exaltation, the sin, and the punishment of Tyre," are, he tells us, to be found in the Bible; and he is about to trace a similar sequence for Venice. When then of England? "It is an age of progress, you tell me. Is your

[43] Rosenberg, *The Darkling Glass: A Portrait of Ruskin's Genius*, p. 7; Hewison, *John Ruskin: The Argument of the Eye*, p. 27.

[44] Ruskin, *Complete Works*, XVIII, 455.

progress chiefly in this, that you *cannot* see the King, the Lord of Hosts, but only Baal, instead of Him?"[45] Whether one looked to art or political economy, the answer, already becoming clear at the time of the writing of *The Stones of Venice*, seemed to be Baal. In the closing pages of the final volume of *Modern Painters*, Ruskin takes care to remind us that the England of his time is infected with "faithlessness, or despair, the despair which has been shown already to be characteristic of this present century, and most sorrowfully manifested in its greatest men; but existing in an infinitely more fatal form in the lower and general mind, reacting upon those who ought to be its teachers.[46]

John Rosenberg remarks that Ruskin ceased to believe in a "divine patterning of history" some time after *The Stones of Venice* and cites an 1864 letter in which Ruskin writes "there is no law of history any more than of a kaleidoscope. . . ."[47] However, the quotation I have cited above seems to suggest that Ruskin never totally abandoned the belief. On the other hand even when he was most confidently interpreting history according to the Old Testament conception of rewards and punishments visited on an entire people, he equally followed the Judeo-Christian tradition in exhorting the individual to righteousness regardless of the state of the nation. Thus, the final chapter of *Modern Painters* also takes care to remind us—with a transcendentalism speaking in religious terms—that the individual man is not bound by temporal history. "This kingdom [of God] it is not in our power to bring; but it is, to receive . . . it is still at our choice; the simoom-dragon may still be served if we will, in the fiery desert, or else God walking in the garden, at cool of day."[48] Though his language within the chapter as a whole implies that God's kingdom will

[45] *Ibid.*, XXVIII, 146–47.

[46] *Ibid.*, VII, 444.

[47] Rosenberg, *The Darkling Glass*, p. 87*n*.

[48] Ruskin, *Complete Works*, VII, 459.

come, this is more an apocalyptic vision than an historical prophecy. As Frederic Harrison wrote in an open letter to Ruskin in the *Fortnightly Review*, "The truth is, that you really forswear 'evolution' and all its works, because you find it difficult to square with the poetic and prophetic scheme of life."[49] That "poetic and prophetic" scheme has the common transcendental structure: history provides effective demonstration of the fate of nations in which evil gains sway, but the necessary righteousness cannot be achieved by institutions but only by individuals. Gaylord Leroy remarks, "Ruskin, like Carlyle, writes constantly in such a way as to imply that social problems have their source in personal ethics and can be solved through an appeal to the individual conscience."[50] I would say that much more than implication is involved—for the transcendentally oriented thinker, no other solution is possible.

William Morris, in whom, despite his reverence for Carlyle and Ruskin, transcendental views flickered at the point of extinction, was able more wholeheartedly to discern progress in history. He finds "inchoate order in the remotest times, varying indeed among different races and countries, but swayed always by the same laws, moving forward ever towards something that seems the very opposite of that which it started from, and yet the earlier order never dead but living in the new, and slowly moulding it to a recreation of its former self."[51] For this reason Morris is more able to admit the evils of the feudal system and less driven to defend the necessity of the control of the many by the few. As Margaret Grennan says, "Morris, unlike others interested in using medieval concepts in the reconstruction of modern society, found little to appeal to him in

[49] Harrison, "Past and Present: A Letter to Mr. Ruskin," rptd. in *The Choice of Books*, p. 132.

[50] Leroy, *Perplexed Prophets: Six Nineteenth-Century British Authors*, p. 99.

[51] Morris, "Architecture and History," in *Collected Works*, XXII, 298.

a hierarchical world."[52] That which he holds up to our admiration is primarily the guild system, so much praised in the later writings of Ruskin. When in need of a model, he looks to the middle ages as an example of a time in which art and work were better integrated into man's life, but he admits the impossibility of going back to an earlier form of society. "To my mind it is a strange view to take of historical knowledge and insight, that it should set us on the adventure of trying to retrace our steps towards the past, rather than give us some glimmer of insight into the future."[53]

MACAULAY might well be taken as the prime example of the empiricist use of history, but Macaulay was eminently the politician and essentially not a metaphysician. He was simply the most articulate spokesman for the type of liberalism most prominent in nineteenth-century England; in Richmond Beatty's words, "His liberalism, in brief, was an economy designed to minister to the materialistic ambitions of a single class, a class whose interests, he came to think, were identified inextricably with the welfare of the entire nation."[54] Beatty seems to be correct in finding Macaulay's increased approval of the utilitarian doctrines to be the result not of agreement with the premises from which these developed but of his having "already lived to see a number of their recommendations enacted into quite practical and sensible laws."[55]

Macaulay's essay on History, published in the *Edinburgh Review* in 1828 (the central doctrines of which are

[52] Grennan, *William Morris, Medievalist and Revolutionary*, p. 63.

[53] Morris, "Architecture and History," in *Collected Works*, XXII, 314.

[54] Beatty, *Lord Macaulay*, p. xiii.

[55] *Ibid.*, p. 245.

summarized in the opening pages of "Hallam's Constitutional History," published four months later), reduces the difficulty in writing history to that of writing imaginatively while remaining within the realm of fact. "A perfect historian must possess an imagination sufficiently powerful to make his narrative affecting and picturesque. Yet he must control it so absolutely as to content himself with the materials which he finds, and to refrain from supplying deficiencies by additions of his own."[56] Excellent advice, but what the material of history is, we are not told, nor, having reminded us that history is "philosophy teaching by examples," does Macaulay pause to explain and justify his belief in *what* philosophy teaches by those examples. Yet, as everyone knows, Macaulay does believe that history teaches a constant lesson—it exhibits the constant improvement in man's ability to supply his wants and to think. Indeed, in the latter task it is hard to see in what way man can go farther: "In our own country, the sound doctrines of trade and jurisprudence have been, within the lifetime of a single generation, dimly hinted, boldly propounded, defended, systematized, adopted by all reflecting men of all parties, quoted in legislative assemblies, incorporated into laws and treaties."[57] Progress flowing, despite eddies and backwaters, like a great river, the roles of individual men, however apparently influential, assume infinitely less importance than for one who, like Carlyle, regards them as the sole conduits provided for new truths. "But we must remember," says Macaulay, "how small a proportion the good or evil effected by a single statesman can bear to the good or evil of a great social system."[58] Such an antiheroic interpretation is the ground of Macaulay's great contribution to the gathering of materials for history: no source of evidence is too mean, too mundane—the house-

[56] Macaulay, *The Complete Writings*, I, 236.

[57] *Ibid.*, I, 265.

[58] *Ibid.*, I, 278.

hold book of the Northumberland family outweighs, for some purposes, any number of royal proclamations.

For a philosophical empiricist's interpretation of history, we do better to turn to John Stuart Mill. Mill was liberated from his father's narrow and unquestioning view of history by the joint influences of Macaulay's attack on the Essay on Government and Saint-Simon's view of human progress. Unlike his father, he saw history as having a major use: the explanation of the causes of the present state of society for the purposes of predicting at least its immediate direction of development and of recognizing the remedies needed for the evils of the present and the immediate future. We find Mill using history in this way in some of his earliest essays. "The Spirit of the Age" is divided into five parts which, though in a sense arbitrary since they are the result of his having had to publish the essay in five numbers of the *Examiner*, are nevertheless convenient as a means of indicating its peculiar structure. In the first section, Mill considers the characteristics that seem to set the age off from earlier ages, especially its lack of fixed opinions, its transitional character (Mill uses the word "transitional" in a rather special sense). The second section argues the necessity of certain accepted principles as the basis of any settled, stable society. The third section begins by explaining more clearly what Mill means by a transitional as opposed to a natural state of society. "Society may be said to be in its *natural* state, when worldly power, and moral influence, are habitually and undisputedly exercised by the fittest persons whom the existing state of society affords." "Society may be said to be in its transitional state when it contains other persons fitter for worldly power and moral influence than those who have hitherto enjoyed them."[59] The remainder of the section examines the mechanisms by which worldly power and fitness have been made congruent in the past and how it is that they

[59] J. S. Mill, *Essays on Politics and Culture*, p. 17.

are not so in the present. Sections IV and V explore the union of moral power and fitness and the reasons for their increasing disjunction.

"The Spirit of the Age" opens with the argument that "since every age contains in itself the germ of all future ages as surely as the acorn contains the future forest, a knowledge of our own age is the foundation of prophecy—the only key to the history of prosperity." Mill pauses to qualify this argument by urging that a knowledge of the present age "also is history, and the most important part of history, and the only part which a man may know with absolute certainty, by using the proper means. He may learn in a morning's walk through London more of the history of England during the nineteenth century, than all the professed English histories in existence will tell him concerning the other eighteen. . . ."[60] But despite this homage to the importance of knowing one's own age, we find Mill devoting a good part of his essay to historical states and processes, particularly in the last three sections in which he examines such questions as why the landed aristocracy were at one time the fittest to exercise worldly power, and why they are so no longer; why the Catholic clergy was at one time the fittest for moral power, and why they are so no longer.[61] As a matter of fact, the essay, which seems quite clearly argued as one reads it but is hard to keep straight in retrospect, constantly plays back and forth between generalizations from history, specific examples from history, analysis of the structure of the society of the present, and arguments based on what are offered as general truths about the operation of the human mind. The influ-

[60] *Ibid.*, p. 3

[61] Everyone knows that part of Mill's interest in history, as exhibited in this essay, is a result of his reading of the Saint-Simonians. However, the interplay between ways of looking at history is apparent in the fact that Saint-Simon's theory of the necessary advance from stage to stage is, in a sense, a secularized version of a religious interpretation of history as stated, for instance, in Burnet's *Theory of the Earth* (1684–1690). See Tuveson, *Millenium and Utopia*, p. 165.

ence of Saint-Simon is certainly there in the insistence on the succession of modes of thought and social structures, but it is closely intertwined with typical utilitarian epistemological preoccupations.

The essay "Civilization" is argued in the same way—generalizations about history and the working of the human mind are used to explain the present, the present is seen to shadow forth the future, and then the best means of coping with the seemingly inevitable direction of the development are discussed. The assumptions behind both essays are (1) that the conditions within society constantly change, (2) that, as they do, new structures of thought are inevitably created, (3) that the new structures of thought initiate further changes in society, (4) that social arrangements and norms perfectly defensible, perhaps almost unimprovable at one time, when they place power in the hands of the fittest, become pernicious at a later time, and (5) that the gradual evolution of states of society in the main represents constant improvement. These assumptions seem perhaps bland enough, but they deny the transcendental assumptions that there is an eternal model for man's emulation which the seers of every age can look to, that moral principles are unchangingly incorporated in the soul and are in harmony with the transcendent model, and that thus the philosopher, seer, or saint can and should, in any age, live at least in approximation to that model. Man is, for Mill, not only forced constantly to correct his beliefs and principles by experience, but in his correction of them he creates new forms of experience which then require further modification of these beliefs and principles.

This empiricist mode of thought runs all through his major essays; a signal illustration is the final portion of *Utilitarianism* in which he argues that what is just in one age is not necessarily just in another, that justice is simply utility. This of course is nothing more than a direct statement of arguments presented throughout "The Spirit of the Age." "To find fault with our ancestors for not having annual parliaments, universal suffrage, and vote by ballot, would be like quarrelling with the Greeks and Romans for not using steam navigation, when we know it is so safe and expeditious; which would be, in short, simply finding fault with the third century before Christ for not being the eighteenth century after. . . . Human nature must proceed step by step, in politics as well as in physics."[62]

But though social and political arrangements of past ages may often have been justified, Mill is as adamant as Bentham against romanticizing the past and thus blinding ourselves to the evils we have outgrown. His essay on "The Age of Chivalry" is devoted to defending the conclusion "that the compound of noble qualities, called the *spirit of chivalry* (a rare combination in all ages) was almost unknown in the age of chivalry; that the age so called was equally distinguished by moral depravity and by physical wretchedness; that there is no class of society at this day in any civilized country, which has not a greater share of what are called the knightly virtues, than the knights themselves; that, far from civilizing and refining the rest of the world, it was not till very late, and with great difficulty, that the rest of the world could succeed in civilizing them."[63]

In Mill's essays, then, we see the working, in somewhat imperfect and undeveloped form, of a method for treating history, and thus society, which is more fully and consciously formulated in his *Logic*: "The fundamental problem . . . of the social science," runs a key passage in the *Logic*, "is to find the laws according to which any state of society produces the state which succeeds it and takes its place. This opens the great and vexed question of the progressiveness of man and society. . . ." Mill's views on this "great and vexed question" are difficult to sum up without considerable reference to the ninety-five percent

[62] J. S. Mill, *Essays on Politics and Culture*, p. 23.

[63] J. S. Mill, *Westminster Review*, VI (1826), 62–103.

of the *Logic* that precedes these final pages. But the essence of the whole argument lies in the following statement: "The circumstances in which mankind are placed, operating according to their own laws and to the laws of human nature, form the characters of human beings; but the human beings, in their turn, mould and shape the circumstances for themselves and for those who come after them."[64] The result is a progressive series of changes (generally, but not necessarily consistently, in the direction of improvement) which are most difficult to explain and predict. Looking back one can find certain principles that seem to explain the order of succession of states of society, but these can only be "empirical laws" (that is, generalizations from observation).[65] The upshot is that while the succession of states of society is too complex to be deduced accurately from the laws of the human mind, no theory founded merely on the summation of observations can have sufficient certainty. The proper method of procedure then is to ascertain empirical laws "and connect them with the laws of human nature, by deductions showing that such were the derivative laws naturally to be expected as the consequences of those ultimate ones."[66] This is the Inverse Deductive or Historical method.[67] To simplify its pur-

[64] J. S. Mill, *System of Logic*, 8th ed., pp. 595–96.

[65] Earlier, Mill defines empirical laws specifically as "those uniformities which observation or experience has shown to exist, but on which [scientific enquirers] hesitate to rely in cases varying much from those which have been actually observed, for want of seeing *why* such a law should exist (*System of Logic*, p. 338).

[66] *Ibid.*, p. 598.

[67] That the Inverse Deductive method was the proper means of pursuing the science of politics (and, by extension, history and all social science) dawned on him, Mill tells us in the *Autobiography*, in 1830, the eventual result of Macaulay's attack on his father's "Essay on Government" (J. S. Mill, *Autobiography*, p. 103). The criticism there sketched out of the methods espoused by Macaulay on the one hand and James Mill and Bentham on the other are much more extensively developed in chapters VII, VIII, and IX of Book Six of the *System of Logic* ("On the Logic of the Moral Sciences"), the summary and the

suit, Mill suggests that there seems one "predominant, and almost paramount" agent of social progress: "the state of the speculative faculties of mankind, including the nature of the beliefs which by any means they have arrived at concerning themselves and the world by which they are surrounded."[68] The method is led up to by the whole of Mill's *Logic*, which is throughout an empiricist manifesto; the empiricist assumptions can be easily traced out wherever Mill turns toward history for verification.

Mill's interpretation of the use of history and his analysis of the proper method of treating it can be found in such empiricist statements on the subject as Harrison's essays collected as *The Meaning of History*, which reproduces, in simpler form, most of Mill's arguments. Like Mill, Harrison argues for the interpretation of history according to principles of human nature that will nevertheless manifest themselves differently within the various social structures that they both create and alter. And he joins Mill in emphasizing the difficulty of determining whether man progresses in any absolute sense, while implying the belief that he does.[69]

John Morley's *On Politics and History* similarly repeats Mill's point about the unpredictability of history; influences that would seem slight and occurrences that appear accidental make prediction by means of general laws impossible. What Mill, Morley, and Harrison are all ultimately opposing is precisely the ransacking of history for illustrative parallels that we find in Carlyle and Ruskin. "History's direct lessons are few, its specific morals rare," says Morley in *On Politics and History*.[70] Seeming paral-

---

anecdote comprising the argument just summarized from chapter X of Book Six.

[68] J. S. Mill, *System of Logic*, p. 604.

[69] On this point, cf. Mill's essay on Coleridge in *Collected Works*, vol. X, and Harrison's essays "A Few Words About the Nineteenth Century" and "Past and Present: A Letter to Mr. Ruskin" in *The Choice of Books*.

[70] Morley, *Notes on Politics and History*, p. 104.

lels may be found for everything, but they are always untrustworthy. All three would say of Carlyle what Morley quoted M. Aulard as saying of Taine: "The document does not speak to Taine; it is he who all the time is speaking to the document."[71]

When Carlyle emphasizes the change toward an ever-higher order of life, he is quite close to Mill's final position. The constant weaving of new clothes to replace ill-fitting ones can serve as a metaphor for Mill's argument in *The Spirit of the Age* that the adequate constitutions of one age are the intolerable ones of the next. Carlyle's view of the relation of right to might, in one of its formulations, is equally close to Mill. "But indeed the rights of man . . . are little worth ascertaining in comparison to the *mights* of man—to what portion of his rights he has any chance of being able to make good! . . . The ascertainable temporary rights of man vary not a little, according to place and time."[72] The whole argument surrounding this statement from "Chartism" implies that "might" means not sheer brute strength, but capacity, within the culture of a particular time, to exercise rights for the good of society. But Carlyle could not hold firmly to such a position because justice or right must exist eternally and unchangingly—they shine forth for the men of vision at all times. So that in "Chartism" we also find Carlyle stating that "an ideal of right does dwell in all men, in all arrangements, pactions and procedures of men: it is to this ideal of right, more and more developing itself as it is more and more approximated to, that human Society forever tends and struggles," and in the next sentence stating "we say also that any given thing either *is* unjust or else just. . . ."[73] with the unmistakable implication that the justness or unjustness is to be known by a transcendental standard, not by an evaluation of the

[71] *Ibid.*, p. 117.

[72] Carlyle, "Chartism," in *Complete Works*, XVI, 68.

[73] *Ibid.*, XVI, 69.

current state of society. The two views continually clash; and when in *Latter-Day Pamphlets* Carlyle proclaims that "no world, or thing here below, ever fell into misery, without having first fallen into folly, into sin against the Supreme Ruler of it, by adopting as a law of conduct what was not a law, but the reverse of one,"[74] transcendental absolutism is triumphing. From this point of view, harmony, order, happiness even, are attainable *now*, not merely in the future—at least the ideal can be descried, and presumably could be obtained were men guided by those who are guided by the ideal. The heroic leader who can see the undistorted idea of justice, conduct, or whatever, and thus transcend, not merely analyze and patch the present social structure, is man's hope. Gather ye statistics where ye may, says Carlyle, looking out on the utilitarians heaping facts into parliamentary reports, the ideal gives life, the arithmetical average killeth. "With what serene conclusiveness a member of some Useful Knowledge-Society stops your mouth with a figure of arithmetic! To him it seems he has there extracted the elixir of the matter, on which now nothing more can be said. It is needful that you look into his said extracted elixir; and ascertain, alas, too probably, not without a sigh, that it is wash and vapidity, good only for the gutters."[75] It is for this reason that almost everything that Carlyle writes, from "Signs of the Times" (1829) to "Shooting Niagara" (1867) is a plea for the right leader. Get the right leader, and all will be added unto you.

THOUGH MATTHEW ARNOLD praised his father's historical sense, he himself seldom speaks directly of the meaning of history, so seldomly that most readers fail to

[74] Carlyle, *Complete Works*, II, 305.

[75] *Ibid.*, XVI, 42–43.

notice that the interpretation of history presents a problem for him. One finds of course a number of passing references to history which echo one or another recognized point of view: "History," he tells us in *Friendship's Garland*, "is a series of waves, coming gradually to a head and then breaking, and . . . as the successive waves come up, one nation is seen at the top of this wave, and then another of the next."[76] And since Hebraism and Hellenism, he tells us in *Culture and Anarchy*, may be regarded as rivals as "exhibited in man and his history," it would seem that we are indebted to history for the discovery of such relationships. One can also, it would appear, judge the adequacy of certain principles and policies by reference to the past; for instance, in his review of Curtius's *History of Greece*, Arnold tells us that "unlimited freedom and the practical school of public life are not enough by themselves, are not self-acting for a people's salvation—this is what we say, and what Greek history and all history, seems to us to prove."[77] Indeed, inasmuch as the value of culture would seem to be in making possible the tracing of parallels, we should expect to find Arnold judging present questions in terms of historic parallels much more often than he does.

That he does not, results perhaps largely from his sense of the way one historical period gives way to the next and the institutions appropriate to a given period are driven out by new social arrangements. Gaylord Leroy presents an Arnold who saw history "as a process of dialectical advance in which the part fulfills itself, only to be superseded by a new mode of development which itself will be superseded in turn," while Peter Allan Dale offers an Arnold fearing history and exhibiting a "melancholic preoccupation with the decline of civilization before the relentless march of the Zeitgeist."[78] Arnold indeed seems at times like Mill

[76] Arnold, *Complete Prose Works*, V, 30–31.

[77] *Ibid.*, V, 283.

[78] Leroy, *Perplexed Prophets*, p. 51; Dale, *The Victorian Critic*, p. 139.

in recognizing the necessary change of institutions, now like Carlyle in regarding the alternation of Hellenic and Hebraic ages, of periods of concentration and expansion as containing as much ground for gloom as hope. In any case, as we shall see, history requires a principle of interpretation external to itself. "Human thought, which made all institutions, inevitably saps them, resting only in that which is absolute and eternal," writes Arnold as the closing words of "Democracy."[79] Mill would have endorsed the first part of that sentence, Carlyle the second. The question is of course how to discover the absolute and eternal by which to judge history.

Actually, the greater part of Arnold's comments on the meaning of history occurs in the context of his examination of what is essential in religion, and specifically in the Bible; looking closely at the most significant of these, one begins to see why Arnold uses history so gingerly. In the first place, we find that "in spite of its containing much that is mere history, and, like all history, sometimes true, sometimes false,"[80] the Bible may properly be called "the Word of God" because it contains "the precepts of the universal divine law written in our hearts." The history given by the Bible is not the source of the authority of these precepts: we recognize their "divinity" because they are the same with an "inly-written and self-proving law." But though "inly-written," the precepts that Arnold finds in the Bible *are* a revelation in that obedience to them leads to discovery that they are indeed written in the heart and do indeed lead to blessedness.

This discovery is to be found both in personal experience and man's accumulated experience. "Now, just as the best recommendation of the oracle committed to Israel, *Righteousness is salvation*, is found in our more and more discovering, in our own history and in the whole history of

[79] Arnold, *Complete Prose Works*, II, 29.

[80] *Ibid.*, III, 166.

the world, that it *is* so, so shall we find it to be with the method and secret of Jesus. . . . Let us but well observe what comes, in ourselves or the world, of trying any other, of not being convinced that this is righteousness, and this only; and we shall find ourselves more and more, as by irresistible viewless hands, caught and drawn towards the Christian revelation. . . . No proof can be so solid as this experimental proof."[81] Personal and historical experience are equally confirmatory of religion and moral precepts, and all history provides the same lesson as Biblical history: "'The nation and kingdom that will not serve thee shall perish, yea, those nations shall be utterly wasted.' It is so; since all history is an accumulation of experiences that what men and nations fall by is want of *conduct*."[82] But, despite these appeals to history and personal human experience, both remain always for Arnold a means of verification, not the source of the discovery, of the religious precepts. For all his emphasis on the experiential verification of the essentials of what religion teaches, Arnold never enters on the empiricists' argument that the *source* of all worthwhile knowledge is experience. Without an awareness of the essential precepts of religion, we will inevitably misread the Bible and history. "It is because we cannot trace God in history that we stay the craving of our minds with a fancy-account of him, made up by putting scattered expressions of the Bible together, and taking them literally. . . . He that cannot watch the God of the Bible, and the salvation of the Bible, gradually and on an immense scale discovering themselves and *becoming*, will insist on seeing them ready-made, and in such precise and reduced dimensions as may suit his narrow mind."[83]

But how does one discover the essential precepts and separate them from "mere history," from inaccurate or mis-

[81] Arnold, *Literature and Dogma*, in *Complete Prose Works*, VI, 401–2.

[82] *Ibid.*, VI, 387.

[83] *Ibid.*, VI, 152.

leading interpretations? How does one, in other words, extract the revelation? Arnold's answer is not unexpected: "We come back to our old remedy of *culture*,—knowing the best that has been thought and known in the world; which turns out to be, in another shape, and in particular relation to the Bible, *getting the power, through reading, to estimate the proportion and relation in what we read*."[84] But, as we have already seen, history does not appear to provide us, in itself, with the means of knowing what *is* the best that is known and thought. Indeed, as Arnold argues in the opening paragraphs of "The Bishop and the Philosopher," any book, including any historical account, must be evaluated by literary criticism, whose "most important function is to try books as to the influence which they are calculated to have upon the general culture of single nations or of the world at large."[85] It also seems clear that what this means is that the value of even an historical work is to be judged in terms of its tendency to bring the present general state of culture closer to the culture that would obtain if all men knew and acted on the best that has been known and thought.

An alternate formulation which Arnold uses in speaking of the study of the Bible is "the history of the human spirit." One gains experience of the history of the human spirit through letters. "For the thing turns upon understanding the manner in which men have thought, their way of using words, and what they mean by them. And by knowing letters, by becoming conversant with the best that has been thought and said in the world, we become acquainted not only with the history, but also with the scope and powers, of the instruments which men employ in thinking and speaking."[86]

What we ultimately find, then, is that history, in which

[84] *Ibid.*, VI, 153.

[85] Arnold, *Complete Prose Works*, III, 41.

[86] *Ibid.*, VI, 196, also see pp. 20, 411.

is imbedded "the best that has been thought and known," must be interpreted by culture, the best that has been thought and known itself: that the "revelation" provided by the Bible, which might presumably be thought to be a guide to the best that is thought and known, requires culture for its discovery, and the personal experience, which confirms the revelation, requires culture, or the revelation which culture separates from the "mere history" of the Bible, for its interpretation. Or again, that the "history of the human spirit" necessary for understanding the Bible, and thus the God of the Bible, is to be separated from history itself by culture. However one looks at it, history, historical events, interpretations of history, the purported historical record which is the Bible, acquire meaning only in the light of culture. The meaning of history will thus depend on what an individual finds to be best among what has been known and thought. Arnold seems to have no doubt that he can identify the best, but the process by which the gold is separated from the dross remains mysterious. Arnold lets us look on while he applies his touchstone, but how does one acquire for oneself a true philosopher's stone? Frederic Harrison's clever satire on *Culture and Anarchy* cuts accurately to the heart of the matter.

> "You have excellently described [says Harrison's Arminius] . . . a very noble condition or state of the soul. . . . Let me now ask you to describe the process by which it is attained."
>
> "Attained? got at?" said I drearily, for I felt stunned by this unexpected question.
>
> "Yes," rejoined he in a resolute tone; "how is it got at?" and he waited for my answer.
>
> "I suppose it comes," said I vaguely.[87]

It is also instructive to compare Arnold's concept of the relation between culture and history with the empiricist

[87] Harrison, "Culture: A Dialogue" in *The Choice of Books*, pp. 100–101; originally appeared in the *Fortnightly Review* (1867).

Morley's advice to his hearers at the Midland Institute in 1876. In the address entitled "On Popular Culture," Morley recommends the study of history as a means of seeing one's way "more clearly through what is happening to-day. I want to know what men thought and did in the thirteenth century, not out of any dilettante or idle antiquarian's curiosity, but because the thirteenth century is at the root of what men think and do in the nineteenth."[88] But ancillary to the study of history, or almost anything else, for Morley is the study of "what constitutes Evidence," with specific recommendation of Mill's *Logic*, Jevons's *Principles of Science*, *Smith's Leading Cases*, and Bentham's *Rationale of Judicial Evidence* and *Book of Fallacies*. The juxtaposition of Morley's recommendations for the acquisition of culture by the populace and Arnold's high standard of acquaintance with the best that has been known and thought (what would Arnold have said to the inclusion of *Smith's Leading Cases* and Bentham's *Book of Fallacies* therein—or to the recommendation of French literature because it comprises "the most amusing and refreshing set of books in the world"?)[89] pretty adequately suggests the gulf between empiricist and transcendentalist, tempered as these positions are in Morley and Arnold. Morley sees history as a source of experience which, when evaluated according to the principles of evidence and reduced to general laws, comprises the core of culture; Arnold reads history by the light of the culture which has somehow already been extracted from it.

Matthew Arnold's historical/cultural doctrine can be seen as the end product of a gradual weakening of the transcendental component of an essentially Anglican tradition extending to him from Coleridge through Thomas

[88] Morley, *Critical Miscellanies*, III, 9.

[89] *Ibid.*, III, 5–6. Another glove in Arnold's face: "The best thing that I can think of as happening to a young man is this: that he should have been educated at a day-school in his own town; that he should have opportunities of following also the higher education in his own town; and that at the earliest convenient time he should be taught to earn his own living" (III, 27).

Arnold. Many a pronouncement of Thomas Arnold's sounds like that of a Coleridge in which transcendental assumptions have been replaced by a combination of common sense and Christian morality, sounds, that is, like Coleridge half-transmuted into the author of *Literature and Dogma.*[90]

Thomas Arnold of course carried on the accommodation of the Bible to human judgments which Coleridge, in *Confessions of an Inquiring Spirit*, had begun.

> Coleridge: "The more tranquilly an inquirer takes up the Bible as he would any other body of ancient writings, the livelier and steadier will be his impressions of its superiority to all other books."
>
> Arnold: "An inquiring spirit is not a presumptuous one, but the very contrary: He whose whole recorded life was intended to be our perfect example, is described as gaining instruction in the Temple by hearing and asking questions: the one is almost useless without the other."[91]

Matthew Arnold's view of history was a step further along this road. For all the efforts devoted to defending that portion of the Biblical message he could accept, he found much less *specific* instruction in the Bible and the religious doctrines derived therefrom than his father. Lacking Coleridgean transcendental convictions, both father and son look back to history; but history is not self-interpretive. Matthew Arnold looks to culture to provide the interpretive light his father found in liberally interpreted doctrines of the Anglican Church.

[90] For instance, we find this quotation in Stanley's *The Life and Correspondence of Thomas Arnold*: "I cannot understand what is the good of a national Church if it be not to Christianize the nation, and introduce the principles of Christianity into men's social and civil relations, and expose the wickedness of that spirit which maintains the gamelaws, and in agriculture and trade seems to think that there is no such sin as covetousness, and that if a man is not dishonest, he has nothing to do but make all the profit of his capital that he can" (I, 247).

[91] Coleridge, *Confessions of an Inquiring Spirit*, ed. H. S. Hart, p. 75; Arnold, "Mutual Relations of Knowledge," in *The Miscellaneous Works of Thomas Arnold*, p. 303.

VII

Philosophy and Form

I HAVE ALREADY had the occasion to remark instances of both success and difficulty in finding literary forms or structures appropriate to the metaphysical views from which the specific message of an author arises. The question indeed can hardly be avoided in treating any prose writer with a systematic set of beliefs, certainly not those of nineteenth-century England. However, I should like here to focus on it more directly. I wish first to consider an intriguing example of a failed structure: Robert Southey's treatment of moral, political, and economic questions in his *Colloquies*. John Ruskin's analysis of the principles of architecture—and, of course, of aesthetic, moral, and economic questions—in *The Stones of Venice* will provide us with an equally intriguing example of a most successful accommodation of thought and structure. Looking then to three very different kinds of autobiographies, I will suggest that the problems every reader encounters in the *Biographia Literaria* are due not only to Coleridge's well-known disinclination to see a major project through, but his more specific failure to find a form compatible with his premises, while Carlyle's *Sartor Resartus* and J. S. Mill's *Autobiography* prove wonderfully appropriate to their authors' respective metaphysics.

For every person who has read Robert Southey's *Sir Thomas More: or, Colloquies on the Progress and Prospects of Society* (1829), there are perhaps a hundred who know Macaulay's famous review of it. However, those whose knowledge of that work is confined to the review will have an inadequate idea of its apparent oddities or the mode of thought that led Southey to produce it. After a general satire on Southey's mind, Macaulay begins his discussion of the *Colloquies* proper by briefly ridiculing its structure. "What cost in machinery, yet what poverty in effect! A ghost brought in to say what any man might have said!"[1] Macaulay's main thrust is directed against Southey's interpretation of the political and economic state of the country and his failure to support that interpretation with logically consistent arguments, or, indeed, any arguments at all. But many are the curious points that Macaulay silently passes over: the lack of an apparent order in the colloquies, the strange intermixture of details of local history and scene-sketching with sweeping pronouncements on the destiny of England, the amount of seemingly inconclusive commentary on historical events, the vagueness of the remedies proposed for the evils which More and Montesinos (as Southey calls himself in the dialogues) agree infect the land, and—perhaps most striking of all to one looking back from the perspective of a century and a half—the absence of any real evidence of the manifold evils the two colloquists deplore.

These peculiarities all fit into a pattern; all are expli-

[1] *The Complete Writings of Thomas Babington Macaulay*, I, 507.

cable as weaknesses typical of the transcendentalist who has failed to overcome the peculiar difficulties inherent in his assumptions. I will try to make this clear by a brief consideration of each of the eccentricities outlined above, beginning with the last.

No one unacquainted with the condition of the factory and agricultural workers in the first half of the nineteenth century could acquire from Southey's dialogues the least idea of the extent and depth of misery afflicting those workers. The state of the lower classes is the central subject of the opening colloquies, and Montesinos is soon brought to admit that "were society to be stationary at its present point, the bulk of the people would, on the whole, have lost rather than gained by the alteration during the last thousand years."[2] Yet not a single fact is brought forward to support this assertion, and the discussion is so colorless that one would imagine the question entirely without human significance. When More answers Montesinos's assertion that war, pestilence, and famine are no more to be dreaded, he goes no further than to argue that all three (and especially pestilence, which is discussed at great length) could again visit the shores of England. The two agree that life was happier for the lower classes in More's time, but only toward the end of the fifth colloquy are any specific references to the degree and extent of the misery of the poor offered. There we find More opining that "not a winter passes in which some poor wretch does not actually die of cold and hunger in the streets of London!"[3] Montesinos replies that "some shocking examples" have occurred

[2] Southey, *Sir Thomas More: Or, Colloquies on the Progress and Prospects of Society*, I, 37. In general, Southey makes his points either by representing the colloquists as in agreement or by having More persuade Montesinos to the proper view. More is represented as an infallible judge, although where Southey disapproves of positions actually taken by the historical More, as on the question of celibacy, More is made to admit that he has learned better since departing this life.

[3] *Ibid.*, I, 112.

to him. "The one of a poor Savoyard boy with his monkey starved to death in St. James's Park. The other, which is, if that be possible, a still more disgraceful case, is recorded incidentally in Ree's Cyclopaedia under the word *Monster*." These are apparently the only examples of the misery of the poor which Southey can offer in the year 1829, though the purpose of the book is to warn against the evils of the time. More than a hundred pages of "Notes and Illustrations" to points made in the colloquies of the two volumes are printed at the end of Volume I: all are examples drawn from literature and history, most of them curiosities; not one an example of present conditions in England. (The disinclination of transcendental thought to descend to examples and illustrations is equally apparent in Coleridge's "Lay Sermon Addressed to the Higher and Middle Classes on the Existing Distresses and Discontents" [1817]. Coleridge refers at one point to having "more than once seen a group of children in Dorsetshire, during the heat of the dog-days, each with its little shoulders up to its ears, and its chest pinched inward. . . ." and of conversations in which Highlanders lamented the depopulation of the countryside and destruction of the rural way of life, but the extent of the very discontent against which he is offering remedies is unchronicled.)[4]

Surely few prophets can ever have been so correct in their conclusions and so shaky in their evidence as Southey is here. The explanation is that the misery of the poor was not the evil which alarmed him, that was simply a corroborative symptom of what he could only regard as an increasing apostasy from the correct moral standards. Recognition of that corruption did not require that one gathered statistics, visited the hovels of the poor, or read parliamentary reports; one need only observe the extent to which certain principles were being eroded. Further, it soon becomes clear to the reader that these principles are

[4] Coleridge, *Complete Works*, VI, 209, 210–12.

all such as follow the belief in a supraphenomenal realm of value which can only be intuited, and directly pursued, by the privileged.

> The fault lies in your institutions, which in the time of the Saxons were better adapted to maintain security and order, than they are now. No man in those days could prey upon society, unless he were at war with it as an outlaw, a proclaimed and open enemy. Rude as the laws were, the purposes of law had not then been perverted: it had not been made a craft; it served to deter men from committing crimes, or to punish them for the commission; never to shield notorious, acknowledged, impudent guilt from condign punishment. And in the fabric of society, imperfect as it was, the outline and rudiments of what it ought to be were distinctly marked in some main parts, where they are now well-nigh utterly effaced. Every person had his place. There was a system of superintendence every where, civil as well as religious. They who were born in villenage, were born to an inheritance of labour, but not of inevitably depravity and wretchedness. If one class were regarded in some respects as cattle, they were at least taken care of; they were trained, fed, sheltered and protected; and there was an eye upon them when they strayed. None were wild, unless they ran wild wilfully, and in defiance of controul. None were beneath the notice of the priest, nor placed out of the possible reach of his instruction and his care.[5]

The necessity of a hierarchy and of a system of superintendence are undoubted, as is the general rightness of the law. There is nostalgia for the past here, but the driving belief is in order; it is the order that is both necessary and possible because there is a universal model which can be known by the few and disseminated to the many. Says More: "Disease, vice, folly and madness are contagious; while health and understanding are incommunicable, and

[5] Southey, *Colloquies*, I, 93–94.

wisdom and virtue hardly to be communicated!"[6] The nature of the diagnosis explains the vagueness of the remedies Southey proposes. Like all transcendentalists he turns from specific laws and programs to the need for proper guidance from above and proper subservience below. Judgment of the correctness of the guidance is to be made in terms of the moral and religious principles of those offering it. Thus, though it is admitted to be in many ways laudable, the system proposed and attempted by Owen of Lanark cannot be supported. More: "He who shows himself grievously erroneous upon one important point, must look to have his opinions properly distrusted upon others. To maintain that the state ought not to concern itself with the religion of the subjects is the greatest and most perilous of all political errors: and to regard religion with indifference is the most dangerous of all moral ones. . . ."[7] Accordingly, Southey prescribes that the Church return to more energetic moral guidance, that care be taken that adherents to the Catholic Church not be given stations in which their false teachings may be spread, that ways be found to counteract the pernicious effects of public opinion as voiced by the press, and that the creation of peers from the middle class (the members of which do not honor those traditions that reflect the model of things as they should be but rather are products of the commercial spirit) be much diminished.[8] As in Coleridge, abuses are to be corrected or the remedial actions undertaken not by fiat but by the fulfillment of their duty by those to whom light has been granted. All these evils are, as Sir Thomas says of the

[6] *Ibid.*, I, 37.

[7] *Ibid.*, I, 133. Cf. another statement by More: "But the principle of nonconformity in religion is very generally connected with political discontent" (*Ibid.*, II, 44).

[8] More: "Ancient and acknowledged privileges have had in European society the effect of disarming pride . . . and in many instances of modifying it, or transforming it into a virtue" (*Ibid.*, II, 21).

"cheapening" of the peerage, ones "which may better be guarded against by usage resulting from clear views of policy, than by a positive statute."[9]

What seems the almost desultory nature of the colloquies is equally the result of Southey's transcendentalism. (That moral, political, and economic issues *could* be treated memorably and excitingly from the transcendentalist point of view was to be shortly proved by Carlyle, who drives home the desperateness of the "Condition of England" in the first six pages of *Past and Present.*)[10] More and Montesinos ransack history from ancient to recent for events which they use not finally as examples to clarify or prove an argument but as chance topics on which to pass judgments, judgments that rest on principles which in turn rest on transcendental assumptions which are never made explicit. The discussion of feudalism leads to a discussion of slavery which glances at Greeks of the Homeric age, the Roman conquest of Britain, the Norman conquest, the Mohammedan world, an Arabian tale, enclosures, the War of the Roses, passages from *Utopia*, the religious views of Latimer, Fish, and Fox, vagabondism, and a number of other matters, none considered long enough for its place in the general argument or the grounds of the *obiter dicta* it occasions to be made clear. This is of course part of what Macaulay meant by Southey's failure ever to use an argument; but the whole form of the *Colloquies* has been specifically adopted as a substitute for argument. Even had Southey felt the importance of, and believed himself equal to, the presentation of an argument from philosophical first principles that would have established the grounds of his belief in feudal order, he had no wish to engage in the Her-

[9] *Ibid.*, II, 213.

[10] In fact, Carlyle's evidence in the opening pages is the 1,200,000 paupers receiving relief, and a single case in which three children are strangled by their parents to defraud a burial society. But Carlyle's imagination and rhetoric do the rest.

culean task of restraining an antilogical transcendental mode of thought within the bounds of logic. His facts were, in their way, as indisputable as the statistics Macaulay called upon. No one in England doubted that the popular press was becoming more powerful, that the authority of the Church was waning, and that the feudal relationship between those with wealth and power and the poor had almost vanished. Southey is responding to the fact that all three violated those conclusions about the proper state of society most naturally drawn from transcendental premises.

What Southey desired was simply some mode of drawing attention to the extent of the decline from "proper" principles. The whole machinery of the volume is specifically designed to avoid the necessity for a long trek back to first principles on the one hand and the (for Southey) superfluous excursion into the swamp of statistical analysis. Instead, he plans a dialogue between two widely read gentlemen with impeccable cultural credentials who in themselves embody the reasonable attitude of those whose whole thought is informed by the ideals which, though embodied in old institutions, are ultimately derived from unchanging, transcendent sanctions and supported by the visible sanctions of the Church.[11]

Southey has chosen Sir Thomas More not for the sum of his opinions on the proper structure of society as set out in *Utopia*, but for his approach to social problems. A good many of the customs of *Utopia* would hardly satisfy Southey: the abolition of private property might still have its theoretical appeal to the projector of Pantisocracy, but by 1830, he would hardly have advocated it for England. As a matter of fact, Southey's views coincide most nearly

[11] The doctrine that government, and all the advantages of civilization, are grounded in religious belief was of course attacked vigorously by Macaulay. Cf. Coleridge's "for it is to the Church assuredly that we owe all the origin, all the groundwork of our present state of civilization" (Coleridge, *The Philosophical Lectures*, p. 259).

with minor points expressed in *Utopia*—the coarsening effect of the butcher's trade for example. But, despite a rather full account of Utopian laws in some areas, the superiority of the Utopian culture rests more on the reasonable and virtuous disposition of its inhabitants than on the precision of its laws. A few clear laws understood by all is the sum of Utopian jurisprudence, but it soon becomes clear that the excellence of the system depends primarily on the assumption that all men will be fair and reasonable. Thus for most crimes "the punishment is assigned by the senate according to the atrocity, or veniality, of the individual crime."[12] Checks against the abuse of power, methods of adjusting the balance between what is good for the nation and what is good for the individual are presumed unnecessary. All, except actual criminals, recognize and obey what is much more a moral than a judicial structure. That is what Southey shares most completely with More.

More is also a convenient choice because he represents a period in history to which Southey can turn for an admittedly imperfect, but nevertheless visible, model of benignly hierarchical society. Montesinos: "Perhaps, Sir Thomas, their condition was better precisely during your age, than it ever has been either before or since. The feudal system had well-nigh lost all its inhuman parts, and the worst inhumanity of the commercial world had not yet shown itself."[13] More, like all whose conception of the perfect society consists in a vision of the society as it will be when it is attained rather than in the steps toward it, must offer a model rather than a program. He places his model in a mythical past of the world of his own time; Southey places his in the past which is More's time. Had England been as happy in More's lifetime as Southey portrays it, there would have been little impetus for More to offer his vision of Utopia. But, of course, the feudal society of about 1500 which Southey admired is as much an ideal vision as

[12] *Yale Edition of the Complete Works of St. Thomas More*, IV, 191.

[13] Southey, *Colloquies*, I, 62.

the Utopian. Both, as a matter of fact, are projecting the same central dream: a society in which every person knows his place and where liberty is circumscribed within limits to which all agree by common consent.

To use a phrase employed by Arnold much later, Southey's colloquists let their minds play freely around various topics that arise out of their starting-point, the decline of the social structure. Philosophical rigor, appeal to empirical data and logical progression are alike out of place in such a discussion—diversification of topics and even the insertion of ornamental discourses on the lake country, on the other hand, seem desirable. Thus Southey regards it as quite natural that "The Manufacturing System," which is the topic indicated by the title of Colloquy 7, should only be arrived at after ten pages on early rising, the appearance of spirits, and the tendencies of the Reformation. Not that the colloquies are wholly without plan. The central question, the present state of English culture, the "condition of England" as it were, is raised at the beginning, and the work ends with a summation, adapted from Kant, of a form of transcendental doctrine that underlies Southey's whole system, a summation of the evils suggested in the earlier colloquies and a denunciation of sinfulness and worldliness as the source of those increasing evils. That in Kant which most interests Southey is the view that "the history of the human race, as a whole, may be regarded as the unravelling of a hidden plan of nature for accomplishing a perfect state of civil constitution for society in its internal relations. . . ." (Of course, the significance of this bit of Kant is transmogrified by its separation from the *Critique of Practical Reason* as it in turn rests on the *Critique of Pure Reason.*) Montesinos is made to say that what Kant calls "the hidden plan of Nature" he would call "the revealed will of God." More replies: "The will is revealed; but the plan is hidden."[14] That well sums up the whole thrust of the *Colloquies*: the plan cannot be set out in concrete

[14] *Ibid.*, II, 411, 411–13.

form, but it does exist, and is to be found by following the will of God. That will, in turn, is taught by the Church of England, and presumably, embodied in the feudal organization of the state. Thus, the way to bring about the perfect society is through resistance to Impiety, Popery, "the levelling principle of democracy," and the growth of the manufacturing system. All four have the same root: "the sinfulness of the nation,"[15] which is to be resisted by strengthening the principles of duty, moral obligation, and religious obedience. There can be no health, no soundness in the State, till Government shall regard the moral improvement of the people as its first great duty."[16]

Southey lands himself in the standard difficulty of the religious believer who couples a providential theory of history with warnings against deviating from those social principles for which he ultimately finds a transcendental sanction. If all history can be viewed as the mysterious working out of an unthwartable providential plan, man's attempt to cooperate by trying to model his institutions on his understanding of the transcendental plan is likely to be supererogatory and presumptuous. Nevertheless, More and Montesinos throughout rely on divine providence while requiring man to cooperate by averting those evils he can oppose, although the mechanism of cooperation remains vague.[17]

Macaulay's wonderment that any man could hold Southey's views or write in such a manner is partly of course a satirical strategy, but the empiricist Whig was likely indeed puzzled. Macaulay found the whole fabric of the *Colloquies* easy to rend and tear; his approach through empirical facts (however artfully chosen) and the canons of logic led his empirical readers (a majority in Macaulay's

[15] *Ibid.*, II, 417.

[16] *Ibid.*, II, 424–25.

[17] One finds the same problem in Carlyle who seems to believe in a divinely ordered program carried out at times by apparently malevolent forces.

time and an increasing majority throughout the century) to a triumphant dismissal of the two volumes. Southey had failed to find an adequate form for what he had to say. But the view Southey wished to set forth was not a series of private eccentricities, nor the form wholly a crochet; behind them lay an unanalyzed and unclarified transcendental worldview that many besides Southey would labor to find means of expressing in the midst of a growing empiricism.

EARLY IN *Praeterita*, Ruskin tells us of his delight in reading Maria Edgeworth's stories about Harry, Lucy, and Frank, and reproduces his first prose effort, an imitation of these written when he was seven years old. Now, Harry, Lucy, and Frank are of course model children created by Miss Edgeworth as a means of exemplifying the proper means of educating children according to utilitarian principles—which in practice generally meant forcing them to learn by personal experiment. The basic pedagogical principle in the kind of "early lessons" Miss Edgeworth advocated is the creation of situations in which the child must solve a problem or work out the answer to a question by trial and error, generally with the help of calculatedly inadequate hints. Thus were these children taught that every problem could be solved, every question answered by dint of hard thought and persistent effort. The method undoubtedly teaches self-reliance, but there are drawbacks to habituating a child to concentrate wholly on the problem at hand and depend almost totally on his own capabilities. He is not encouraged by such a system to go beyond the problem he is exploring, nor to order his acquired knowledge according to first principles. I should not like to argue that Ruskin's life-long method of investigating questions is wholly indebted to his reading Miss Edgeworth's stories, but they do serve as a paradigm for his almost invariable approach to any problem, and many of the strengths and weaknesses of his work are precisely those endemic to that method.

No one who has read Ruskin can have doubted his extraordinary ability to see clearly both the larger pattern and the consistent detail of whatever he looked at in nature or art, nor his ability to describe what he had seen both accurately and vividly. But the writer of essays and treatises, however perceptive he may be as an observer, must be able to organize his perceptions, give order and form to the reports of his observations, and point the significance of that which he describes. Ruskin never shirks these responsibilities, but he generally meets them as Miss Edgeworth's model children would—by organizing and manipulating the limited phenomena with which he is then dealing as expediently as possible in view of his purpose at the time. He rarely pushes back to first principles and feels no need of axioms, postulates, or series of deductions. He has no system with which the subject he is investigating must be brought into line. He approaches each subject, each collection of phenomena, each book freshly. His faculty for seeing remains undarkened by the filters of theory.

That Ruskin does not construct axioms, postulates, and systems may at first sight seem untrue. One recalls for instance, the five kinds of "Ideas" that are given at the beginning of *Modern Painters* as the sources of pleasure in art, the three systems of architectural ornament, the six "Divisions of Architecture" discussed in Volume I of *The Stones of Venice*, and the seven "lamps" of architecture. But the air of logical development given to Ruskin's work by his habit of briskly dividing a subject into divisions, heads, or kinds should not blind us to the extent to which these sets of divisions or principles represent immediate convenience, not ultimate verities. That they are not related to a coherent total structure becomes clear as soon as one tries to compare lists of principles taken from different works or even different sections of the same work. The reader who tries to work out exact correspondences between the five kinds of "Ideas" in *Modern Painters*, the seven architectural "lamps," and the three virtues of architecture stated early in *The Stones of Venice* will find the exercise more puzzling than profitable. That Ruskin's treatment of geology offended the professional geologists because his classifications were more fanciful than systematic is well known. The fact is that in none of his work was he concerned that his divisions of a subject be logical, complete, or coordinate. Convenience in handling and amenability to elaboration are his concern, not rigid principles of taxonomy.

For the most part, each of his works was a new start. The first two volumes of *Modern Painters*, *The Seven Lamps of Architecture*, and *The Stones of Venice*, for example, were published within a ten-year period. All three treat the relationship between beauty, morality, truth, art, and nature, yet the later works make surprisingly little use of the earlier ones. References from *The Stones of Venice* back to *Modern Painters* or *Seven Lamps* are infrequent and generally unhelpful. Just as Ruskin disapproved of an architect directly imitating a previous building—the new would have no life to it—he appears to have begun each of these works on a new foundation. The analyses of the greatness of Turner, the principles of good architecture, and the relation between the moral and architectural powers of Venice are each developed independently. The basic materials are the same, but they are rearranged in a new design. A principle or concept that serves as a supporting buttress in one plan becomes a bearing wall in another; the materials that form a central arch in one are divided to form two arches, or perhaps lintels, elsewhere.

However, though Ruskin's works are not interrelated in an ordered system of thought of the kind one might be led to expect by their surface organization, that one feels a general coherence in reading Ruskin's work can hardly be denied. There is indeed one ultimate principle on which he depends as on a master-key to unlock all doors, a principle presented in various ways by transcendentalists as divergent as the Cambridge Platonists and Schelling. It is simply that man's faculties and nature's beauty and meaning were created in harmony with each other by God.[18] It is a helpful and comforting doctrine, but one which allows for a great deal of imprecision of thought because it can be used to explain almost anything. The essence of a harmony between two things is that each completes the other but neither is the cause of the other. When P is shown invariably to cause or imply Q we do not say that they are in harmony; only if the existence of P is given significance by the existence of Q and vice versa do we speak of harmony. Thus to say that man's moral nature, external nature, and art are intended to fit into an harmonious interrelationship that has a transcendental guarantee is to free oneself from the necessity of explaining the relationships in terms of the logical categories of cause and effect, necessary and/or sufficient conditions, or the rules of the syllogism. Ruskin is able to disregard almost all of the usual metaphysical questions—what is real? what is truth? how is truth known?—and rely on his one interpretive principle—that all which man does is an expression of his understanding of God and of God-ordained moral laws.[19] The good, the true, and the beautiful are terms that describe different ways of knowing God.

But though his constant dependence on this principle makes precise analysis of his arguments difficult, the prin-

[18] Cf. Coleridge's "nature itself is to a religious observer the art of God," *Biographia Literaria*, ed. J. Shawcross, II, 254.

[19] Ruskin, of course, distinguishes between that in nature which is merely adapted to man's practical life and that which is in harmony with his moral and aesthetic life, it being the function of art, as he states in Volume II of *Modern Painters*, to call man's attention to the aesthetic and moral and away from the practical, for man's function is "to be the witness of the glory of God." See Ruskin, *Complete Works*, IV, 28.

ciple is enormously suggestive, making practically everything a potentially significant symbol. The flexibility of Ruskin's sense of the relationship between morality, nature, and art allows him endless creativity in interpreting individual phenomena. Natural objects are symbols of God's nature and plan; objects built by man are symbols of man's moral and mental constitution and thus ultimately symbolic of his reading of the divine symbolism. Any subject may at any moment be raised to a higher level of interpretation and invested with symbolic meaning. The structure of his volumes is thus like that of a good Gothic building, separate features of which may be so elaborated as to become individually worthy of contemplation.

Gothic architecture, says Ruskin, "can fit itself most easily to all services, vulgar or noble"; it allows each man to express as completely as possible his thought and imagination, his *thoughtful* part, "whatever faults and errors we are obliged to take with it," and its builders "never suffered ideas of outside symmetries and consistencies to interfere with the real use and value of what they did."[20] An analogous structure in prose has obvious advantages for the man who wishes to be able, at any point, to move from art to morality, from natural beauty to divine intention, from works of art to economics, and we indeed find that the structures of most of his works become like the system of architecture he came to admire above all others. Thus it turns out that Ruskin's lack of systemization becomes for him almost a method, a method made possible by an underlying transcendental structure. Ruskin's resulting, highly flexible intellectual system is, I think, the key to his prose structure.

The Stones of Venice, which I wish to use to exemplify this way of viewing Ruskin, is, appropriately, the most Gothic of the earlier works. (The five volumes of *Modern Painters* might seem to have a better claim to this place,

[20] Ruskin, *Complete Works*, X, 212, 191, 212.

but the metaphor of a single building seems hardly adequate to them. What was intended as a modest gallery in which to hang a one-man show grew into a housing development for the more comfortable accommodation of Ruskin's rapidly diversifying interests.) The "Gothic" structure of *Stones of Venice* allows Ruskin to make certain main points and pursue a variety of other matters as they arise, avoiding what he would regard as the beautiful but limiting symmetry of the Byzantine or the sterile regularity and perfection of the Renaissance. The structure of the work is indeed odd and irregular enough: a volume setting forth the principles on which walls, shafts, arches, apertures, roofs, and ornaments should be designed; a second volume describing the founding of Venice and the architecture of the Byzantine and Gothic periods; and a third short volume treating, or rather, dismissing, the Renaissance, the examples of Renaissance work (which make up more than one half the volume) being restricted almost entirely to tombs and grotesque ornaments.

The keystone of the work, the chapter entitled "The Nature of Gothic," is, if read in its entirety (as it too seldom is), a miniature model of the way in which Ruskin applies a veneer of system over a disorderly mass of perceptions. The six characteristics of Gothic buildings are to be seen as corresponding to six "moral elements" of the builder. But to the immediate confounding of order and consistency, the first characteristic, Savageness, is given a dual explanation. It is the result of the "magnificence of sturdy power, put forth only the more energetically because the fine finger-touch was chilled away by the frosty wind, and the eyes dimmed by the moor-mist,"[21] but it is also a result of the recognition of individuality in the Christian system

[21] One finds a similar explanation of the Gothic mind marked by having been shaped "in rude forests amid the inclemencies of outward nature" in Coleridge's *Philosophical Lectures*, p. 291. See also Lectures I and II of the course of lectures reprinted in Volume IV of *Complete Works of Samuel Taylor Coleridge*, pp. 232–39.

of ornament that is able "out of fragments full of imperfection . . . indulgently [to] raise up a stately and unaccusable whole."[22] We are provided with two causes for one effect, both apparently sufficient for the effect, neither uniquely necessary to it. The second characteristic, Changefulness, is described, on the one hand, as the product of the moral element of love of change and on the other as the reward for "allowing independent operation of the inferior workmen," on which grounds Changefulness and Savageness would seem to become almost identical. The section on Naturalism leads to a long discussion of two triple divisions of kinds of men and artists, just as the discussion of Savageness had led to a consideration of the role of the worker in all manufacturing. On the other hand, the Grotesque proves to be unimportant enough to the understanding of Gothic to be postponed to the third volume, and Rigidity and Redundancy can be very briefly defined and explained, especially since the last seems partly a result of Naturalism. In short, the six characteristics are not of the same order or equal rank, as is suggested by the fact that Ruskin's interest in a particular characteristic is sometimes claimed by its cause, sometimes by its immediate result, sometimes by its larger ramifications.

When, more than two thirds of the way through the chapter, Ruskin begins to discuss the specific structural features of Gothic—the pointed arch, the gable, foliation, etc.—he makes almost no attempt to relate these features to the six characteristics. Rigidity has something to do with the arch, and Naturalism influences both foliation and surface-sculpture, but cause and effect are never distinguished in these instances; and, on the whole, little correlation can be discovered between the earlier argument and this latter portion of the chapter with its four rules for determining whether a building is Gothic and its four other rules for determining whether the building is an example

[22] Ruskin, *Complete Works*, X, 188, 190.

of good architecture, it having rather surprisingly turned out that, after all, impure Gothic may be "noble" architecture and pure Gothic may be "bad" architecture.

But given Ruskin's whole method of thought, his "Gothic" prose structure proves, in this as in other works, a wonderfully adequate way of embodying a message that does not depend on and never was intended to be judged by the conventional canons of logic or consistency. In equating the vices and virtues of states of national culture, he was engaged in explaining architecture in terms of God-implanted, that is transcendent, values, and transcendent values in terms of architecture, a circular procedure possible only on his assumption of the God-established harmony. On the one hand the significance of architectural features is vastly increased by relating them to the transcendent; on the other, he has found a way, to use a Carlylean metaphor, of "clothing" his belief in transcendent values in architectural forms. He is not only discussing the ultimately transcendental implications of architecture but building for the transcendent a local habitation.

To state the matter this way is to make the structure of *Stones of Venice* sound complex and abstract, but we do not feel it to be so in the reading. Never does the treatment seem esoteric or "metaphysical" because the links between Ruskin's symbols and God's creation—mankind's architectural symbols and God's natural symbols—bridge the palpable inane. Ruskin explicitly points out the error of looking for an abstruse symbolism not based on these links. Of the theory that the pointed roofs and spires of Gothic cathedrals express "aspiration" and "devotional sentiment" Ruskin declares:

> We may now, with ingenious pleasure, trace such symbolic characters in the form; we may now use it with such definite meaning; but we only prevent ourselves from all right understanding of history, by attributing much influence to these poetical symbolisms in the formation of a national style. The hu-

> man race are, for the most part, not to be moved by such silken cords; and the chances of damp in the cellar, or of loose tiles in the roof, have, unhappily, much more to do with the fashions of a man's house building than his ideas of celestial happiness or angelic virtue. . . . the direct symbolisation of a sentiment is a weak motive with all men.[23]

Architecture does not directly symbolize a human sentiment; rather, by basing itself on God's symbolization of His nature and commands in external nature, it expresses feelings which man recognizes as inspired in him by natural phenomena. Architecture has two virtues, says Ruskin, "strength or good construction" and "beauty or good decoration."[24] The goodness of the construction reveals man's knowledge and character (which indirectly depend on an understanding of God's plan); the beauty of the decoration reveals a strong liking for "God's work, which he made for our delight and contentment in this world." "So then, these are the two virtues of building: first, the signs of man's own good work; secondly, the expression of man's delight in God's work."[25] Thus from Ruskin's point of view, he is not creating symbols, but interpreting the symbolism inherent in all man's work. Architecture is a visible symbol of man's grasp of the meaning of divine symbolism; a treatise on architecture by Ruskin becomes a visible symbol of Ruskin's grasp of the meaning of man's symbolization of the meaning of God's symbolization of His intentions. Ruskin's transcendentalism is thus much closer to Carlyle's than to Coleridge's in its emphasis on the symbolic function of the objects of our experience; revelation in the theological sense is thus pretty much eliminated from the general scheme of things, as is traditional theology.

The statement Ruskin later gave of the purpose of *The*

[23] *Ibid.*, IX, 186.

[24] *Ibid.*, IX, 64.

[25] *Ibid.*, IX, 70.

Stones of Venice is merely a special formulation of his belief in an underlying harmony grounded in God's plan; it had, he tells us, "from beginning to end, no other aim than to show that the Gothic architecture of Venice had arisen out of, and indicated in all its features, a state of pure national faith, and of domestic virtue; and that its Renaissance architecture had arisen out of, and in all its features indicated, a state of concealed national infidelity, and of domestic corruption."[26] Read in the light not only of that purpose but of the belief that all relationships were grounded in a divine harmony out of which that purpose grew, *The Stones of Venice* becomes considerably less chaotic.

The initiation to the principles of construction and decoration which Ruskin provides in the first volume gains for him the confidence of the average reader who, delighted to be conducted into the mysteries of architecture in a fashion at once so sprightly and authoritative, is pleased to take Ruskin for a guide. For many a reader the description of piers as the "gathering up" and pillars as the "concentration" of the wall veil was simultaneously novel, helpful, and indubitable. Why shouldn't a man who can make complicated architectural matters so clear be correct when he describes the Christian system of ornament as the recognition of "the individual value of every soul"?[27] While pursuing this cram course the reader also becomes accustomed to thinking of architectural planning as a series of choices; he is thus prepared for Ruskin's explanation in the later volumes of the way these choices are to be made. Joan Evans remarks, in her biography of Ruskin, how singular it is that nowhere in his discussion of the principles of construction does Ruskin ever treat the actual roofing of a building. It *is* singular, but it doesn't matter.

[26] *Ibid.*, XVIII, 443.

[27] *Ibid.*, X, 190.

The reader is not to be required ever to roof, or indeed raise, an actual building; he is simply to build up in his own mind a body of doctrines regarding the relationship between architecture and morality, that is, between man's works and God's guidance as given through nature. Ruskin will roof *that* structure for him in the "Conclusion" to *The Stones of Venice.*

In the first half of the second volume, which treats Byzantine architecture, Ruskin can indulge in painting the romance of the founding of Venice in its wondrous location, praising all that has delighted him in Byzantine work, and defending that work by the adroit use of the mass of detailed study he has given it. Since for Ruskin the Gothic represents the highest moral perfection, all Gothic work must be seen in the light of its total moral, economic, and religious significance. Accordingly, the second portion of the second volume leaps over the transition from Byzantine to Gothic in order to open with the great central chapter "The Nature of Gothic." This done, Ruskin can take the reader on a tour of Gothic palaces, climaxed by the great Ducal Palace, confident that the reader will try to work out for himself, or take on faith, the existence of the moral equivalents of architectural features and practices whenever Ruskin omits to supply them. The third volume, with its truncated treatment of the Renaissance, is an offense to the systematic mind, but it nevertheless fulfills Ruskin's purpose. The proper principles of architecture and their result had been set forth in the treatment of the Gothic. To show how these were violated by the Renaissance would have been tedious repetition and meant the careful description of an architecture he found valueless. Besides, defining Renaissance architecture as "the school which has conducted men's inventive and constructive faculties from the Grand canal to Gower street; from the marble shaft, and the lancet arch, and the wreathed leafage, and the glowing and melting harmony of gold and azure to the square cavity in the brick wall,"[28] Ruskin could be sure his readers were familiar enough with it.

The Gothic functionality of the total structure of the work is paralleled by the seemingly unpredictable way in which Ruskin moves from topic to topic within individual sections. Since he does not develop general architectural theories deductively, working from theory to illustrative material, but moves from fact or detail to the elaboration of theory, he is free at any moment to explain architectural detail by reference to the state of the builder's mind, its "expression of man's delight in God's work." This is essentially what Ruskin really means by "reading" the architecture. Thus the sculpture of the Virtues and Vices on the capitals of the Ducal Palace leads to observations on Christian symbolism and to the difference between symbolism and personification; a comparison of types of cornices leads to the struggle of the "Christian element" with the "Formalism of the Papacy."[29] Throughout, the system of symbolic correspondences makes possible the dual reference of words like "false," "noble," "base," and "honest"; these adjectives may be applied indifferently to man or his works because the moral quality of the man is directly expressed in his work. Further, Ruskin's whole style is integral to the structure of his thought in that he continually vivifies or personifies both architectural and natural features; they are not to be conceived as lifeless; all express the force and energy of the creator at either first or second remove.[30]

[28] *Ibid.*, XI, 4.

[29] *Ibid.*, X, 377; IX, 371.

[30] For instance: "Until at last, as if in ecstasy, the crests of the arches break into a marble foam, and toss themselves far into the blue sky in flashes and wreaths of sculptured spray . . . "; "There one poor abacus stretched itself out to do all the work: here there are idle abaci getting up into corners and doing none"; "the vast tower of St. Mark seems to lift itself visibly forth from the level field of chequered stones; and, on each side, the countless arches prolong themselves into ranged symmetry. . . ." *Ibid.*, X, 83; IX, 149; X, 82.

Of the Gothic architects, Ruskin says, "If they wanted a window, they opened one; a room, they added one; a buttress, they built one."[31] Ruskin similarly feels free to carve his topic elaborately in one place, merely suggest its outline in another. He can ornament with a word-frieze here, rely on plain workmanlike prose there. He can develop the full symbolic implications of one part of his subject, leave the interpretation of the significance of another part to the sagacity of his reader. Working like the Gothic sculptor who takes delight in the creation of a novel and unique form under his chisel, Ruskin constantly creates new forms out of the subject matter before him, pursuing what beckons, scorning regularity.

Despite all irregularities, the plan of *The Stones of Venice* is solid, meeting Ruskin's purposes with entire adequacy. But one must always recognize that the system of correspondences between God's will, nature, art, and man's morality lacks any truly logical structure. Not only does one have to take Ruskin's word for any particular "reading" of an architectural feature, but one can never be sure how Ruskin will "read"—that is, interpret—a previously unexamined architectural form. The degree to which the symbolic interpretation of architecture in *The Stones of Venice* is arbitrary, or at least subject to unknown rules never explained in the work, can be made clear by an experiment that will illustrate the degree to which, despite the exhaustiveness with which Ruskin sets forth the principles of meeting the major architectural problems, he is free to interpret with seeming capriciousness any particular form that these features may take.

Suppose Ruskin to have been transported to the American Southwest and asked to investigate and interpret the moral meanings of the system of adobe and wood construction so prevalent there. Will anyone undertake to say whether he would have praised or condemned? Innu-

[31] *Ibid.*, X, 212.

merable are the passages that might be cited on either side, but since Ruskin has not spoken directly on the matter, we cannot be sure how he would pronounce. One can hear him praising: "Accept this then for a universal law, what material a builder uses is unimportant so long as he goes honestly to work to shape that material to noble ends. Though necessity demand that he build with soil and straw, the soul of man can nevertheless express itself. What though true corners and sharp sculpture be denied? The workman may shape an adobe tower with as much thought as he gives to a stone gargoyle." One can, however, equally well imagine Ruskin condemning: "Understand this clearly: the man content to yield to the first difficulty, to build his place of worship with the commonest of materials, degrades himself and his deity. The builders of Venice had no quarries convenient to their hand, but they built of marble and stone. Scorning to plead force of circumstance, they exulted in difficulty surmounted."

That one feels one can judge of Ruskin's position on a political, religious, or economic question much more easily than on the value of an architectural style he had not discussed is a paradox full of significance. If we can know only *a posteriori* his interpretation of an architectural system, the arbitrariness of his symbolic use of art and architecture is clear, as is the source of his inconsistencies in evaluating art. The Gothic structure of *The Stones of Venice*, which, in imitating the architecture he most admired, provided the perfect framework in which to develop his personal interpretation of the symbolic meaning of architectural features becomes a model of Ruskin's habitual mode of thought. What one may call his Edgeworthian manner of approaching a problem is perfectly appropriate to his Gothic prose structure and central intention: to offer interpretations through prose of men's interpretations through art of God's self-interpretation through nature.

A similar lack of system, of a structure of intermediate deductions lying between his one great premise and all the areas in which he wishes to apply it, can be found in almost all Ruskin's writing. Coleridge, as we have seen, found difficulty in explaining how any mediation might occur between the noumenal realm of ideas and the phenomenal world. Ruskin doesn't so much as attempt such an explanation—he simply examines the meaning of man's works and announces, after measuring them against the invisible set of moral weights and measures in his own mind, whether they are congruent with God's intentions. He never claims privileged communication with the Deity, but he nevertheless assumes that his intuitions reflect God's purposes.

Ruskin's indifference to philosophical principles is quite clear, incidentally, in his heterogeneous approval of portions of systems of thought in themselves incompatible. Thus, the Platonic elements of Ruskin's thought have been amply cited—for instance, his editors comment that Ruskin "sought to reconstruct society on the Platonic concept of Justice—assigning to each man his due place, and requiring for each man the fulfullment of his duties. To him, as to Plato, the health and happiness of all the citizens was the sole end of legislation, and the role of the wisest was the surest method of securing it."[32] And they point out the Platonic tradition behind such a sentence as "there is an ideal form of every herb, flower, and tree, it is that form to which every individual of the species has a tendency to arrive, freed from the influence of accident or disease."[33] But the fact is that Ruskin's capacity for absorbing aspects of all art, artists, and thinkers into his own system is equal to Coleridge's; his absorption is indeed more complete—he fails to recognize even the possibility of a conflict between Bacon and Plato. He calls Bacon "the wisest of Englishmen"—and goes on immediately to link him with "the wisest of all other great nations," in which group he here

[32] *Ibid.*, XXVII, lix.

[33] *Ibid.*, III, 27*n*.

explicitly places Plato.[34] Plato and Bacon are both in the list of great thinkers upon whose support he calls in his definition of "Political Economy."[35] "The Philosophy I teach is Plato's and Bacon's," he writes to the editor of the *Oxford University Herald.*[36] The great document of this eclecticism is perhaps his summary of the rules he intends to establish for St. George's society; these are to be the laws of fourteenth-century Florence qualified by rules from Bacon and Sir Thomas More "under sanction always of the higher authority which of late the English nation has wholly set its strength to deny, that of the Founder of its Religion; not without due acceptance of what teaching was given to the children of God by their Father," which latter teaching he exemplified by quoting from the conclusion to the ninth book of the *Republic.*[37] But if metaphysically untenable, Ruskin's eclecticism is effective—the structure of his work proved adequate both to that eclecticism and his inexactly formulated transcendentalism.

THE DIFFICULTIES Coleridge experienced in writing the *Biographia Literaria* and the shifts and expedients to which he was driven in order, after many delays, to supply the printer with sufficient material to fill out its two volumes are notorious. Neither the peculiarities of Coleridge's temperament nor the complexities of the composition of the *Biographia* need be rehearsed here. These help to explain how Coleridge was led to give the *Biographia* its ultimate form, but concentration on them has perhaps ob-

[34] *Ibid.*, XVIII, 513.

[35] *Ibid.*, XVII, 148.

[36] *Ibid.*, XXXIV, 547

[37] *Ibid.*, XXVIII, 23.

scured the problems which were inherent in that form once it had been chosen. Few have denied that Coleridge was a brilliant thinker but an ineffective propagandist: he was almost never able to hit upon the appropriate form for the expression of his ideas, and the god of form has had his revenge.

Coleridge's decision to write (as the subtitle has it) a series of "biographical sketches of my literary life and opinions" ran into two interrelated problems: (1) the attempt was premature in that Coleridge's "literary life" had not proceeded far enough, and (2) his opinions, to the extent that they were "transcendental," were too foreign to the prevailing mode of thought to be offered in such a form.

New views carrying sweeping consequences require careful introduction to the public; transcendental views by the very nature of the incommunicability of the whole of a transcendental vision require even greater care. J. S. Mill could rely throughout his *Autobiography* on brief references to the well-known and logically argued works he had previously published in almost all the areas of thought that particularly interested him. Carlyle constructed a fictional biography which, for the most part, is only metaphorically dependent on events in his own life to serve as the vehicle for presenting his personal, transcendental interpretation of life. Coleridge's attempt in the *Biographia* falls uncomfortably between the forms adopted in these two works. When the *Biographia* appeared in 1817, the publication of the "lay sermons," in which he would try to give an unmystical and unmetaphysical definition of the "idea" and diagnose the ills of England were just appearing; the formal statement of his concept of the method by which the mind grasps the world as set forth in the introduction to the *Encyclopaedia Metropolitana* and in an altered form in the final version of *The Friend* lay a year ahead, as did the great lectures on Shakespeare; and the union of his philosophical and religious beliefs as presented in *Aids to Reflection* lay eight years away.

Coleridge, then, was presented not with the usual task of the autobiographer, the tracing of the steps by which he has arrived at the set of beliefs associated with his name, but at setting forth the beliefs as well as the steps which led to them. He had arrived at his position through a gradual rejection of Hartleian psychology and the assimilation of Kantian and post-Kantian speculation. But the retracing of this route was hardly the form which could best commend his conclusions to the world. An argument from metaphysical principles must be rigorously developed, will appeal and can be grasped only by a small group of readers, and mixes ill with autobiography. Moreover, Coleridge had not merely to repudiate Hartley and establish Kant, but to lead reluctant readers beyond Kant's misleadingly named "transcendental" philosophy toward the realms of what has traditionally been known as transcendence.

Nevertheless, in Chapter IV, having found it necessary to set forth the distinction between fancy and imagination and being aware that what he saw as the true ground of that distinction could be set forth only after a philosophical disquisition, Coleridge set bravely out to present his metaphysical principles, with the results we all know. Nine chapters, making up three fourths of the first volume of the *Biographia*, proved insufficient for Coleridge's purpose.

The insights Coleridge had to offer were of course of sufficient value to make their way in the world and ultimately have great influence. Initially, however, that influence appears to have come very largely through his direct contact with his admirers during the years he was the Sage of Highgate. Moreover, the one passage expressive of his philosophical views which the great majority of readers carry away is the famous definition of the Imagination in the antepenultimate paragraph of the thirteenth chapter. Here, attempting to sum up the key principle toward which his argument had been driving, Coleridge turns toward the metaphorical formulas through which the great mysteries and paradoxes beyond the reach of the ordinary human logical processes of the mind have traditionally been stated. "The primary imagination I hold to be the living Power and prime Agent of all human Perception, and as a repetition in the finite mind of the eternal act of creation in the infinite I AM."[38] For a moment Coleridge lifts a corner of the veil of appearance and custom and invites the reader imaginatively to accept the reality which he believes lies behind it. There is a sad irony in Coleridge's failure in the midst of his exaltation of the imagination to recognize that if he wished his readers to distrust the ordinary associations of use-and-wont and grasp the possibility of transcending them through the imagination, he must appeal to the imagination by means of metaphor, symbol, and the total structure of his prose.

To regard *Sartor Resartus* as in essence autobiographical leads to crude enough errors; nevertheless, it is a spiritual autobiography. *Sartor* has been the subject of several important studies, in particular George Levine's treatment of it as a novel and G. B. Tennyson's examination of its background in Carlyle's early work and its style and structure.[39] Both make its total form clearer by analyzing the formal elements that make it up: the novelistic devices, the editorial mechanism, the repetition of key metaphors, etc. However, we still have to ask why Carlyle's use of these methods seems to have been the right choice *for him*, why the methods he used *were* effective in presenting his view of the world.

In presenting his vision, Carlyle was faced with the special problem which faced Coleridge. In Carlyle's famous account of Coleridge in *The Life of Sterling*, he described the momentary glimpses of Coleridge's meaning which emerged out of his talk only to be lost again. "Glorious islets, too, I have seen rise out of the haze; but they were few, and soon swallowed in the general element again.

[38] Coleridge, *Biographia Literaria*, in *Complete Works*, III, 363.

[39] Levine, *The Boundaries of Fiction*; Tennyson, *Sartor Called Resartus*.

Balmy sunny islets, islets of the blest and intelligible . . . till once your islet got wrapt in the mist again. . . ."[40] The danger that mists will shroud his own message in *Sartor* was evidently present in Carlyle's mind, and one finds Teufelsdröckh's Editor describing early impressions of Teufelsdröckhian philosophy in much the same imagery. "The Philosophy of Clothes is now to all readers, as we predicted it would do, unfolding itself into new boundless expansion, of a cloudcapt, almost chimerical aspect, yet not without azure loomings in the far distance, and streaks as of an Elysian brightness. . . ."[41] By the end of *Sartor*, those uncertain glimmerings must be transformed into truths permanently intelligible to the reader.

The total structure and style of *Sartor Resartus* represents a solution to this difficulty. That there is an invisible structure and order behind the visible world is the message to be conveyed. The reader is therefore to be taught to think of the visible world as a revelation of the infinite, and, as a limbering-up exercise for his mind, he is constantly offered highly metaphorical explanations, clarifications, and commentary. A great many of these metaphors also vivify what we ordinarily think of as inanimate; since the visible world symbolizes the transcendent, it is pregnant with meaning and a living organic whole, not a dead mechanism, and the reader must become accustomed to thinking of it in this way. The reader is thus weaned away from reliance on logical deduction and sense experience, from "common school Logic, where the truths all stand in a row, each holding by the skirts of the other,"[42] and made to think imaginatively. There can be no agreed starting point from which to suspend a chain of linked syllogisms, for the basic premise, the existence of a transcendent structure, is precisely the matter in question. Ordinary

[40] Carlyle, *Complete Works*, II, 56.

[41] *Ibid.*, I, 53.

[42] *Ibid.*, I, 39.

logic being irrelevant to the vision of the transcendental realm Carlyle wishes to offer, the reader must be kept occupied with sudden insights, metaphors, glimpses into quaint turns of the Professor's mind, and felicitous descriptions, in the hope that at some point the whole mode of alogical, transcendental thought for which the clothes philosophy is a metaphor will be imaginatively grasped. The words "at some point" are important here: one of the peculiarities of *Sartor* is that, unlike the book or essay in which the writer attempts to carry his reader with him from point to point until they mutually arrive at the climactic conclusion toward which everything in the piece converges, *Sartor* is in a sense a book without a climax, without a focal point. The reader who comes to understand *Sartor* will at some point begin to see Carlyle's general drift, at some point see the real significance of the Clothes Philosophy, at some point begin to feel comfortable with the whole structure of the book, and at some point make up his mind finally whether to assent to, deny, or qualify the transcendental doctrines it presents. Neither the chapters in which a given reader will reach these points nor the order in which they will be reached by that reader can be predicted; some may not be reached until a later reading. In *Sartor*, Carlyle is very much like a juggler: he keeps an astonishing number and variety of things in the air before our eyes until we begin to see the patterns they weave in their flight.

Indeed, whether one looks at individual works like "Characteristics" and "Chartism," or *Latter-Day Pamphlets* and *Past and Present*, or the whole corpus of Carlyle's prose, he seems always circling around his central points, using his ostensible topic as a means of leading to these in new ways, contributing ingenious variations on a minimum number of themes. This method of immersing his readers in a series of beliefs derived from a vision they could not directly see invites tedium; in *Sartor* it is more successful than anywhere else in Carlyle's writing on the condition of England and the condition of the human soul. What seems irascible in the later Carlyle is partly a failure in ingenuity—meeting the same message presented in forms which fail to evoke the sense of a transcendent force that we get in *Sartor*, we find Carlyle's nostrums less palatable, more disturbing.

In *Sartor*, the repetition that results from the tripartite form gradually immerses the reader into transcendentalism and accustoms him to think in Teufelsdröckhian (transcendental) terms by offering the same contentions again and again in diverse but picturesque and intriguing forms until they become familiar, until they come to seem revealing ways of looking at the world. Further, the task set the Editor functions as the framework within which all the other devices are made operative. To challenge the reader to follow Carlyle in solving the riddle of the universe would be not only to warn away many but to induce the wrong frame of mind in those who accept the challenge. To allow the reader to follow the Editor in solving the riddles of the biography and philosophy of a quaint German Professor of Things-in-General is to offer the delights of fiction, mystery, and humor. To speak in his own person Carlyle must either write a dryer, less imaginative prose (a self-defeating course) or run the risk of seeming at best frivolous, at worst mad. The device of the Editor not only allows Carlyle to gain all the advantages of irony but to retain the most outrageous metaphorical language as a spur to the reader's imagination. The accumulation of glimpses into the mode of thought of the transcendentalist is made possible by the fiction of the gradual accumulation of data by the Editor.

The entire book is thus itself a metaphor for the way in which the mind comes to accept that there is an invisible structure, an underlying set of norms, a world-direction, a vast complex of interacting forces which are not mechanical. It is of interest to see the elements of Carlyle's biography which make their way into *Sartor*; it is of value to see the ways in which *Sartor* approaches the novel. But to see *Sartor* as neither novel nor autobiography but as metaphor for the mind's fitful wrestling with the fact of transcendence is to see it most nearly whole. The editor's wrestling with intractable materials which nevertheless promise fascinating revelations once mastered is a metaphorical representation of the spiritual biography of all men who struggle toward a vision beyond ordinary experience. The fragmentary form in which, after all his efforts, the Editor must leave the biography and Clothes Philosophy of Teufelsdröckh is a metaphor for the incapacity of mortal man to comprehend the transcendental realm. The exceptional man, the great man, sees beyond experience more steadily, but even he cannot see the whole, nor can he discursively describe what he sees. That is why he must lead, inspire, and not merely report back. Plato's ideal forms are not what Carlyle has to offer his readers; what he offers are the symbols and metaphors which will keep their imaginative acceptance of a transcendental world alive and remind them of the poverty and error of those who would deduce all from sense-experience.

John Stuart Mill's *Autobiography* is a much more typical representative of the autobiographic genre than *Sartor Resartus*, but most readers notice that it is nevertheless odd enough. It is a commonplace that one of the major sources of interest in the *Autobiography* is the description of the way in which James Mill attempted to mold his son into an error- and emotion-proof thinking machine, and the best-known portion is the account of the mental crisis that led the son to discover the importance of the emotional faculties. Nevertheless, it is striking that despite the account of that crisis, the *Autobiography* is written in a style and form which seem uninfluenced by that experience. The book *is* a report of the thoughts of a thinking-machine.[43] This is not to say that the personality of John

[43] Such a description need not be taken in the pejorative sense in which Carlyle used similar phrases. Morley's eulogy in "The Death of Mr. Mill" quoted,

Stuart Mill which emerges seems inhuman but rather that the autobiography records only one portion of Mill's life, his intellectual development. On the whole, the work remains faithful to the aims set forth in the first paragraph, to record his own "unusual and remarkable" education as an example of how much can be taught in the early years, to describe the successive phases in his own thought, and to acknowledge the debts which his "intellectual and moral development" owed to others. Indications of emotion are not lacking; no reader has, I think, failed to feel the strength of emotion behind his references to Harriet Taylor, but Mill's emotions enter the pages of the *Autobiography* only after they have been transformed into intellectual equivalents. Thus, though Mill records his discovery of the importance of the "culture of the feelings,"[44] his own emotional responses to nature, to beauty, to human personality, to the major events of his own life, are always decently draped in the folds of intellectual analysis. It is possible that Mill's excessive regard for Harriet Taylor's intellect is to be explained by his need always to explain all things intellectually. Harriet Taylor must appear to the reader not as a sympathetic woman but as an intellectual force. Therefore, though he speaks of "her gifts of feeling and imagination," the reader is likely to remember, however much he may doubt, only such sentences as this: "Alike in the highest regions of speculation and in the smaller practical concerns of daily life, her mind was the same perfect instrument, piercing to the very heart and marrow of the matter; always seizing the essential idea or principle."[45]

Now clearly this suppression of the emotional and personal in his life is partly due to a feeling that a man can be

---

with approval, the comment of an "eminent American" that Mill's mind "worked like a splendid piece of machinery; you supply it with raw material, and it turns you out a perfectly finished product" (*Critical Miscellanies*, III, 40).

[44] J. S. Mill, *Autobiography*, p. 96.

[45] *Ibid.*, p. 120.

expected to share only so much of his life with readers. But it is not unreasonable, I think, to regard that feeling as a corollary of a larger explanation, the deeply ingrained belief that only ordered thought is finally of value. Not only is ordinary experience—experience defined as something that arises in the stimulation of the senses and ends in being incorporated by the mind in a logical system—the only source of knowledge, but received stimuli and one's emotional responses to them *require* to be intellectually grasped and ordered. There are passages enough in which Mill seems to be going beyond the apparently dry intellectualism that he criticized in both his father and Bentham. But the results of the "conversion" of Mill, the leavening of his thought through the influence of Wordsworth, Coleridge, and the Coleridgeans, which occurred during the years 1826–1830 and which he describes in the famous Chapter V, "A Crisis in My Mental History," have, as I have argued above, been exaggerated. That chapter itself merits a close look.

Having asked himself the fatal question—whether the realization of all changes he is working for would bring "a great joy and happiness"—and found the answer negative, he attempted to analyze his unhappiness. His education had formed "associations of pleasure with all things beneficial to the great whole, and of pain with all things hurtful to it."[46] The central aim of education as defined by his father had been achieved. But since these associations are somewhat "artificial and casual" they can be worn away by analysis. Perhaps the key sentence is "for I now saw, or thought I saw, what I had always before received with incredulity—that the habit of analysis has a tendency to wear away the feelings: as indeed it has, when no other mental habit is cultivated, and the analysing spirit remains without its natural complements and correctives." Three points are, I think, essential to the proper estimation of this

[46] *Ibid.*, p. 88.

sentence. First, Mill is using the words "feeling" and "association" almost interchangeably here, as he is correct in doing on the basis of his description of "all mental and moral feelings and qualities" as the results of association. Second, the qualification "or thought I saw" indicates that Mill later modified his interpretation and is one of many similar phrases sprinkled through the paragraph to warn that he has done so. Third, that part of the sentence which follows the colon explains the nature of the modification: the "analysing spirit" must be complemented and corrected by other "mental habits."

All three points must be borne in mind in interpreting the two cardinal moments in the recovery from his mental crisis as described in the immediately succeeding pages. The first moment was the discovery that he still could feel strongly—it is, I think, especially important to note that not only did Mill experience strong feeling at this, but the feeling he experienced was the one that he knew he should feel, that had been inculcated by the proper associations; he felt "the pleasure of sympathy with human beings" which he had thought he had lost. The second moment was of course the reading of Wordsworth's poems; this was a "medicine" for his mind, he tells us, because "they expressed, not mere outward beauty, but states of feeling, and of thought coloured by feeling, under the excitement of beauty." That is, as I interpret the passage, they strengthened the associations worn down by analysis, providing one of "the natural complements and correctives" needed.[47] What Mill discovers is the *utility* of poetry; it cultivates the feelings by renewing and strengthening our habits of association. It should be noted that Mill records that poetry had been of value to him even before the crisis

[47] The doctrine that aesthetic or imaginative pleasures are very largely denied to the man of business or to a philosopher Mill would have known from the work of Archibald Alison, whose *Essay on the Nature and Principles of Taste* James Mill cites approvingly in his *Analysis of the Phenomena of the Human Mind.*

as a source of strengthening the proper association. "Long before I had enlarged in any considerable degree, the basis of my intellectual creed, I had obtained in the natural course of my mental progress, poetic culture of the most valuable kind, by means of reverential admiration for the lives and characters of heroic persons; especially the heroes of philosophy."[48] Mill's account here of the role of Wordsworth's poetry is consistent with the view set forth in his essays on poetry of 1833. Poetry—and, by extension, all art, all immediate stimuli to the emotions rather than the intellect—are valuable as a source of pleasure and associative renewal only. They tell us nothing about the world, reveal nothing that man needs to know.

The discovery that "those only are happy (I thought) who have their minds fixed on some object other than their own happiness" is really hardly different from the Utilitarian theory Mill cites as held by "all those to whom I looked up" that "the pleasure of sympathy with human beings, and the feelings which made the good of others, and especially of mankind on a large scale, the object of existence, were the surest sources of happiness."[49] And the application of the discovery itself is qualified by the last sentence of the paragraph in which it is announced. The modifications to his father's theory of political philosophy, which he finds necessary at this time, though attributed partly to the influence of transcendentalists, amount mainly to "a conviction that the true system was something much more complex and many-sided than I had previously had any idea of"[50] and a recognition that the steps in human progress must be taken in a certain order. (The ease with which his father's formal deduction of the proper form of government is restated as a historical development in

[48] J. S. Mill, *Autobiography*, p. 73.

[49] *Ibid.*, pp. 92 and 90.

[50] *Ibid.*, p. 104.

the first pages of *On Liberty* indicates how little this disturbed his basic premises.) All in all, Mill retains his distrust of imaginative language for the conveyance of intellectual content.

The result is reflected in Mill's style as much as in his choice of material. Metaphor, simile, and figure of speech are rarely employed, and when they do appear they are little developed and so integrated into the course of the straightforward narrative or argument that they are scarcely noticed. A typical example is the familiar paragraph:

> After 1829 I withdrew from attendance on the Debating Society. I had had enough of speech-making, and was glad to carry on my private studies and meditations without any immediate call for outward assertion of their results. I found the fabric of my old and taught opinions giving way in many fresh places, and I never allowed it to fall to pieces, but was incessantly occupied in weaving it anew. I never in the course of my transition, was content to remain, for ever so short a time, confused and unsettled. When I had taken in any new idea, I could not rest till I had adjusted its relation to my old opinions, and ascertained exactly how far its effect ought to extend in modifying or superseding them.[51]

The felicitousness of the metaphor on which the third sentence is based perhaps accounts for the fact that this is one of the better-known passages in the *Autobiography*, but even here one notices that Mill is careful immediately to restate in plain language the meaning he has clothed in a metaphor.

Even more rarely does Mill attempt strongly to evoke the external physical appearance of anything. Perhaps it is as well that he does not; in the few passages in which he attempts a somewhat heightened description, the result is a bit like a parody of the eighteenth-century grand style. One is grateful that Mill seldom ventured on the ornamen-

[51] *Ibid.*, p. 101.

tal diction of the closing portion of the following sentence: "The middle-age architecture, the baronial hall, and the spacious and lofty rooms, of this fine old place, so unlike the mean and cramped externals of English middle class life, gave the sentiment of a larger and freer existence, and were to me a sort of poetic cultivation, aided also by the character of the grounds in which the Abbey stood; which were riant and secluded, umbrageous, and full of the sound of falling waters."[52] But such infelicities are rare; for the most part, Mill, like Carlyle, was able to mirror his philosophy in his prose.

[52] *Ibid.*, p. 37.

VIII

Aesthetic Theory

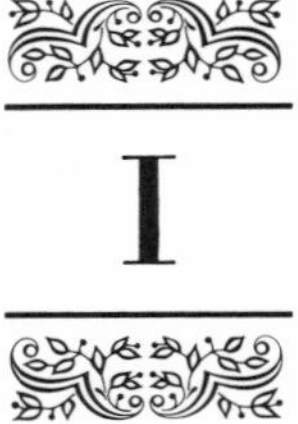

IT IS HARD for one living in the twentieth century to give full weight to the interest in aesthetic theory in the nineteenth. It was discussed as regularly, as seriously, and over the same dinner tables and in the columns of the same journals as economics, politics, or international relations. The regular contributors to the quarterlies and reviews were men of letters in the older, quite honorific sense of the phrase, and men of letters find questions of aesthetics perennially interesting. Educated Victorians in general felt the same way. Ruskin's views were the great force to be reckoned with by mid-century, but there were Classicist, Neo-Classicist, Wordsworthian, Coleridgian, and Benthamite arguments ready to hand (as shortly there would be art-for-art's sake and evolutionary) to support one's individual response to art, whatever it might be.

Of particular interest is the long and winding series of attempts by "Vernon Lee" (Violet Paget) to construct a personally satisfying theory of aesthetics, first by modifying Ruskin and later by taking a new, empirical approach. She also thus exemplifies once again the difficulties of harmonizing principles drawn from the two reigning metaphysical camps. Of equal interest, I believe, is the aesthetic theorizing of E. S. Dallas, who, by regarding the Imagination as an *unconscious* activity of the mind, arrived at a true *via media* between the usual forms of empiricist and transcendentalist aesthetics. Vernon Lee and E. S. Dallas are, I believe, still less known than they deserve to be. Dallas, though a loyal disciple of Sir William Hamilton, in fact planted his banner in a region outside both metaphysical traditions; Lee eventually found her way to new intellectual territory beyond the old metaphysical battlegrounds. Both explored views of the mind and of the function of art which anticipate I. A. Richards and subsequent twentieth-century critics. And finally, Lee has written some of the most stimulating and delightful essays of the nineteenth century.

On the other hand, George Henry Lewes exemplifies something like the lowest common denominator of empiricist aesthetics; his lack of cogency and trenchancy in *The Principles of Success in Literature* follows from his not having thought it necessary to connect the superficial empiricism at work here with its deeper philosophical moorings. I shall close by briefly contrasting Lewes's attempt with another empiricist investigation of an aesthetic question, Herbert Spencer's well-wrought "Philosophy of Style."

I HAVE SKETCHED Ruskin's moral aesthetics in the process of analyzing the structure of *The Stones of Venice*; for all the waywardness of his arguments and lack of compatibility in certain of his key conceptions, the identification of the beautiful with the good, and of both ultimately with the true, was assumed to be what God had arranged and man was intended to recognize. The applications of this can be gathered in profusion from Ruskin's works.

We cannot say that a painter is great because he paints boldly, or paints delicately; because he generalizes or particularizes; because he loves detail, or because he disdains it. He is great if, by any of these means, he has laid open truths, or aroused noble emotions. . . . So that true criticism of art . . . can be just only when it is founded on quick sympathy with the innumerable instincts and changeful efforts of human nature, chastened and guided by unchanging love of all things that God has created to be beautiful, and pronounced to be good. (1856)[1]

This then is the great enigma of Art History,—you must not follow Art without pleasure, nor must you follow it for the sake of pleasure. And the solution of that enigma, is simply this fact; that wherever Art has been followed *only* for the sake of luxury or delight, it has contributed, and largely contributed, to bring about the destruction of the nation practicing it; but wherever Art has been used *also* to teach any truth, or supposed truth—religious, moral, or natural—there it has elevated the nation practicing it; and itself with the nation. (1858)[2]

The art of man is the expression of his rational and disciplined delight in the forms and laws of the Creation of which he forms a part. (1877)[3]

. . . and, now, in writing beneath the cloudless peace of the snows of Chamouni, what must be the really final words of the book which their beauty inspired and their strength guided, I am able, with yet happier and calmer heart than ever heretofore, to enforce its simplest assurance of Faith, that the

[1] *Modern Painters*, vol. III, in *The Complete Works of John Ruskin*, V, 41–42.

[2] Ruskin, "Inaugural Address," Cambridge School of Art, in *Complete Works*, XVI, 197.

[3] Ruskin, *The Laws of Fésole*, in *Complete Works*, XV, 351.

> knowledge of what is beautiful leads on, and is the first step, to the knowledge of the things which are lovely and of good report; and that the laws, the life, and the joy of beauty in the material world of God, are as eternal and sacred parts of His creation as, in the world of spirits, virtue; and in the world of angels, praise. (1888)[4]

Ruskin's authority, much enhanced by the grandeur of his prose, helped support such identifications of the true, good, and beautiful almost to the end of the Victorian period.

The signal influence of Ruskin's aesthetic theory, the central weakness of that theory, and the difficulty of asserting the importance of art without falling into his errors are all apparent in the work of Vernon Lee. Born in 1856 into a cultivated, art-loving, and continent-clinging English family, she had from childhood constant association with the fine art of Europe. Aesthetic questions had common dining-table and drawing-room currency, and Ruskin's name led all the rest. From the composition of her first book, *Studies of the Eighteenth Century in Italy* (1880), Lee struggled to unite immediate reactions to art and life which we should expect only within the context of a transcendentalist philosophy, with constant introspection, the latest doctrines of empirical psychology, and a strong bias toward evolutionary explanations.

Tension, conflicts, and inconsistencies are almost inevitable in such a program; the basic conflict faced by Vernon Lee is represented as clearly in the forms as the arguments of her speculations. She writes two very different kinds of essays. One is Pateresque; half-speculative, half-impressionistic, it begins with observations on a particular work, event, or intellectual problem and winds its way through impressions, analyses, and second thoughts to a conclusion less significant, perhaps, than the route taken to come to that conclusion. Such, for instance, are the es-

[4] Ruskin, "Epilogue" to *Modern Painters*, in *Complete Works*, VII, 464.

says gathered in *Belcaro*, *Juvenilia*, *Euphorion*, and *Renaissance Fancies and Studies*. That Vernon Lee was conscious that the vagaries of such essays gave them much of their charm is clear from the half-serious closing paragraph of "In Umbria," the seventh essay in *Belcaro*.

> This is the end of our long wandering up and down, round and round, the question of artistic personality, even as we must wander up and down, round and round, before we can reach any of these strange Umbrian towns. And, as after long journeying, when we enter the city, and find that that which seemed a castle, a grand princely town, all walled and towered and battlemented, is in reality only a large, rough village, with blackened houses and fissured church steeples, and a place containing nothing of any interest: so also in this case, when we have finally reached our paltry conclusion that this painter of saints was no saint himself, we must admit to ourselves that to arrive at this conclusion was scarcely our real object; even as while travelling through this country of Perugino we make our guide confess that what, in all this expedition, we were meant to see and enjoy, was not the paltry, deceptive hill-top village, but the sere-brown oakwoods, tinged russet by the sun, the grey olive hills through which we have slowly ascended, and the glimpses of undulating grey-green country and distant wave-blue mountains which we have had at every new turn of our long and up-hill road.[5]

However, some of her later books are cast in the form of straightforward treatises, bristling with references to psychological and physiological theories and buttressed with reports of personal experiments. In these, for reasons to which we shall have to return, the charms of style and subtle organization totally disappear.

Her difficulty in reconciling divergent tendencies of thought is apparent even in the most happily constructed essays—in fact, it is most noticeable in those essays in

[5] Lee, *Belcaro*, p. 196.

which Lee is striving to express her total response to her subject. The heart of her own difficulties can be found analyzed in the fine essay on "Ruskinism" published in *Belcaro.* Though she has a sincere admiration for Ruskin, Vernon Lee sees clearly how much of the inconsistency and confusion in his work is caused by his desire, perhaps even compulsion, to find a moral explanation for the beauty of whatever appeals to his aesthetic sense. He errs, she finds, in constantly trying to identify the true, the good, and the beautiful; an error she constantly but never wholly successfully guarded against in her own thought. Ruskin had himself warned against confusing the three quite as emphatically as does Lee, but for both it was a most difficult thing to avoid. Much of Vernon Lee's writing centers on three topics: the source of what we call beauty, the relation of art to morality, and the value of art. All three topics constantly tempt her, as they had Ruskin, into the explanation of the beautiful in terms of the good and true. The resulting tension between unreconciled positions is in itself often intriguing; we see a new aesthetic arising out of the clash of the two major lines of nineteenth-century aesthetic thought.

Vernon Lee's initial positions on these three related topics are to be found in *Belcaro* (1883). The first essay in the volume, "The Child in the Vatican," records her realization that the subjects of painting and sculpture serve no other purpose than that of suggesting forms which can be presented beautifully. Taking a Niobe group in sculpture as her example, she finds that "there is not, in this group, any movement, any effect, of which we could decidedly say that it would not arise in a scene like this; but, in a scene like this there would certainly be a great many movements and effects which cannot be found in the group."[6] That is, only that which can be rendered by pleasing lines and harmonious groupings is admitted into the representation of

[6] *Ibid.*, p. 36.

this scene of violence and pain. Her analysis seems simple and obvious enough, but what she is facing here is of course the question of the relation between accuracy of representation and beauty of design, which Ruskin wrestled with on more than one occasion, most notably perhaps in his discussion of "naturalism" in "The Nature of Gothic," in which the Gothic architects are praised for being able to unite "fact with design." Ruskin, however, is embarrassed by the consequences of his total identification of beauty in art with the truthful representation of nature, which in turn represents the goodness of God, for this raises the question of how the artist is to be truthful without including the ugly and unpleasant that exists in the world, as well as the question of the existence of the ugly and unpleasant. By making the subject only a means of suggesting form and insisting that it is the beauty of the form rather than the entire truthfulness of the representation that is central to art, Vernon Lee attempts to skirt the morass into which Ruskin more than once sinks. "The highest intrinsic quality of form is beauty; and the highest merit of the artist, of the mere form creator, is to make form which is beautiful."[7]

The next essay, "Orpheus and Euridyce," is an attempt to meet the question that the argument of the first essay naturally suggests: is it not true that we find pleasure in much besides pure form, especially in associations suggested by the subject matter of art, associations with one's own life, with one's intellectual interests, with one's stock of knowledge? Of course, says Vernon Lee, but this is nevertheless to be, if not regretted, at least sternly controlled. No associations should override our appreciation of form as form. This is followed by two essays, "Chapelmaster Kriesler" and "Cherubina," which in diverse ways extend to music the argument for the centrality of mere form in painting and sculpture—music is "intellectually meaningless," in fact, it is in essence emotionally meaningless.

[7] *Ibid.*, p. 41.

Lee is now in a position to advance to the consideration of the second question, the relation of art to morality. She begins by discussing (in the essay "In Umbria") the work of Perugino. The saints in his masterly paintings appear ethereal, wholly devoted to heaven; Perugino himself is thought to have been personally sordid and selfish. The contradiction cannot be resolved unless, denying Ruskin's equation of the great man with the great artist, we insist that a man's moral state and his skill as a painter have no relation. She can then go on, in the previously mentioned essay on "Ruskinism," to deny the whole movement of Ruskin's thought. It is not true "that the basis of art is moral; that art cannot be merely pleasant or unpleasant, but must be lawful or unlawful, that every legitimate artistic enjoyment is due to the perception of moral propriety; that every artistic excellence is a moral virtue, every artistic fault is a moral vice; . . . and that the aim and end of art is the expression of man's obedience to God's will, and of his recognition of God's goodness." Instead we must recognize that "the true state of things is by no means always the noblest or the most beautiful; our longing for ineffable harmony is no proof that such harmony exists: the phantom of perfection which hovers before us is often not the mirage of some distant reality, but a mere vain shadow projected by our own desires, which we must follow, but may never obtain."[8] Venice did not fall because of moral corruption but because the Mediterranean and its cities lost their importance as other nations learned to conquer the ocean beyond it. But this position leaves Lee face to face with the question of the value of art; if the true and the good are not necessarily the beautiful, has the beauty created by art any value beyond immediate pleasure? Yes, she says, "For, though art has no moral meaning, it has moral value; art is happiness, and to bestow happiness is to create good."[9] This formula is repeated in the final essay, "A Dialogue on

[8] *Ibid.*, pp. 205, 206.

[9] *Ibid.*, p. 229.

Poetic Morality": "art in general has a definite function in our lives; and if it attempts to perform the work of philosophy, or practical benevolence, or science, or moralizing, or anything not itself, it will merely fail in that, and neglect what it could do."[10]

The introductory chapter of *Belcaro* states the same thing in other words: "My own art philosophy is . . . simply to try and enjoy in art what art really contains, to obtain from art all that it can give, by refraining from asking it to give what it cannot."[11] By the end of the volume, the reader is able to see how much is implied in that statement. All art that achieves the beauty which is its goal, she finds, offers a form which gives a deep and refreshing pleasure and sense of harmony. This form makes no statements about morality, nor does it reflect the morality of its creator; but the sense of pleasure and harmony it gives are good in themselves and thus have a moral value. Focused as they are on particular works, artists, or anecdotes, the individual essays that make up *Belcaro* seem at first reading only tenuously related, but they turn out to be so many steps in setting forth a reasonably comprehensive view of art.[12]

Nevertheless, certain half-hidden inconsistencies will occur to any reader of *Belcaro*. If, for instance, the pure form divorced from subject matter is the central consideration in painting, why so much discussion of the saintliness of Perugino's saints? If Ruskin's mistake was the attempt to legitimate his aesthetic responses on moral grounds, his errors of judgment about art are not the result, as she claims, of his moral concerns but of his aesthetic responses. Why, if both subject and the associations it awakens are irrelevant to our pleasure in a work, does she devote such full and fond description to the subject? Despite

[10] *Ibid.*, p. 247.

[11] *Ibid.*, p. 13.

[12] The possible exception to this is "Faustus and Helena: Notes on the Supernatural in Art."

all her efforts, her aesthetic theory is still in conflict with her personal tendency to judge art on moral grounds. In the abstract, the general theory she develops in *Belcaro* is reasonable, if not air tight, but she betrays in her very presentation of the theory that it does not explain all of her own responses to art. Her own uneasy recognition that such vexing problems remain led to a series of restatements and modifications of these positions in the two volumes of *Juvenilia*, subtitled "Being a Second Series of Essays on Sundry Aesthetical Questions," published in 1887. However, the various adjustments and qualifications attempted in these essays, too complex to trace here, fail to solve the problems. It is important to recognize that Lee's moral preoccupations are not mere Puritanism; it is clear throughout that something of the typical transcendentalist assumption of the high purpose of art as somehow intended to improve mankind is in question.

Another of Vernon Lee's early major interests was the evolutionary nature of art. Her first book, *Studies of the Eighteenth Century in Italy*, had assumed an inevitable but unpredictable progression from technique to technique, form to form in the arts; and the evolutionary assumption, although not central to *Belcaro*, is easily traced there. In *Euphorion* (1884) and its sequel *Renaissance Fancies and Studies* (1895), Lee uses the sort of personal essay she had developed in *Belcaro* to explore instances of this kind of progression which led toward the Renaissance. In *Belcaro* and *Juvenilia* one can see her struggling to establish the primacy of form—lines, colors, balances, tones, groupings and progressions—in art, while nevertheless frequently distracted by an interest in subject matter, the pleasures that come from association, and the moral value of art. In *Euphorion* and *Renaissance Studies*, her intentions are no less complex. Part of her impatience with Ruskin as expressed in "Ruskinism" arose from his failure to see that certain kinds of change were evolutionary necessities, not the expression of moral qualities. The excessive delicacy of the tracery in late Gothic stonework was a natural development of an artistic technique; the decay of Venice was a natural result of a series of economic developments. Her theory of the evolution of the arts owes something to J. A. Symonds but much more to Pater, whose *Renaissance* is an obvious model both in its evolutionary approach to the Renaissance and its form—a series of carefully styled essays each working out a personal interpretation of its subject.[13]

In joining with Symonds and Pater in the later nineteenth-century enthusiasm for the Renaissance and the classical culture it joyously rediscovered, she was turning away not merely from Ruskin's praise of the Gothic, but from the whole Carlyle-Ruskin-Morris admiration for the spiritual and moral virtues of the middle ages. Lee is perfectly willing to admit the immorality which permeated the Italian culture at the time of the Renaissance, but the "sacrifice" and expense that accompanied the breaking of old patterns were well worthwhile.[14] Not only was the sculpture of the Renaissance much finer than that which it replaced, and the idealization of love in Dante a great advance for the human spirit made possible by the evolution of courtly love (an evolution partly the result of changing economic structures and domestic arrangements), but the economic and political changes of the Renaissance were an enormous advance. The deadening feudal tyranny gave way to democracy and freedom; the narrow medieval literary conventions gave way to an appreciation of all men, all nature. "The Love of the Saints" (*Renaissance Fancies*)

[13]Her style in *Euphorion* and *Renaissance Fancies* approaches Pater's more closely than in any of her other works; the essay "A Seeker of Pagan Perfection" in *Renaissance Fancies* is a truly Paterian "imaginary portrait." Her description of what she tried to do in *Euphorion* could equally well have been applied by Pater to the writing of his *Renaissance*: "My *dramatis personae* have been modes of feeling and forms of art."

[14]We recall that Lee argues in "Ruskinism" that Ruskin failed to understand the way in which good often grows out of evil.

traces the coming of human love into the arid monastic religion of the earlier middle ages to "greater liberty and prosperity, to the growing importance of honest burgher life." Quoting specific passages from medieval writers, Lee denies the benevolence, charity, and imaginative freedom that Ruskin had imputed to the feudal structure. The lot of the peasant was wholly miserable. "For a man it is difficult to call him, this medieval serf, this lump of earth detached from the field and wrought into a semblance of manhood, merely that the soil of which it is part should be delved and sown, and then manured with its carcass or its blood, nor as a man did the Middle Ages conceive it."[15] The medieval period, she finds, was "rich in beginnings," poor in achievement, wasteful of what is important.

Nevertheless, the old Ruskinian attitudes haunted her. Though the doctrine that beauty of form is independent of the moral content of the work or moral worthiness of the artists, as developed in *Belcaro*, is implied throughout, she is much more concerned with moral values than Pater. It is the value of Dante's idealization of love, not the form of the *Divine Comedy*, which she chooses to discuss. Nor, it turns out, are form and content totally independent of the moral and cultural climate. The "fruitfulness" of the Renaissance in which she rejoices results, she says, from its freedom—a cultural, and, for her, a moral attribute. And when she salutes Pater in the close of *Renaissance Fancies*, she praises him as one who "began as an aesthete, and ended as a moralist."

With so strong a sense of moral imperatives, it is not surprising that two of her earlier volumes (*Baldwin*, 1886, and *Althea*, 1894) are devoted to the direct consideration of moral issues. In these volumes, another source of the constant tension in her thought emerges; the ethics she urges are strongly empiricist. They are, in fact, very largely those of John Stuart Mill salted with a stronger evolution-

[15] Lee, *Renaissance Fancies and Studies*, pp. 129–30.

ary belief than Mill was ever able consistently to hold. Mill's arguments that morality consists of opposing the structure of nature, that the terms right and wrong have no meaning except as purely human judgments, that such judgments are ultimately based on the criterion of human happiness, and that belief in a God both omnipotent and benevolent must make the existence of evil a constant torment to the consistent thinker are all urged. Combined with these in Lee's mind is the belief that moral standards are not only constantly improving, but, somewhat mysteriously, somehow becoming hereditary.

However, just as Lee's analysis of aesthetic problems never remains clear of ethical questions, her examinations of ethics frequently returns to questions of aesthetics. Thus "On Novels," while mainly concerned with the moral content of novels (her spokesman defends the restriction of what may be represented in the novel to that which will not corrupt or offend a female reader), turns also to the value of the novel in making mankind more sensitive and, more importantly, begins to discriminate between literature and all other forms of art. The subject matter of literature, she here implies, is much more important in its effects than the subject matter of the other arts. In the last essay of the volume this is developed into the doctrine that since literature brings one into contact with the personality of the author, all but ennobling personalities should be rejected. Writers like Baudelaire cannot be recommended, whatever their literary skill. Thus, in literature at least, Vernon Lee finds she must endorse a directly moral evaluation of art. The difficulty of separating ethics and aesthetics can be seen even more clearly in the penultimate essay, "The Value of the Ideal," where "idealism" is defined in terms of aesthetic harmony rather than an ethical imperative. "To me, idealism does not imply deliberate alteration in conformity to an abstract notion; it does not even necessarily imply alteration of any sort whatever. It means merely the attempt, conscious or unconscious, to obtain for the soul a special sort of satisfaction . . . which may . . . be obtained by mere selection, or by mere accident, or, again may be obtained by what you call the alteration of things."[16]

Just as Vernon Lee attempted in *Juvenilia* to resolve some of the problems and inconsistencies patent in *Belcaro*, she found it necessary to attempt in *Althea* (1894) modification of both the doctrines of *Baldwin* and the assurance with which these are urged. The message of this dilated sequel seems to be simply that one should recognize an ongoing evolution of the race and cooperate with it by improving one's own thought. The final sentence of the volume sums up this semimystical attitude: "Let us see to our thought being as good as it can be, thorough, sincere. We shall take as much of it [apparently the tendency toward good] into our life as we can; or, rather, it will take as much of our life as is worthy."[17]

Thus are Vernon Lee's six major topics developed in the essays gathered in three curiously symmetrical pairs of books. In each case, the first of the pair is more definite in its pronouncements, better finished stylistically, and altogether more confident. The announced sequels seem to reflect both a loss of imaginative force and dissatisfaction with the earlier conclusions. As an apparent result of this dissatisfaction, Vernon Lee began, in a group of essays first published in periodicals in the late 1890s, to try to adjust the relationship between morality and art along new lines.

Those essays, later collected as *Laurus Nobilis*, attempt to link the beautiful, good, and true while preserving distinctions between them. The three are not the same, but the "energies which express themselves in their pursuit . . . have become indissoluably woven together by a number of great and organic coincidences."[18] Lee's rejec-

[16] Lee, *Baldwin*, p. 261.

[17] Lee, *Althea*, p. 278.

[18] Lee, *Laurus Nobilis*, p. 10.

tion of the transcendental assumptions that make possible the Platonic staircase from love of concrete beauty to a vision of absolute truth is still clearly at war with her belief in the moral power of art. Accordingly, she has recourse to the postulation of a number of somewhat vaguely stated coincidences and correspondences: between the development of the aesthetic faculties and altruistic instinct, between one's sense of aesthetic harmony and one's sense of the higher harmonies of universal life, between the preference for aesthetic pleasure and the nobler growth of the individual. Essentially, the argument turns on the assertion that in training all one's faculties to appreciate art and denying lower pleasures in order to appreciate higher, we acquire virtues necessary elsewhere. "As every great writer on art has felt, from Plato to Ruskin, but none has expressed as clearly as Mr. Pater, in all true aesthetic training there must needs enter an ethical element, almost an ascetic one."[19]

The second essay fills in certain details of these arguments, insisting on the unselfishness of aesthetic enjoyment and its capacity to enliven the mind and spirit by causing the beholder to participate in the process of creation. By such a route she reaches Ruskin's conclusion about the relation between aesthetic and economic morality, a conclusion she can never bring herself to abandon however much she tries to adhere to empiricism, logic, and the doctrine of the centrality of aesthetic forms; the more aesthetically aware we are, the less we tolerate any form of living that creates dull and dirty work for others. Her intellectual road passes indeed beyond this point, reaching Wilde's conclusion in the *Soul of Man* that aesthetic sensibility demands the proper distribution of the good things of life to all.

That Vernon Lee is wholly conscious that she is trying to rebuild the Platonic stairway out of new material is made

[19] *Ibid.*, p. 17.

quite clear in the third chapter, which opens with a passage from Diotima's speech on the use of the "beauties of the earth" as steps to higher things. This Lee reinterprets as a series of steps in which the harmony one feels in aesthetic responses creates or strengthens a desire for greater harmony elsewhere in our experience. Especially to be noticed is her substitution of a physiological for a transcendental explanation of the importance of harmony. "Now man requires organic harmony . . . because his existence, the existence of every cell of him, depends upon it."[20] This argument leads her to return to a Ruskin-like sternness about the morally permissible subject matter of art since an art that does not suggest a higher harmony is not morally valuable. "It is a question not of what we *are*, but of what we shall be." But she is perfectly clear that art is not to be propagandistic, not to suggest specific programs. Art for her, like culture for Arnold, is to improve man through leavening his thought and action in unpredictable ways. Unable to rest in her earlier argument that the moral value of art derives simply from the pleasure it gives amidst the evils of the world, Lee, like Arnold, Pater, and Wilde, has found herself driven to argue that love of art leads to the love of harmony and humanity. These essays in effect close the first phase of Vernon Lee's assault on the six questions that occupied her most serious thought: the source of beauty, the relation of art to morality, the value of art, the evolution of artistic forms, the importance of intellectual honesty, and the evolution of human thought.

That the second phase of her writing on these matters, a phase which looked toward quite a different method of solving the difficulties she faced, had been initiated while she was still attempting new maneuvers with elements of her old methods is an indication of the degree of dissatisfaction she felt during these years. In 1894 she had begun,

[20] *Ibid.*, pp. 88–89.

in collaboration with her friend C. Anstruther Thomson, a series of empirical observations which attempted to isolate and describe specific psychological and physiological reactions to the form of objects of art. The results appeared toward the end of 1897 in *The Contemporary Review* under the title "Beauty and Ugliness." The theory there worked out is essentially that aesthetic response arises out of physical reactions to the following of the form of the object by the appropriate sense.

The whole project had immense attraction for Lee. Some way of separating the response to form from the response to subject, with its inevitable moral overtones, had been one of the goals toward which she had, however inconsistently, been driving. Moreover, the theory took account of the evolutionary doctrines she had accepted by assuming that a "special instinct" has evolved which causes one "to court or to shun those opposite qualities of Form which we call beauty and ugliness."[21] Finally, the theory introduced a moral value that was not dependent on the subject matter of the work of art. For the aesthetic instinct, itself a product of evolution, could be regarded as having become one of the powers by which evolution proceeds, "setting the active impulses of man to work for its sole and single gratification, and to create out of reality a world more consonant with the most deeply organized and most unchanging modes of man's bodily existence."[22] The goal was to differentiate the pleasure (or irritation) produced by sheer form from the more consciously formulated reaction to the subject or context of the work, and, as far as possible, explain the source of the former.

The precise form of the theory as formulated in 1897 did not long seem satisfactory. How hard she struggled with the problem for the next fifteen years is apparent in *Beauty and Ugliness* (1912), which sandwiches the origi-

[21] Lee and Thomson, *Beauty and Ugliness*, p. 176.

[22] *Ibid.*, p. 177.

nal *Contemporary Review* article between three rambling, repetitious essays which try to provide context, support, and necessary correction for the original essay, and a hundred pages of extracts from Vernon Lee's diaries together with commentary which exhibits the empirical basis from which the essay had been developed.

Both the 1912 edition of *Beauty and Ugliness* and the introduction to *Art and Man* are tortuous. The awkward fact that becomes more and more apparent as one wearily plods the rounds between "Lange-James" theory, the various arguments of Theodore Lipps, Karl Groos, and Professor Titchener, and the examination of the meaning of such terms as "empathy," and "miming," is that, feeling forced to fit her aesthetic theory within still-debated and still-developing physiological and psychological theories, she became overwhelmed by the tedious process of adjusting the details and ramifications of constantly modified scientific hypotheses, the validity of which lie outside her competence.

Fortunately, however, in a volume contributed to The Cambridge Manuals of Science and Literature, Lee found it possible to restate the central theories of *Beauty and Ugliness*, as modified by second thoughts, in a form free of the encumbrances of the theories of Lipps, Groos, Lang *et al.* In *The Beautiful* she simply reported the results of her own observations and contemplation. The result is a clear statement of her distinction between purely aesthetic response to form and the other feelings which are called up both by the subject of the work and personal association. Moreover, we here find the clearest statement of the link between perception of the beautiful and the larger moral and spiritual effects of that beauty, effects which she has been at pains to distinguish from the response itself. The central argument is that aesthetic pleasure has to do with our active response to aspects, not things: "what we contemplate as beautiful is an Aspect of a Thing, but never a Thing itself." For instance, the beauty of shape, one aspect of a thing, depends on the activity both of the eye and the mind: "Ours are the energy, the effort, the victory or the peace and cooperation. . . ."[23] While avoiding Coleridgean metaphysics, she is echoing his "we receive but what we give, /And in our life alone does Nature live: /Ours is her wedding garment, ours her shroud!" Lee follows Ruskin, and Morris, in finding that man naturally wishes to add beauty to even the most utilitarian of the objects he makes, but she is very clear that the object's beauty is not to be confused with its utility (its "good") or its "value for fact-transmission" (its "truth"). To think about the utility or truth of an object is to think away from its shape—the whole purpose of art (the creation of beauty) is to cause us to "think back to the shape." Finally, however, art has an indirect utility, or moral value:

> But, as the whole of this book has tried to establish, the contemplation of beautiful shapes involves perceptive processes in themselves mentally invigorating and refining, and a play of empathetic feelings which realise the greatest desiderata of spiritual life, viz. intensity, purposefulness and harmony; and such perceptive and empathetic activities cannot fail to raise the present level of existence to leave behind them a higher standard for future experience.[24]

This may seem to be dragging morality in through the back door, but one must notice how far Vernon Lee has been able to move from the Ruskinian view of the beautiful as the preeminent manifestation of God's goodness—and how far toward I. A. Richards.

In the new century, Vernon Lee also adopted a new method of doing battle for her conception of intellectual honesty. The earlier dialogues on abstract questions of ethics are abandoned for direct attack on what she feels are pernicious doctrines. A collection of such critical essays

[23] Lee, *The Beautiful*, p. 81.

[24] *Ibid.*, p. 149.

which analyzes contemporary topics and figures in the interest of strict intellectual discipline appeared in 1908 as *Gospels of Anarchy*. The title is derived from the general drift of all these essays: they protest against moral and intellectual anarchy, by which she means the tendency to free oneself from strict empirical and logical thought and leap over the fence into more spacious intellectual pastures.

Her defense of truth, the empiricist truth, continued with the two volumes of *Vital Lies* (1912). Vitalism, Intuitionism, and Transcendentalism are all attacked as attempts to preserve the remnants of primeval chaos in the mind. The common element of all these formulations, which arouses Vernon Lee's alarm and irritation, is what she sees as an appeal to something known to be untrue as a source of motivation, comfort, and inspiration. No doctrine that is not objectively, empirically true can lead man to better his condition. Thus we find in the brief notes which close Volume II a section entitled "Humanism" which confesses:

> If I have shown, peradventure, lack of moderation and sweetness towards *Will-to-believe Pragmatism*, it is due in part to the exasperated recognition that this doctrine, and these doctors, have distorted views which are mine, or which resemble my own: utilitarianism, relativism, and the idea vaguely roughed out in the saying that *Man is the Measure of all things.*[25]

Lee is correct in pointing out that her thought is strongly influenced by utilitarianism: the discussion of evil throughout *Vital Lies* maintains, for instance, the same views of man's relation to evil and to nature that we find in J. S. Mill. But both her thought and strategies remain too eclectic to accept any simple label.

Proteus, Or, The Future of Intelligence, Lee's last sig-

[25] *Ibid.*, p. 186.

nificant essay on human thought and culture, draws together in a very simple statement the final forms of her views of evolution, the relationship between mind and reality, and the value of art. This essay has nothing strikingly profound about it, nor does it delight by felicitous illustration or the sprightly pursuit of a speculation wherever it may lead. Yet as a document which reflects the amalgamation of traditions of thought which flow from Ruskin, from Bentham and the Mills, from Comte, it has considerably more claim to our interest than commentators on Vernon Lee have made clear. Like many intelligent Victorians and Edwardians, Lee recombined portions of all three modes of thought while refusing to become a doctrinaire disciple of any.

Defining human thought and its history as the pursuit by intelligence of a reality which, like Proteus, is multiform and ever elusive, Lee denies that Reality is either an eternal model hidden behind a veil which the seer at times pierces or that it is a simple structure to be traced by logic and dealt with by formulae. Transcendentalists are blinded by superstition; utilitarians are trapped by the narrowness of their logic. "Intelligence," which is limited neither by "reason and logic" nor by metaphysical assumptions about the one and the many, the real and the apparent, etc., is simply the constantly increasing ability of the mind to combine memory and perception, to recognize the difference between desire and experience, between oneself and the not-oneself which "has ways of its own and does not exist merely to suit our liking." Intelligence so defined has now evolved far enough, hopes Lee, for man to think in terms of change and otherness rather than of the eternal and the self, to regard the "problem of evil" as "the problem not of its toleration by God, but of its diminution by man"[26] and to understand that the proper means of satisfying man's craving of art, not of religious creeds. Reading this

[26] Lee, *Proteus, Or, The Future of the Intelligence*, pp. 14, 28.

essay as the culmination of the wisdom of the author of some twenty books on aesthetics, culture, and morality, one is likely to be disappointed to recognize so many echoes of previous writers. We encounter a combination of Macaulayan contempt for philosophical dialectics, Ruskinian moral earnestness, Paterian sense of experience as flux, Millian discounting of the benevolence of nature, and Arnoldian urging that art is the true source of what men have sought in orthodox religion. But what these voices blend into is simply the intellectual creed of the twentieth century. Gone is the assumption that the beautiful is the expression of God's nature (that ancient view given its definitive nineteenth-century form by Ruskin), gone is the rationally elaborated empiricism that resulted in complex and comprehensive schemata (like that of Bentham's *Principles of Morals and Legislation*), gone are the attempts to evoke such shadowy essences as the "being not ourselves which makes for righteousness," gone are the certainties that simplify the evolution of human thought into three stages. The core of what remains is the assertion of man's constantly increasing power of understanding the world and the concomitant possibility, though not the certainty, of solving the problems it poses. That might seem to sum up rather well the predominant mode of thought which the twentieth century inherited.

THIRTY YEARS before Vernon Lee began her series of struggles against Ruskinism, Eneas Sweetland Dallas had published the first of two attempts to put aesthetics on a wholly new basis. "We must, like receivers of stolen goods, accept our pleasures and ask no questions. Pleasure says to every one of us what we say to our children, Open your mouth and shut your eyes. She turns from the man that woos her, and to the heedless child flies unbidden.

She seldom gives note of her coming; she comes like an angel, unheard, unseen, unknown, and not till she is gone or is parting from us, are our eyes opened, to see what we have enjoyed."[27] This statement on the nature of pleasure, the doctrine of which is essential to E. S. Dallas's theory of art, well represents the felicity of Dallas's writing. The vivacity of his treatment of aesthetics in *The Gay Science* goes far to convince one of the appropriateness of the title.[28] His aesthetic theory is as appealing as the style in which he presents it. The operation of unconscious powers of the mind is the key with which he unlocks the problems of aesthetics; the novelty of that solution at that time is perhaps just about equal to its obviousness to post-Freudian generations. That he was able to take a new line is adequately explained, I think, by the fact that his intellectual father is Sir William Hamilton, whose attempt to combine Scottish common sense empiricism with Kantian idealism provided Dallas with an approach not likely to suggest itself to the orthodox empiricist or transcendentalist.

Dallas, whose work on aesthetics seems to be perennially "discovered" but never placed securely amidst the classics of nineteenth-century thought, began the formulation of his theories in *Poetics: An Essay on Poetry*, published in 1852. The book is dedicated to Sir William Hamilton "in token of the admiration, the regard, and the obligations of a pupil." A good many passages in the volume are memorable in themselves,[29] but its real signifi-

[27] Dallas, *The Gay Science*, II, 112.

[28] Presumably from the Provençal *Gai saber* as well as in obvious allusion to Carlyle's description of economics as the Dismal Science.

[29] For instance: "The lyric is an aspiration; its banner has the strange device, Excelsior"; "Conscience can belong only to a fallen being; it is the jurymast of a wreck, mast and rigging borrowed from all parts of the vessel"; "The shows of the sensuous world fall upon the mind, like oil dropt upon water, to spread a film of glorious colouring on the surface of every thought and every feeling"; "Like the conjuror's bottle that will at pleasure produce wine or water, milk or

cance is as a first approximation to the more thoroughly developed argument of *The Gay Science*, which incorporates whole passages from the earlier work. In the *Poetics*, Dallas expresses his dissatisfaction with Aristotle's definition of poetry in terms of imitation and Bacon's definition in terms of feigning and begins to marshal arguments for regarding poetry as a record of the writer's pleasure which is intended to produce pleasure in the reader and for defining pleasure as "the harmonious and unconscious activity of the soul."[30] These will become the major hinges on which the whole of *The Gay Science* turns, though they remain undeveloped in the *Poetics* where Dallas's intellectual energies soon become diverted into the construction of an ingenious schematic outline of the arts.[31]

The Gay Science opens with a frequently witty survey of the deficiencies of all earlier aesthetic theories. Aristotle's view of art as imitation, says Dallas, "has transmitted to all after criticism a sort of hereditary squint." Of Schiller, Dallas comments, "After every sober bit of argument, he breaks off into inarticulate rhapsody, which we can only interpret as the fol-de-diddle-dol at the end of a song." Of Coleridge: "He rather prided himself on his anatomy of thought and expression, but he hardly ever made a clean dissection."[32] Dallas then narrows his survey of aesthetic problems and theories down to their relation to what is generally called the imagination, his figurative account of

vinegar; fiction, truth, reality, are words any of which will express ideas the most opposite" (*Poetics*, pp. 150, 37, 46, and 281).

[30] Dallas, *Poetics*, p. 17.

[31] The scheme, reminiscent of similar bits of joyous castle-building by nineteenth-century German thinkers, is much more provocative than definitive: Dallas labors, for instance, to identify the Present with Beauty and Plurality, the Past with Truth and Totality, and the Future with the Good and Unity (*Poetics*, pp. 95–106).

[32] Dallas, *Gay Science*, I, 26, 157, 109.

the current theories of which is no less accurate than evocative:

> Imagination is the Proteus of the mind, and the despair of metaphysics. When the philosopher seizes it, he finds something quite unexpected in his grasp, a faculty that takes many shapes and eludes him in all. First it appears as mere memory, and perhaps the inquirer lets it escape in that disguise as an old friend that need not be interrogated. If, however, he retain his hold of it, ere long it becomes other than memory; suddenly it is the mind's eye; sudden again, a second sight; anon it is intuition; then it is apprehension; quickly it passes into a dream; as quickly it resolves itself into sympathy and imitation; in one moment it turns to invention and begins to create; in the next moment it adopts reason and begins to generalize; at length it flies in a passion, and is lost in love.[33]

There follow four chapters devoted to establishing grounds for the belief in activities of the mind of which we are not consciously aware. "The thing to be firmly seized is, that we live in two concentric worlds of thought,—an inner ring, of which we are conscious, and which may be described as illuminated; an outer one, of which we are unconscious and which may be described as in the dark. Between the outer and the inner ring, between our unconscious and our conscious existence, there is a free and a constant but unobserved traffic for ever carried on."[34] Dallas then arrives at one of his two major points: "I propose this theory, that the imagination or fantasy is not a special faculty but that it is a special function," that is, "the free, unconscious play of thought."[35] The imagination, in short, as Dallas attempts to establish in a variety of ways, is the name we give to the unconscious activities of the mind. Unable to draw on appropriate psychological termi-

[33] *Ibid.*, I, 179–80.

[34] *Ibid.*, I, 207.

[35] *Ibid.*, I, 193–94, 305.

nology, Dallas gives the name "Hidden Soul" to the sum of these unconscious activities. The unconscious affords him explanations of what others variously call the coadunative, reconciling, or integrative power of the mind: "the mind in free play works more as a whole than in conscious and voluntary effort. It is the very nature of voluntary effort to be partial and concentrated in points. Left to itself the mind is like the cloud that moveth altogether if it move at all; and this wholeness of movement has its issue in that wholeness of thinking which we find in true works of imagination."[36]

The transition from this definition of the imagination to his other major argument is best given in Dallas's own words. "We started with the common doctrine, that art is the opposite of science, and that, as the object of science is knowledge, so that of art is pleasure. But if the reader has apprehended what I have tried to convey to him as to the existence within us of two great worlds of thought—a double life, the one known or knowable, the other unknown and for the most part unknowable, he will be prepared, if not to accept, yet to understand this further conception of the difference between science and art that the field of science is the known and the knowable, while the field of art is the unknown and unknowable." In other words, "The object of art is pleasure—a sensible possession or enjoyment of the world beyond consciousness. We do not know that world, yet we feel it—feel it chiefly in pleasure, but sometimes in pain, which is the shadow of pleasure."[37]

By this route we come back to Dallas's belief as expressed in the *Poetics* that poetry "on the one hand, is the record of pleasure, and, on the other, is intended to produce pleasure in the reader's mind."[38] The poet initially and the reader ultimately are thus tapping the "Hidden Soul."

[36] *Ibid.*, I, 305.

[37] *Ibid.*, I, 312, 313.

[38] Dallas, *Poetics*, p. 12.

In order to defend this position, Dallas finds it necessary to distinguish between types of pleasure. "Mixed pleasure," in which pleasure arises out of pain, is produced by art that treats of action, especially the drama. "Pure pleasure," arising out of a sense of harmony and repose, is given by those kinds of art which we think of as beautiful. But most important of all is "hidden pleasure" which arises out of the unconscious. "Here, at last, we reach the most wonderful, the most vital, of all the elements of art—the element of mystery, that sense of the unseen, that possession of the far-away, that glimmer of infinity, that incommunicable secret, that know-not-what, of which I tried to give some account in the first volume of this work. It is the suggestion of this unknown something in art which we are in the habit of signalizing as in a peculiar sense poetical."[39] Having reached this, the climax of his theoretical argument, Dallas turns aside to answer the question that haunted nineteenth-century aesthetic theory: "if art is the pursuit of pleasure, is it not inimical to morality?" As he enters on the question (discussed below) he indicates that he will return to applications of his definition of the imagination and the goal of art,[40] but Volume II ends in the consideration of ethical and social tendencies of contemporary life and literature. Almost certainly a third volume was intended but never given to the printer. Even in its truncated form, however, *The Gay Science* intriguingly anticipates a wide variety of later theories.

Dallas's loyalty to Sir William Hamilton is manifest throughout the *Poetics* and *The Gay Science*, especially in his defense of Hamilton against the strictures of J. S. Mill, whom he regards as merely a reviver of Hume's philoso-

[39] Dallas, *Gay Science*, II, 134–35.

[40] "And now it may be expected, in the course of this inquiry, that we should proceed to apply the principles which have thus been worked out to a solution of the great problems of criticism. That is a task which in due time will have to engage our attention; but in the meantime it may be right to complete the psychological view. . ." (*Ibid.*, II, 143–44).

phy.[41] By modifying Hamilton, Dallas avoids having to begin his studies with essentially philosophical arguments; for that reason, however, Dallas's theory is not wholly free standing. To a significant extent his aesthetic theory thus becomes a hostage to Hamilton's metaphysical one, and certainly Hamilton's somewhat improbable attempt at combining Thomas Reid's "common sense" empiricism with Kant's critical philosophy has not been judged successful. (Dallas's only objection to Hamilton was that he too severely limited the extent of the unconscious realms, and in *The Gay Science* he defends Hamilton against J. S. Mill.) Of course, as it happened, psychology has provided support for the existence of an active unconscious that would have made the dependence on Hamilton unnecessary.

Hamilton, Dallas argues, believed in Hidden Thought;[42] if the same arguments are applied to aesthetics, they prove the existence of Hidden Feeling, that is, feelings that originate in the "Hidden Soul" or unconscious, the possibility of which Hamilton had denied. The existence of unconscious activities within the mind explains a number of things in new ways. What was it that Wordsworth really felt when he saw into the life of things? It was indeed a world beyond consciousness; that is, it was the unconscious. And all that Plato tried to explain by the "hypothesis of a previous life passed in a previous world" can be better explained, Dallas argues, by reference to the unconscious realm of the mind.

The Kantian portions of Hamilton's thought emerge in various ways—Kant's insistence on the activity of the mind is assimilated in Dallas's theory, for instance. But just as Kant had substituted a possible noumenal realm for the transcendental realm of pure Ideas, Dallas replaces the noumenal realm by the unconscious. While true to the em-

[41] See *Gay Science*, II, 23–24; I, 333; and chapter XIII of volume II.

[42] See Hamilton's Lectures XVII and XVIII in *Lectures on Metaphysics and Logic.*

pirical tradition in denying that there is anything which can be known in the world by means other than reason, that is, denying to art unique cognitive powers, he is able to give the imagination as autonomous a realm as any transcendentalist.

Early in *The Gay Science* Dallas argues that Aristotle is wrong in thinking of art as imitation, Plato wrong in thinking it the manifestation of one great idea such as beauty or truth. His alternative avoids, and, if accepted, invalidates both kinds of explanation. He also states early in his survey of other aesthetic theories that "if the first of all lessons in art is that art is for pleasure, and the second is that this pleasure has nothing to do with falsehood, the third is that art is not to be considered as in any sense opposed to utility."[43] By making art in a sense a report from the appeal to the unconscious, he avoids all questions of the truth or falsity of art, whether raised by moralists or utilitarians.

By implicitly denying the transcendentalists' identification of the good, the true, and the beautiful, he also avoids many of the pitfalls of more orthodox defenders of the arts and can calmly say that art is no friend to virtue but no foe to morality. Art can nevertheless lay claim to fulfilling an essential function: "man leads a double life, and . . . the laws and the needs of the one which flourishes in imagination, or as I have ventured to name it, the 'Hidden Soul,' are not less imperative and importunate than those which rule in our work-a-day consciousness."[44]

Though partially inspired by Hamilton's lectures on metaphysics, Dallas's approach effectively severs aesthetic from metaphysical questions. The aesthetic imagination neither reveals a transcendent world nor falsifies our knowledge of the empirical world. No one else writing on

[43] Dallas, *Gay Science*, I, 78, 112.

[44] *Ibid.*, II, 239.

aesthetic theory in mid-nineteenth-century England finally gives the poetic imagination a true autonomy and at the same time a ground in a universal human need.

THOUGH GIFTED with a lively appreciation of literature, deserving of at least some of the credit for George Eliot's success as a novelist, and credited by William Archer and Robert Lowe with having written, in *On Actors*, "one of the not too numerous classics of English dramatic criticism,"[45] George Henry Lewes's general view of aesthetics, and his discussions of the history of literature, are surprisingly pedestrian. Lewes included in his *Life of Goethe* a clever little parable which sums up his own endeavors with perhaps unconscious aptness.

> A Frenchman, an Englishman, and a German were commissioned, it is said, to give the world the benefit of their views on that interesting animal the Camel. Away went the Frenchman to the *Jardin des Plantes*, spent an hour there in rapid investigation, returned and wrote a *feuilleton*, in which there was no phrase the Academy could blame, but also no phrase which added to the general knowledge. He was perfectly satisfied, however, and said, *Le voila, le chameau*! The Englishman packed up his tea-caddy and a magazine of comforts; pitched his tent in the East; remained there two years studying the Camel in its habits; and returned with a thick volume of facts, arranged without order, expounded without philosophy, but serving as valuable materials for all who came after him. The German, despising the frivolity of the Frenchman, and the unphilosophic matter-of-factness of the Englishman,

[45] Archer and Lowe, *Dramatic Essays by John Forster and George Henry Lewes*, p. xiv.

> retired to his study, there *to construct the Idea of a Camel from out of the depths of his Moral Consciousness.* And he is still at it.[46]

Significantly, the parable omits the possibility of a systematic empiricism like that of Bentham and the Mills; Lewes's empiricism, in its lack of rigor, is rather strikingly like that assigned to his Englishman.

Lewes was early influenced by Comte, but over the years his thought moved from a specifically Positivist orientation to a more general empiricism. His first important publication, *Aristotle: A Chapter from the History of Science* (1864), opens with a statement on the importance of the "objective" or empiricist method. In his *Biographical History of Philosophy* (first published in 1845), after placing metaphysics in opposition to "positive Science," he characterizes it "as a great power that *has been*, and no longer *is*. . . . The only interest it can have is an historical interest."[47] His condescending chapter on Plato follows J. S. Mill's essay in distinguishing in Plato a valuable method and an untenable metaphysics. The chapter on Aristotle, which draws heavily on Mill's *Logic* (published just two years before), develops the argument presented in his earlier book that Aristotle's great contribution was in his grounding of science in experience. But because Aristotle nevertheless at times leaped to conclusions beyond those that could legitimately be drawn from experience and attempted to penetrate beyond laws "to the mystery of existence," the secure founding of Positive Science had to await the coming of Bacon, whose mind "was averse to all metaphysics." Lewes's praise for Bacon's method is quite as full as that of Macaulay, on whom he has clearly drawn. Lewes explained in the 1882 London edition that the *Biographical History of Philosophy* was "written with the avowed purpose of dissuading the youth of England from

[46] Lewes, *Life of Goethe*, p. 397.

[47] Lewes, *Biographical History of Philosophy*, p. xxii.

wasting energy on insoluble problems, and relying on a false method. With this object of turning the mind from Metaphysics to Positive Philosophy, it employed History as an instrument to disclose the successive failures of successive schools."[48]

Lewes's own most direct contribution to philosophy is a series of volumes entitled *Problems of Life and Mind.*[49] The first series, entitled "The Foundation of a Creed" is an attempt to show how scientific method may be applied to all those problems of metaphysics which can be rationally stated: metaphysics being defined here, somewhat trickily, as "the ultimate generalizations of Research."[50] With this as his goal, Lewes drives straightforwardly to the positivist's position that all things about which we can talk rationally are derived from experience. "When metaphysicians tell us that we can never know things in themselves, and therefore all knowledge of the Absolute is necessarily excluded, our reply must be, that, in any rational sense of the terms, things *are* known; and that if the Absolute is the sum of things, then this Absolute is known, both in the known concretes, and in the abstraction framed from them."[51] Lewes's terminology is frequently novel, but his arguments are traditional and empiricist. "Phenomena exist, but it is impossible to deduce their manifold variety from the postulate of a Noumenon in its formless monotony; whereas we can well understand the genesis of the abstraction Noumenon from the concrete Phenomena, as the symbol of what is common to them all."[52] We recognize Bentham's explanation of Platonic ideas as simply gener-

[48] Lewes, *Biographical History of Philosophy*, 4th ed., I, vi–vii.

[49] In his 1876 essay "Philosophy at Oxford," Mark Pattison cites *Problems of Life and Mind* as "the ready-made rejoinder to T. H. Green's 'declaration of war . . . against the reigning empirical logic.'"

[50] Lewes, *Problems of Life and Mind*, I, 16.

[51] *Ibid.*, II, 441.

[52] *Ibid.*, II, 440.

alizations produced by abstraction. Even in his most apparently unique and striking argument, that the "*Thing in Itself*" is simply feeling, we can recognize a close kinship with James Mill's *Analysis of the Phenomena of the Human Mind*. "I simply mean that Feeling is our ultimate: it is that in which all knowledge begins and terminates. We can express all phenomena whatever only in its terms, for whether these phenomena are objective or subjective, they are, in a last analysis, seen to be forms of Feelings; and the remote abstractions of Matter, Motion, Space, and Time are symbols of sensible concretes." Or, more simply, "Does it not follow that Feeling is the much sought *Thing in Itself*—the ultimate of search? All things can be reduced to it; but it can be referred to nothing more general."[53] What we have here, as the conclusion of Lewes's analysis, is of course the starting point of Mill's *Analysis of the Mind*: all experience begins in varieties of feeling. What Lewes essentially does is restate the major empiricist propositions in new ways which do not so directly rely on the theory of association.

Alice Kaminsky, whose *George Henry Lewes as Literary Critic* is the only full-dress treatment of Lewes's writing on literature, had no difficulty in finding tributes to the quality of Lewes's mind in general and to his ability as a critic in particular. G. B. Shaw, for instance, called Lewes "the most able and brilliant critic between Hazlitt and our own contemporaries."[54] But, despite his undeniable good sense, clarity, and occasional illuminating insights, Lewes's criticism deserves its neglect. To read his *Principles of Success in Literature*, or a series of his essays, or even Mrs. Kaminsky's well-chosen selection, is an exercise in tediousness. One may chafe at the quirks and crochets that adherence to a philosophical system is likely to introduce

[53] *Ibid.*, II, 493.

[54] Quoted by Alice Kaminsky, *George Henry Lewes as Literary Critic*, p. 184.

into a critic's work, but it is much worse to feel oneself sinking into a bottomless morass of inadequately grounded commentary.

Lewes occupies many of the positions we would expect of an empiricist. It is a "superstitution" to believe "the Ancients to have discovered all wisdom, so that if we could only surprise the secret of Aristotle's thoughts and clearly comprehend the drift of Plato's theories (which unhappily was not clear) we should compass all knowledge." "That art is the mirror of eternal truths is one of the pompous imbecilities into which ignorance has led the critics." "The boasted benefits of 'intellectual training' which are claimed for the classic languages would be far more efficiently secured by Science. But Science is not dead; if it were Oxford would teach it." And when he uses such a term as "organic" in his discussion of the novel it turns out to mean no more than "the rejection of whatever is superfluous."[55]

But for all his allegiance to empiricism and the cognate associationist doctrines, Lewes never seems to have asked himself where his literary principles led; that is, what ultimate meaning an empiricist could assign to them. It has been argued that there *is* a direct correlation between Lewes's philosophical and aesthetic theories in the concept of relativism.[56] But Lewes's literary "relativism" is simply the doctrine that infallible rules for art could not be formulated, a position that can equally well be defended by any variety of empiricist or transcendentalist.

The Principles of Success in Literature, first published in the *Fortnightly Review* in 1865, is Lewes's most ordered presentation of his critical views, bringing together most of the major theoretical principles enumerated by the way in his other books and his many periodical essays. It will, therefore, not be unfair to focus on Lewes's critical and

[55] Lewes, *The Principles of Success in Literature*, p. 117; other quotations cited from Kaminsky, *Lewes as Literary Critic*, pp. 30, 32, 82.

[56] See Kaminsky, *Lewes as Literary Critic*, chapter II.

aesthetic principles as there formulated. He begins by laying out the groundwork methodically enough:

> The laws of Literature may be grouped under three heads. Perhaps we might say they are three forms of one principle. They are founded on our three-fold nature—intellectual, moral, and aesthetic.
>
> The intellectual form is the *Principle of Vision.*
> The moral form is the *Principle of Sincerity.*
> The aesthetic form is the *Principle of Beauty.*[57]

The relationship among these three principles is shortly after summed up thus:

> Books minister to our knowledge, to our guidance, and to our delight, by their truth, their uprightness, and their art. Truth is the aim of Literature. Sincerity is moral truth. Beauty is aesthetic truth.[58]

We thus appear to have a set of three equations. The first defines one purpose of literature as the provision of knowledge, that is, truth, by means of the writer's Vision. The second purpose is the provision of guidance, or moral truth, by means of the writer's Sincerity. The last is the provision of delight, that is aesthetic truth, by means of the writer's grasp of Beauty. Lewes would appear to be setting out an ambitious program which will require definition of intellectual, moral, and aesthetic truth and the means by which the writer first perceives and then presents each of these. However, what the reader of *Principles of Success in Literature* at last emerges with is a reduction of all three "Laws of Literature" to the single rule that one must always be sincere. The doctrine of the chapter entitled "The Principle of Vision" is that "personal experience is the basis of all real Literature. The writer must have thought the thoughts, seen the objects (with bodily or mental vision),

[57] Lewes, *Principles of Success in Literature*, p. 35.

[58] *Ibid.*, p. 36.

and felt the feelings; otherwise he can have no power over us."[59] This is a theme to which Lewes returns again and again, though he never directly faces the problems which it raises. For we find that the writer with vision is able to organize his past experience so as to have a mental vision of situations he has not experienced. "A fine poet has no need of the actual presence of men and women under the fluctuating impatience of emotion, or under the steadfast hopelessness of grief; he needs no setting sun before his windows, under it no sullen sea. . . . He sees the quivering lip, the agitated soul; he hears the aching cry, and the dreary wash of waves upon the beach."[60]

There is nothing unfamiliar in Lewes's belief that one can extrapolate from one's experience, but that belief, especially in the form in which Lewes presents it, poses problems as to what Lewes really means by the adherence to personal experience. In explaining how such extrapolation is possible, Lewes postulates four intellectual operations: Perception, Inference, Reasoning, and Imagination. Perception "is the presentation before Consciousness of the details which once were present in conjunction with the object at this moment affecting sense." Reason "presents an *ideal series*, such as would be a series of sensations if the objects themselves were before us. A chain of reasoning is a chain of inferences. . . ."[61] "Vision" is then the power of calling up, through the ascending series of Perception, Inference, and Reasoning, that which is absent. The relation between the Imagination and these three other powers is not entirely clear, but it appears that the Imagination has the power of calling up images rather than signs at each stage. Imagination, offering clear im-

[59] *Ibid.*, p. 38.

[60] *Ibid.*, p. 49.

[61] *Ibid.*, pp. 43–44. In the introduction to his *Biographical History of Philosophy*, Lewes defines Perception as "inferential respecting objects *present*" and Reasoning as "inferential respecting objects *absent*" (p. xxv).

ages rather than abstract signs, is of great value to the writer, though whether it is an addition to or part of what Lewes thinks of as clear vision is not altogether apparent. Indeed, in Chapter III, the value of the other powers seems to depend on the extent to which they are enlivened by the Imagination, though Lewes specifically indicates earlier that there are types of reasoning in which signs are essential because images would be too confusing. A further problem arises in determining what Lewes really means by images—Newton and Shakespeare, we are told, both had "intensely active" imaginations, but where Shakespeare fastened on concrete facts, Newton grasped "the abstract relation of things."[62] How one sees abstract relations without moving from images to signs is puzzling.

The fact is that Lewes never explores the relation between vision and truth. Clearness of Vision is wearisomely insisted on, but it is not apparent whether "the born seers" who compose the highest class of writers[63] are celebrated for seeing truth or simply seeing things uniquely. The ambiguity increases the further one goes. Consider the following: "As all Art depends on Vision, so the different kinds of Art depend on the different ways in which minds look at things. The painter can only put into his pictures what he sees in Nature; and what he sees will be different from what another sees. A poetical mind sees noble and affecting suggestions in details which the prosaic mind will interpret prosaically. And the true meaning of Idealism is precisely this vision of realities in their highest and most affecting forms, not in the vision of something removed for or opposed to realities."[64] One could well ask what is meant by "highest form," but at least it is clear that Lewes recognizes that art will represent different ways of looking at

[62] Lewes, *Principles of Success in Literature*, pp. 58–59.

[63] *Ibid.*, pp. 54–55.

[64] *Ibid.*, pp. 82–83.

things. Sincerity, it turns out in the next chapter, is the honest and accurate presentation of one's own Vision.

What then, gives Beauty to that presentation? Lewes does not have to look far to answer the question, for it turns out that Beauty is mainly reducible to style, and style to the honest and accurate presentation of one's vision. "No style can be good that is not sincere. It must be the expression of its author's mind."[65] The use of such words as "truth" and "beauty" in the first passage quoted above from *Principles of Success*, and the intimate relation there implied between the good, true, and beautiful, are misleading in their vaguely transcendental connotations. One recalls that in his 1842 review of "Hegel's Aesthetics" for the *British and Foreign Review*, Lewes had tried to adapt Hegelian terminology to express empiricist views, and had not scrupled to describe poetry as "the beautiful phasis of a religious Idea," where "religious" turns out to mean only "the formula of any truth leading to new contemplation of the infinite, or to new forms in our social relations." Thus "liberty, equality, and humanity" are religious Ideas.[66]

The final chapter of *The Principles of Success in Literature* offers us five laws of style: Economy, Simplicity, Sequence, Climax, and Variety. But the application of these is, for Lewes, determined by the Vision which is to be presented, and these laws can in fact also be reduced, almost without remainder, to Sincerity. For instance: "And how is Variety to be secured? The plan is simple, but like many other simple plans is not without difficulty. It is for the writer to obey the great cardinal principle of Sincerity. . . ."[67]

All finally reduces to the sincere expression of the writer's vision—a vision that will vary from writer to writer

[65] *Ibid.*, p. 115.

[66] Quoted in *Literary Criticism of George Henry Lewes*, ed. Alice Kaminsky, pp. 50, 56–57 from "Hegel's Aesthetics," *British and Foreign Review*, XIII (1842).

[67] Lewes, *Principles of Success in Literature*, p. 158.

and thus is hardly to be conceived of as giving objective truth. What does it then report that is of value? How does it offer "guidance"? Why are such reports the source of pleasure and delight? We are not told. Arnold had difficulty in establishing how one knows the "best," but Lewes has even more difficulty in establishing the value of literature once he has placed it outside any evaluation of what is known and thought.

Lewes's position, attentively considered, is really very close to that of Pater's equation, as set forth in his essay on Style, of beauty to truth and both to the "finer accommodation of speech to that vision within." But Pater recognizes that he is using "truth" in a curious way and that art, as he views it, conveys impressions, not unchanging, ontologically verifiable realities. Pater does not go far enough to be fully self-consistent, but he is clear about the ultimate significance of what he is doing and is quite aware that he is employing empiricist doctrine in a way that radically undercuts the orthodox aesthetic theories of both empiricists and transcendentalists. There is a very real irony in the fact that the aesthetically oriented Oxford Don rather than the scientifically oriented Lewes saw that scientific method implied the uniqueness of the individual response as reported, for instance, through art.

LEWES FAILED TO SEE how much rethinking was necessary for the consistent formulation of an empiricist aesthetic which asked about the truth of art. Neither, apparently, did he see the advantage of restricting his inquiry to the sort of aesthetic questions that could conveniently and consistently be treated on available empiricist principles. For comparison, we may look at a work in which the latter tactic was adopted, Herbert Spencer's brief "Philosophy of Style," an essay which Lewes cites and to some extent incorporates, in a diluted form, in *The Principles of Success in Literature.* Spencer no more than Lewes sets out all of his philosophical premises before entering on the subject at hand, but these nevertheless determine the way the subject to be investigated is formulated: "whether economy of the recipient's [reader's] attention is not the secret of effect, alike in the right choice and collocation of words, in the best arrangement of clauses in a sentence, in the proper order of its principle and subordinate propositions, in the judicious use of simile, metaphor, and other figures of speech, and even in the rhythmical sequence of syllables."[68] Spencer is able to treat all of these questions in less than forty pages, because his explanatory principle, the "economy" of the reader's attention, is derived directly from his assumptions about the laws of the mind, and these in turn are derived directly from his empiricism. That all thought consists of trains of association in which language calls up ideas, that abstractions are simply convenient fictions which must be translated into concrete instances to be meaningful (both taken directly from the Bentham-Mill tradition), and the corollary that the importance of images lies in the fact that "when an abstract word is used, the hearer or reader has to choose from his stock of images"[69] give an exact meaning to the concept of "economy." Now it may well be argued that Spencer's treatment compensates for the narrowness of its base by over-ingenuity, but the fact is that it is striking and memorable in a way that Lewes's discussion is not; and the reason, I think, is that the consistency of the argument derived from basic philosophical and psychological beliefs which gradually emerges affords a purchase for the reader's mind conspicuously lacking in Lewes's treatment. Had Lewes begun with the argument that the principles of success in literature are reducible to "sincerity" he would have pro-

[68] Spencer, *Philosophy of Style*, p. 12.

[69] *Ibid.*, p. 15.

duced a clearer argument and avoided several confusions, but even so he could hardly have given the concept of sincerity the weight of meaning necessary for it to be the center of a theory of aesthetics without grounding it in a developed epistemology.

IX

The Long Decline

THE CONFLICTING ISSUES, personalities, and literary maneuvers swirling through every decade of the nineteenth century partially conceal the steady decline of transcendental belief. If it were possible to chart something called transcendental allegiance on a graph, the line, while descending on the whole, would exhibit a series of peaks and valleys. However, one can observe certain kinds of temporal sequences that highlight the decline of the anti-empiricist beliefs. I should like to call attention to two.

The Carlyle-Ruskin-Morris sequence provides a sweeping paradigm of the gradual abandonment of the high ground of transcendentalism and the effect of this retreat on the tone and style of prose literature. It is apparent, for instance, in the decline from Carlyle's piercing vision to Ruskin's uneasy reliance on traditional Christian belief and interpretation of nature and thence to William Morris's socialist doctrine. The dawn of a new era is announced by the *Weissnichtwosche' Anzeiger*; the dusk is fast gathering in *News from Nowhere.* Carlyle bids defiance to the utilitarians trapped within their empirically certain iron laws of economics like a goose in a chalk circle and therein drearily grinding their logic mills, because he is in no doubt "that all forms whereby Spirit manifests itself to sense, whether outwardly or in the imagination, are Clothes," and that he, like Teufelsdröckh taking his stand on the new science of clothes as on a "prophetic height," looks down on all below "as on so many weaving-shops and spinning-mills, where the Vestures which *it* has to fashion . . . are, too often by haggard hungry operatives who see no farther than their nose, mechanically woven and spun."[1]

Ruskin, however, hardly tries to press his attack to the empiricist postulates behind the economic theory and utilitarian calculation he so much despised. And the attacks themselves, for all the force of their rhetoric, meet the empiricists on their own ground: the celebrated opening of the first essay of *Unto This Last* argues not that the economists have been misled by phenomena that mask transcendental realities, but that their theories fail to square with ordinary, empirically observable facts. "Assuming, not that the human being has no skeleton, but that it is all skeleton, it founds an ossifant theory of progress on this negation of a soul; and having shown the utmost that may be made of bones, and constructed a number of interesting geometrical figures with death's head and humeri, successfully proves the inconvenience of the reappearance of a soul among these corpuscular structures. I do not deny the truth of this theory: I simply deny its applicability to the present phase of the world."[2] Mill, Ruskin writes to Charles Eliot Norton, is "in truth an utterly shallow and wretched segment of a human creature, incapable of understanding *Anything* in the ultimate conditions of it,"[3] but he sees Mill as a "segment" because he lacks moral and

[1] Carlyle, *Sartor Resartus*, in *Complete Works*, I, 204.

[2] *The Complete Works of John Ruskin*, XVII, 26.

[3] *Ibid.*, XXXVI, 579.

aesthetic principles not because he should have transcendental vision.

Morris, the disciple of Ruskin and Carlyle in many ways[4] takes his stand on purely phenomenal grounds. English taste is degraded, the countryside is growing ugly, the cities are unhealthy, the economic system is not only unjust but absurd. One knows this empirically simply by looking around; one improves the world by imagining the opposite situation and setting that imagined alternative as a goal. Thus Morris's definition of Socialism, visionary as it may be, appeals to nothing transcendent, revelatory, or God-ordained: "Well, what I mean by Socialism is a condition of society in which there should be neither rich nor poor, neither master nor master's man, neither idle nor overworked, neither brain-sick brain workers nor heart-sick hand workers, in a word, in which all men would be living in equality of condition, and would manage their affairs unwastefully, and with the full consciousness that harm to one would mean harm to all—the realisation at last of the meaning of the word COMMONWEALTH."[5] Similarly, the complex web of thought, the highly charged prose through which Carlyle finds it necessary to urge his vision is replaced by the rhetorically striking but much more straightforward commentary of Ruskin, and then by Morris's simply phrased appeal to common sense and common humanity through the quiet-toned essay and the simple device of the dream-vision. One does not expect Morris, or any other man, to write like Carlyle or Ruskin, but surely the lowering of rhetorical pressure in a passage like the following is not unrelated to the fading of the transcendental imperatives. "I cannot refrain from giving you once again the message with which, as it seems, some

[4] Morris's discipleship is implicit and explicit throughout his work, but see especially "How I Became a Socialist" in *The Collected Works of William Morris*, XXIII, 279.

[5] *Ibid.*, XXIII, 277.

chance-hap has charged me: that message is, in short, to call on you to face the latest danger which civilisation is threatened with, a danger of her own breeding: that men in struggling towards the complete attainment of all luxuries of life for the strongest portion of their race should deprive their whole race of all the beauty of life. . . ."[6]

For Carlyle, life is a sphinx, continuously and peremptorily demanding that we answer her riddle rightly. "Answer her riddle, it is well with thee. Answer it not, pass on regarding it not, it will answer itself; the solution for thee is a thing of teeth and claws; Nature is a dumb lioness, deaf to thy pleadings, fiercely devouring."[7] For Ruskin, the necessary answers have been given through Nature and the Scriptures by the author of life; man must simply have the wit to seek them. His metaphors tend to be based on the revealed Christian scheme, not transcendentally assured correspondences as, for instance, in his appeal against human apathy in "The Mystery of Life": "For just suppose I were able to call at this moment to anyone in this audience by name, and to tell him positively that I knew a large estate had been lately left to him on some curious conditions; but that though I knew it was large, I did not know how large, nor even where it was—whether in the East Indies or the West, or in England, or at the Antipodes. I only knew it was a vast estate, and that there was a chance of his losing it altogether if he did not soon find out on what terms it had been left to him. Suppose I were able to say this positively to any single man in this audience, and he knew that I did not speak without warrant, do you think that he would rest content with that vague knowledge, if it were anywise possible to obtain more?"[8] Ruskin maintains of course that it *is* possible to obtain more, through revelation and nature. He emphasizes especially

[6] Morris, "The Beauty of Life," in *Collected Works*, XXII, 51.

[7] Carlyle, *Complete Works*, XII, 9.

[8] Ruskin, *Sesame and Lilies*, in *Complete Works*, XVIII, 154.

the latter; nature, through what Ruskin calls "natural myths," offers guidance. But Ruskin's emphasis is on the wisdom rather than the terrible necessity of regarding these. "The dark sayings of nature will probably become clearer for the looking into, and will very certainly be worth reading."[9] Nature offers us "living hieroglyphs" which it is better to read than pass by—but they are unlike Carlyle's sphinx who offers no choice in the matter. In neither case is it "who runs may read," but for Carlyle clearly who doesn't read aright will not run far.

For Morris there is no supra-human force or power which either imperiously demands or clearly urges answers—there is simply purely human perception. The final sentence of "How We Live and How We Might Live" reflects this quiet hope in gradually increasing clear-sightedness: "As the working classes—the real organic part of society, take in these ideas [the socialist economic principles], hope will rise in them, and they will claim changes in society . . . which indirectly will help to break up our rotten sham society, while that claim for equality of condition will be made constantly and with growing loudness till it *must* be listened to, and then at last it will only be a step over the border, and the civilized world will be socialized; and, looking back on what has been, we shall be astonished to think how long we submitted to live as we live now."[10]

As one looks from Carlyle to Ruskin and Morris, one finds the same decreasing pressure behind the doctrine of work. No one ever doubted the intensity of Carlyle's dedication to work: "I too could now say to myself: Be no longer a Chaos, but a World, or even Worldkin. Produce! Produce! Were it but the pitifullest infinitesimal fraction of a Product, produce it, in God's name!" Everyone knows that for him pleasure and happiness are mere by-products: "The

[9] Ruskin, *The Queen of the Air*, in *Complete Works*, XIX, 361.

[10] Morris, "How We Live and How We Might Live," in *Collected Works*, XXIII, 26.

only happiness a brave man ever troubled himself with asking much about was, happiness enough to get his work done."[11] Ruskin, however, celebrates work with arguments which hover somewhere between recipes for happiness and counsels of perfection, as in his prescription for girls suffering from over-strained religious enthusiasm. "Give such a girl any true work that will make her active in the dawn, and weary at night, with the consciousness that her fellow-creatures have indeed been the better for her day, and the powerless sorrow of her enthusiasm will transform itself into a majesty of radiant and beneficent peace."[12] Morris transforms work neither into awful responsibility, praise of God, simple duty, nor an ordained road to happiness; he translates all work simply into the production of art and thus makes it "a joy to the maker and user." All men are to be workers, all work is to be at once enjoyable and to bring into being that which will give joy to others. "Now, these works of art are man's expression of the value of life, and also the production of them makes his life of value. . . ."[13] Work becomes a right rather than a duty, a means of creating happiness rather than of shaping the Cosmos: "It is right and necessary that all men should have work to do which shall be worth doing, and be of itself pleasant to do; and which should be done under conditions as would make it neither over-wearisome nor over-anxious."[14] Carlyle's sphinx who demands "What thou canst do today; surely attempt to do?" has become the little girl of the tobacconist's shop in *News from Nowhere* who introduces the narrator to the advantages of a world simultaneously emptied of money and filled with beautiful, useful things.

[11] Carlyle, *Sartor Resartus*, in *Complete Works*, I, 149; XII, 150.

[12] Ruskin, *Sesame and Lilies*, in *Complete Works*, XVIII, 186.

[13] "Gothic Architecture," in *William Morris: Artist, Writer, Socialist*, I, 266–67.

[14] Morris, "Art and Socialism," in *Collected Works*, XXIII, 194.

Similarly, the intensity with which errors are condemned lessens as the meaning of error changes; for Carlyle, all error ultimately violates the design of the universe, for Morris, error simply violates common sense. Everyone remembers Carlyle's indignation at the man who advertised by means of "a huge lath-and-plaster Hat, seven feet high, upon wheels." The Hatter "has not attempted to *make* better hats, as he was appointed by the Universe to do . . . but his whole industry is turned to *persuade* us that he has made such!"[15] "Nature requires no man to make proclamation of his doings and hat-makings; Nature forbids all men to make such." Ruskin finds the bills stuck on every wall ugly and is concerned when they violate truth, one of the seven lamps not merely of architecture but of all man's endeavour. However, his irritation satisfies itself with satirizing the contemporary mode of advertising through a mock-advertisement for *Fors Clavigera*: "Just published, the —th number of *Fors Clavigera*, containing the most important information on the existing state of trade in Europe; and on all subjects interesting to the British Operative. Thousandth thousand. Price 7d. 7 for 3s. 6d. Proportional abatement on large orders. No intelligent workman should pass a day without acquainting himself with the entirely original views contained in these pages."[16] In a lecture on Cimabue he comments in passing on the illustrations in the advertisements for Mrs. Allen's hair-restorer: "the great Madonna of the nineteenth century, with flowing hair and equally flowing promises; but even she palls on repetition."[17] Morris's objections—on the grounds of aesthetic and common sense—are more quiet: "I suppose 'tis early days in the revival of the arts to express one's disgust at the daily increasing hideousness of the posters with which all our towns are daubed. Still we ought to be

[15]Carlyle, *Past and Present*, in *Complete Works*, XII, 138.

[16]Ruskin, *Fors Clavigera*, in *Complete Works*, XXVII, 354.

[17]Ruskin, *Complete Works*, XXIII, 207.

disgusted at such horrors, and I think make up our minds never to buy any of the articles so advertised. I can't believe they can be worth much if they need all that shouting to sell them."[18]

We find, of course, a stylistic progression as well. Carlyle's metaphors are intended to evoke an awareness of far-reaching interrelationships, of the complex structure that transcends formulation into language and that is more distorted by straightforward, purely denotative language than by symbolic and hyperbolic expression. The richness of Ruskin's prose constantly reminds the reader of the great moral absolutes against which he compares all things. In Morris, the metaphor, divorced from any underlying structure of thought, becomes lifeless—witness the deadness of the metaphors of "slavery" and "war" in "Art and Socialism" and "How We Live and How We Might Live" where these terms, merely pejorative labels, suggest no new interpretation of fact.

A MUCH LESS SWEEPING but nevertheless extremely significant series of steps in the dissolution of the transcendental view is to be found by returning to the aesthetic doctrines of the second half of the century.

The influences of Arnold on Pater, and of Arnold and Pater on Wilde, are so clear, and so openly acknowledged, that scholars have for the most part been reluctant to belabor the obvious.[19] There is, however, a tendency to forget

[18] Morris, "The Beauty of Life," in *Collected Works*, XXII, 72. It is not surprising perhaps to find that Jeremy Bentham was so far from questioning the use of advertisements that he once proposed to make it easier for readers and advertisers to find each other. See *The Works of Jeremy Bentham*, X, 322.

[19] The influences have been constantly alluded to, but comments generally reach no further than the enumeration of the differences and similarities

the obvious: Richard Ellmann has recently felt it necessary to remind us that "there are not two but three critical phases in the late nineteenth century, with Pater transitional between Arnold and Wilde."[20] Moreover, since the obvious is that which we feel the least need to account for, obvious relationships at times effectively screen more complex ones. Taking the position with which Arnold opens "The Function of Criticism at the Present Time," his broadest statement of his theory of criticism, as a point of departure for their own quite different major aesthetic doctrines, as set forth in *The Renaissance* and "The Critic as Artist," Pater and Wilde offer the reader neatly packaged statements of their divergences from the Arnoldian position which stimulated their rebellion. However, the grounds of the necessity felt by Pater and Wilde for developing and insisting on these divergences are easily overlooked. Thus, T. S. Eliot's influential essay on Arnold and Pater[21] is too preoccupied with protesting what Eliot sees as the perni-

relevant to the particular study the critic has in hand. Major exceptions are Eduard J. Bock's *Walter Pater's Einfluss auf Oscar Wilde* (Bonn: P. Hanstein, 1913) and Ernst Bendz's *The Influence of Pater and Matthew Arnold in the Prose Writings of Oscar Wilde* (Gothenburg: Wettergern and Kerble, 1914). The comparisons they offer are to some extent analytical, but neither attempts to penetrate to the philosophical problems that generate the differences.

[20] Ellmann, "The Critic as Artist as Wilde," *Wilde and the Nineties*, p. 3.

[21] "Arnold and Pater," *Bookman*, LXXII (1930), 1–7; reprinted as "The Place of Pater," in *The Eighteen-Eighties*, ed. Walter de la Mare (Cambridge: Cambridge University Press, 1930), pp. 93–106. Paul Elmer More had emphasized the line from Arnold to Wilde in his essay on "Criticism" in the Seventh Series of the *Shelburne Essays* (New York: G. P. Putnam's Sons, 1910); he regards Pater and Wilde as erring disciples, and, like Eliot, prefers a moral judgment against them. In his important and stimulating "The Divided Tradition of English Criticism" (*PMLA*, XXXIII [1958], 69–80), William Madden explores the bearing of theological assumptions on the critical positions of Arnold and a number of important later critics, including T. S. Eliot. However, from one point of view at least, a theological assumption is ultimately one kind of philosophical assumption; here I am attempting to push back to the metaphysical assumptions of Arnold, Pater, and Wilde, subsuming theological in philosophical differences.

cious displacement of religion by aesthetics to examine the grounds and significance of Pater's reasons either for citing Arnold's statement of the goal of criticism or for drastically qualifying it, and he makes Wilde simply an erring disciple whose deviations from the Paterian position are due to misinterpretation.

To trace the development and alterations in the major doctrines of each of the three and then to compare their explicit and implicit statements of each of these doctrines would require the unweaving of an enormous web, the individual strands of which, untangled and spooled up in critical categories, still require interpretation.[22] On the other hand, Arnold's "The Function of Criticism at the Present Time," Pater's Preface and Conclusion to *The Renaissance* together with the essay "Style," and Wilde's "The Critic as Artist" are the seminal documents, later qualified but never repudiated, from which the critical theories of each have most strongly spread, and between which the strands of the web are most clear. Looking primarily to those works, and avoiding as many as possible of the derivative and ancillary questions of aesthetics, morality, culture, and religion addressed by the three writers, one can discern a basic, ultimately metaphysical, problem lurking behind their successive formulations of the roles of artist and critic. I have no wish to claim that Arnold, Pater, or Wilde consciously attempted to follow a logically irrefragable path from metaphysical first principles. All three found metaphysics dreary. Rather, I think it important to recognize that the three exhibit in a general way the almost inevitable direction of development of aesthetic principles behind which lie certain implied metaphysical assumptions.

It is easy to regard Pater and Wilde's successive trans-

[22] For a very able analysis of a complete series of borrowings, qualifications, and adjustments, see David DeLaura's "The 'Wordsworth' of Pater and Arnold: 'The Supreme Artistic View of Life,'" *Studies in English Literature, 1500–1900*, VI (1967), 651–57.

mogrifications of Arnold's doctrine that the goal of criticism is "to see the object as in itself it really is" as strategic moves toward the ultimate positions at which they, in their own critical statements, wish to arrive. However, if we explore in the first instance not the regions to which Pater and Wilde were bound, but that from which they were escaping, if we turn, as it were, from final to efficient causes, the significance of their reformulations looms large.

Arnold's argument in "The Function of Criticism" involves the evident assumption that it is indeed possible to "see the object as in itself it really is." That Arnold is giving full weight to every word in the famous statement and stating unequivocally that it is at least possible to see objects as they actually exist, without any distortion arising from the constitution of the mind of the viewer, is apparent from the argument that leads up to its original formulation in the second lecture of "On Translating Homer."[23] His summation of his argument at the end of that lecture begins by reiterating that the overwhelming defect in F. W. Newman's translation of the *Iliad* (Arnold's principal target) is that Newman's conception of Homer is arbitrary and eccentric. Arnold then links Newman's failure to "the great defect of English intellect," that against which so much of his writing is directed, the arbitrariness and eccentricity that result from the neglect of the cultivation of the critical spirit as found in France and Germany, the neglect of "the endeavour, in all branches of knowledge . . . to see the object as in itself it really is." The mind must be disciplined to avoid personal eccentricities and thus, by striving for "simple lucidity of mind," move beyond the personal estimation to an objective one.

[23] That "The Function of Criticism at the Present Time" grew out of the Colenso controversy and not immediately out of the lectures on translating Homer has been clearly established by Sidney M. B. Coulling in "The Background of 'The Function of Criticism at the Present Time,'" *Philological Quarterly*, XLIII (1963), 36–54. However, the Arnoldian attitudes lying behind "The Function of Criticism" are as much to be found in the lectures on translating Homer as in "The Bishop and the Philosopher."

To the attentive reader of these lectures, Arnold will be found already to have involved himself in unhappy confusions. For from the beginning, the means of comparing the translation with the original have been assumed to be by comparing the *effects* of the translation with the *effects* of the original, and once it is admitted that one must judge by the effects, one has already dropped a veil over the work "in itself." Moreover, Arnold argues that the effect of the translation cannot be judged by comparison of its effect on modern readers with that of the *Iliad* on its original Greek hearers, since the latter can never be known; therefore, the proper comparison is between the effect of the original and that of the translation on the modern scholar. But this is an admission that the same work (object) produces different effects in different ages, and one is farther than ever from knowing how to come at the work as in itself it really is.

The philosophical shadows cast by Arnold's doctrine are not at all lightened in "The Function of Criticism at the Present Time." Beginning with the attempt to establish the importance of the fruits of criticism for the creative artist, Arnold moves on to the topic which so preoccupies him, the lack of the critical spirit in England, and then to the importance of a disinterested criticism of political and religious institutions and party programs. Criticism must be patient, must redress the balance when any element of thought receives undue emphasis, must above all "maintain its independence of the practical spirit and its aims." Criticism thus becomes for Arnold the "disinterested endeavour to learn and propagate the best that is known and thought in the world." The difficulty in disinterestedly and unpractically propagating anything has been well examined by Geoffrey Tillotson.[24] However, quite another and

[24]"Matthew Arnold: The Critic and the Advocate," *Essays by Diverse Hands*, n.s. XX (1943), 29–41; reprinted in *Criticism and the Nineteenth Century* (London: Athlone Press, 1951).

more basic problem is raised by the intent of this formula in supplying a recipe by which criticism (either literary or cultural) can see the object as it really is. By comparison of one's own view with the views which make up the best that is known and thought, personal aberrations and eccentricities can be overcome. But this only pushes the matter back one step: what *is* the best that is known and thought? Since the best that is known and thought is itself a set of objects, one of a contentious nature might even ask how one is sure one really knows these and not merely one's own impression of them. Arnold's method of judging poetry by comparison with established touchstones provides a working model of the operation of all criticism as he envisions it. For just as criticism judges the slogan "The Dissidence of Dissent" by reference to St. Peter, and the pilgrim fathers by comparing the assumed personalities of the pilgrims with those of Plato and Virgil, it judges a poem by comparison with selected lines from Shakespeare, Virgil, Milton, Dante *et al.* But is not what the Arnoldian critic performs really a comparison of the effects, the impressions, made on him by the things compared? And are not the original touchstones chosen because they make the strongest impression on the chooser? Arnold's own bias, his preference among types of effects or impressions, is as obvious in the elegiac tone of most of his touchstones as in his praise of high seriousness and eviction of Chaucer from the heights of Helicon. There seems no reason that what is true of the attempt to avoid misleading estimates in judging poetry would not be equally true of the attempts to see any object as it really is. The veil remains, as Frederic Harrison had wittily insisted in his parody in the style of *Friendship's Garland*, "Culture: A Dialogue." In his essay of 1896 on Arnold, Harrison wrote: "I said what I had to say nearly thirty years ago. . . . We are most of us trying to get what of Culture we can master, to see things as they are, to know the best, to attain to some little measure of Sweetness and Light—and we can only regret that our great master in all these things has carried his secret to the grave. The mystery still remains, *what* is best, *how* are things to be seen really as they are, by *what* means can we attain to perfection?"[25]

Had Arnold been a philosophical realist, he might have made the case for the possibility of seeing "the object as in itself it really is" which necessarily must precede the injunction that we should endeavor so to see it. Had he followed the Romantic doctrine of the imagination, at least as that doctrine is set out in D. G. James's *Matthew Arnold and the Decline of English Romanticism*, that all perception depends on imagination, he might have argued that, in James's words, "to be a man of imagination, is to see the object in exceptional degree as it really is."[26] Had he been an idealist believing that there is a realm of truth that transcends experience and yet is accessible to man,[27] he might have argued for its availability through a higher form of the imagination such as Coleridge has been interpreted by some as believing, or through ascending the Platonic stairway, or through a Carlylean vision vouchsafed after the recognition of an "Everlasting Yea."

In *Culture and Anarchy*, while lightly admitting the charge that he lacks "a philosophy with coherent, interdependent, subordinate and derivative principles"—a charge the wording of which begs his mockery—Arnold, wielding his urbane modesty as a weapon, makes a virtue of "a plain man's expedient of trying to make what simple notions I have, clearer and more intelligible to myself." Nevertheless, though Arnold may have been well advised not to "affect the metaphysics," one who advances the importance

[25] Harrison, *Tennyson, Ruskin, Mill and Other Literary Estimates*, pp. 121–22.

[26] James, *Matthew Arnold and the Decline of English Romanticism*, p. 5.

[27] That he did not so believe is of course nowhere better demonstrated than by his definitions of religion in *Literature and Dogma* as "morality touched by emotion" and God as "the not ourselves which makes for righteousness."

of knowing anything as it really is has need of recourse to some sort of system which will explain what really exists, how we know that which exists, and how we know what we think about that which exists is true. That is, we need answers to the primary questions to which metaphysics addresses itself.

Nothing in the above analysis is, I think, either startling or altogether novel, but if we bear the results in mind it becomes evident that Pater was being neither wilful nor capricious in amending Arnold's doctrine in the Preface to *The Renaissance*: "'To see the object as in itself it really is,' has been justly said to be the aim of all true criticism whatever; and in aesthetic criticism the first step is to know one's own impression as it really is, to discriminate it, to realize it distinctly." Pater is recognizing and accepting the implications of Arnold's position. All we have, finally, as an object of contemplation is the effect, the impression. Pater, of course, is not simply reacting to the absence of a metaphysical base to Arnold's idea of criticism. The relativism implied and never directly contradicted (but never admitted) in Arnold is explicitly adopted in that conclusion to *The Renaissance* which is too well known to require much comment here. If it is true that experience "is ringed round for each one of us by that thick wall of personality through which no real voice has ever pierced on its way to us," we can only know the object as a personal impression, and to speak of knowing "the object as in itself it really is" can only be a rhetorical adjuration to compare notes with impressions expressed by others (that, primarily, is what culture makes possible), in the attempt to clear away as much of the personal as possible.[28] But for Pater the critic simply records his impression: "What is this song or picture, this engaging personality presented in life or in a book, to

[28] It is worth noting that in Pater's metaphor it is not the individual mind that is ringed by personality, but experience itself—the effect of this inversion of the expected metaphor is to put emphasis on the importance and "reality" of the individual mind, not on the object.

me?"[29] The aesthetic critic will distinguish and analyze "the virtue by which a picture, a landscape, a fair personality in life or a book, produces the special impression of beauty or pleasure, to indicate what the source of that impression is, and under what conditions it is experienced." But the immediate raw material of this analysis is the impression, not the object that produces it. The impression may be an eccentric or arbitrary one, but nevertheless it is the starting point. For Arnold, the highest intellectual life is the attempt to increase the range and power of the ability to see things as in themselves they really are; for Pater, "the wisest, at least among 'the children of this world'"[30] will attempt to increase the intensity of their impressions.

Now in Pater's aesthetic doctrine, of course, it is not only the critic who begins with an impression, but the creative artist. The Conclusion to *The Renaissance* provides the philosophical base for the Preface and was in fact written several years earlier, appearing originally as a pendant to Pater's 1868 review of three volumes of William Morris's poems. There it stands as a justification of the earthly paradise created by Morris's poetry, "a kind of poetry which . . . [assumes] artistic beauty of form to be an end in itself," a justification drawn from the "sad-coloured world of abstract philosophy." It serves there as a defense of "art for art's sake" in the most innocent sense of that slogan, but it implies not only that one should not look in poetry for the accurate presentation of the truths of which the modern world is in possession but that neither art nor any other endeavor of the human mind gives us unqualified truth (the object as it really is). Thus, as he makes clear in the

[29] Madden, "The Divided Tradition of English Criticism," *PMLA*, LXXIII (March 1958), 69–80, has reminded us that Pater's very phrasing here echoes the Goethean formulaic question for ascertaining truth on which Arnold had built: "Is it so to *me*?" The differences in the uses to which the question is put sum up Pater's revision of Arnold.

[30] The qualifying phrase, "at least among 'the children of this world,'" was added in the edition of 1888.

Preface written some five years later, the critic is concerned not with the degree of truth but the kind of beauty, the formula of the beauty, in a given work.

The Preface states a theory of criticism; the later essay "Style" (1888) states a theory of creation which is also based largely on the Conclusion: "all beauty is in the long run only *fineness* of truth, or what we call expression, the finer accommodation of speech to that vision within." And by "vision" Pater means, as the whole passage makes clear, the writer's "sense of fact rather than the fact." At this point Pater allows himself to be inconsistent with his earlier position, for he goes on, "as being preferable, pleasanter, more beautiful to the writer himself." If one is truly bound to "the narrow chamber of the individual mind," and experience ringed round by the "thick wall of personality," the artist must *necessarily* be limited to transcribing his "sense of fact," that is, his impressions. In emphasizing the importance of recognizing that the artist's role is to be conscious, that it is the uniqueness of his "sense of fact" that is worth conveying, Pater is moving from a purely relativistic position, a tendency both Helen Young and Ruth C. Child have documented in his later works.[31]

But the larger question to which I wish to call attention remains unaffected. Whether all humans, and thus all artists, are limited to their personal impressions, or whether artists choose to transcribe personal impressions by choice; what critics have to work with are their impressions of the artists' impressions of experience. The artist, says Pater, attempts accurately to transcribe or translate his impression (or vision), but the critic cannot judge the degree of his success in being accurate. Not only are the immediate materials on which the critic has to work his own impressions, but there is no way of getting behind these

[31] Young, *The Writings of Walter Pater*; Child, *The Aesthetic of Walter Pater*. One finds a considerable amount of dallying with the thought of what might be hidden "behind the veil" in Pater's later essays, but he never completely commits himself to the belief that there is a veil, or anything behind it.

impressions to compare either the artist's work with his impression or that impression with the object "as in itself it really is" which gave rise to it.

Pater was enough of a Platonist to accept the view that our experience is of appearance only, not enough of one to believe that there is a transcendent world of forms. Had he believed the latter, in one form or another, he might have tried to develop in his own terms Carlyle's view of the poet as prophet (and thus hero), or Coleridge's struggle to give the creative imagination the high destiny of seeing beyond appearance. But he did not, and he refused to follow Plato in reconciling Heraclitean Flux with the Parmenidean Absolute through the assignment of the first to the world of appearance and the second to the world of ideal forms.

Helen W. Young's *The Writings of Walter Pater*, a useful study not only of Pater's writings but the philosophical climate of the time, makes clear how strongly during the period in which *The Renaissance* was written, despite his imaginative rhetoric and his acquaintance with the new British idealism being formulated by T. H. Green and Edward Caird, Pater's relativism is a reflection of British empiricism and interest in scientific method. She is able to see the critical approach set forth in the Preface as, "in its emphasis on analysis into simples," an adaptation of the methods of physical science.[32] His sense of the relativism of all things reinforced by scientific empiricism, Pater drops curtains between the object and the artist's impression of it, between the artist's impression as embodied in the work of art and the critic's impression of that work. The stage is set for Wilde.

ERNEST: I seem to have heard another theory of Criticism.

GILBERT: Yes: it has been said by one whose gracious memory we all revere, and the music of whose pipe once lured Proserpina from her Sicilian fields, and made those white feet

[32] Young, *The Writings of Walter Pater*, p. 20.

stir, and not in vain, the Cumnor cowslips, that the proper aim of Criticism is to see the object as in itself it really is. But this is a very serious error, and takes no cognisance of Criticism's most perfect form, which is in its essence purely subjective, and seeks to reveal its own secret and not the secret of another.

Wilde's gracious tribute to Arnold's poetry precedes a denial of Arnold's theory of criticism and, after purple passages proclaiming that the prose in which Ruskin treats Turner or Pater describes the *Mona Lisa* has its value solely in its own perfection without reference to accuracy, leads to its clear reversal:

ERNEST: The highest Criticism, then, is more creative than creation, and the primary aim of the critic is to see the object as in itself it really is not; that is your theory, I believe?

GILBERT: Yes, that is my theory. To the critic the work of art is simply a suggestion for a new work of his own, that need not necessarily bear any obvious resemblance to the thing it criticises.

Ernest's "I seem to have heard another theory of Criticism" is Wilde's recognition of the importance of Arnold's influence, but his readiness to bring in Arnold's formula may also be the result of his sense that the juxtaposition of the two views, in combination with reference to Ruskin and Pater, will remind at least some of his readers that they turn to critics like these for something besides an accurate description of the object. Wilde's presentation of his position proceeds by his usual method of paradox, but the number of direct references to and echoes from Arnold and Pater indicate that Wilde had been pondering both critical theories. Moreover, indications that Wilde had been giving at least some thought to the philosophical cruxes which historically underlie aesthetic debates are not lacking.

For instance: "All artistic creation is absolutely subjective. The very landscape that Corot looked at was, as he said himself, but a mood of his own mind. . . ." Wilde is indicating an acceptance of Pater's subjectivism and relativism which, as I have tried to show, implies not merely that the artist does not imitate, but that the role of critic is not to imitate either. For both are in receipt only of impressions. As he states earlier in the essay, "it is rather the beholder who lends to the beautiful thing its myriad meanings, and makes it marvelous for us, and sets it in some new relation to the age. . . ."

Wilde's whole central paradox can perhaps be illuminated by the way in which he stands Plato on his head. As everyone knows, Plato condemns art for being merely an imitation of appearance, which in itself is only a poor imitation of the ideal. There are two obvious lines of rebuttal: one can argue that art is not an imitation but a means of transcending experience and gaining direct access to the world of ideal forms, or one can argue that art is not an imitation but a wholly new creation which is of interest in itself. Wilde accepts the position that imitation *per se* is paltry—"Criticism is no more to be judged by any low standard of imitation or resemblance than is the work of poet or sculptor"—and takes the second route, that art and criticism are valuable precisely because they create something wholly new. Art and criticism thus become identified, except that criticism, being further removed from experience, is more creative. Plato is inverted, and the further one moves from immediate experience, the more creative one is.

Wilde is not simply being paradoxical and ingenious when he goes beyond Arnold's claim for the importance of criticism to the creator (which Wilde himself asserts fairly early in the essay: "But there has never been a creative age that has not been critical also"). Criticism becomes more creative than creation primarily because the relativism implied by Arnold and made explicit by Pater is here carried to a conclusion. Neither Wilde nor Pater is consistent enough directly to assert that since it is impossible in any case to see the object as in itself it really is, the only basis for judging either art or criticism is the degree of its creativity. Rather, Pater simply sees the artist as leaving fact for the sense of fact, Wilde the critic as aiming at seeing the object as in itself it really is not.

Wilde was, of course, often inconsistent in following out the consequences of his basic principles. For instance, at one point in "The Critic as Artist" he regards the work of art as an object that can be depended on always to produce the same effect on a given reader. Yet in passages both preceding and following, he builds on the view that the effect of a work will change both with the mood of the reader and his familiarity with the work.[33] The first argument has its charms, but, if what art offers us are impressions, why should these not change, at least within limits? However, such inconsistencies, into which one feels Wilde is led by the force of his own rhetoric, scarcely touch his basic aesthetic, and ultimately metaphysical, commitments.

Wilde was clear about the alternatives he was rejecting, and he seems to follow Pater in believing their acceptance impossible to the modern mind. Pater's "to regard all things and principles of things as inconstant modes or fashions has more and more become the tendency of modern thought" is echoed by Wilde:

> Metaphysics do not satisfy our temperaments, and religious ecstasy is out of date. The world through which the Academic philosopher becomes "the spectator of all time and existence" is not really an ideal world, but simply a world of abstract ideas. When we enter it, we starve amidst the chill mathematics of thought. The courts of the city of God are not open to us now. . . . We cannot go back to the philosopher, and the

[33] The passages referred to are those beginning, respectively: "How different it is in the world of art! On a shelf of the bookcase behind you stands the *Divine Comedy* . . ."; "Sometimes, when I listen to the overture of Tannhauser . . ."; "The aesthetic critic, constant only to the principle of beauty in all things, will ever be looking for fresh impressions." These may be found in the one-volume *Complete Works of Oscar Wilde*, pp. 1035, 1029, and 1045, respectively.

> mystic leads us astray. Who, as Mr. Pater suggests somewhere,[34] would exchange the curve of a single roseleaf for that formless intangible Being which Plato rates so high? What to us is the Illumination of Philo, the Abyss of Eckhart, the Vision of Bohme?

Not only is art not an imitation, as Plato thought, but neither is the object experienced an imitation of anything, for all that it may be ringed around by the personality of the beholder. An imitation of an imitation of an imitation would indeed be valueless, but an impression of an impression of an impression is to be celebrated as the most unalloyed expression of creativity.

But for Wilde, as for Arnold, finally, criticism offers more than delight. For Arnold, the value of criticism is in discovering the object as it really is; for Pater, who, in emphasizing the impression offered by the artist rather than the critic, considered the results of criticism rather than its larger possible functions, its value is in increasing our delight in art; for Wilde it offers both insight and delight. For although we may not know the objects of experience, the impressions reported by the artist and critic reveal what the soul is and is capable of. Wilde's rhetorical development of this idea has all the qualities of mystical rapture which he had earlier dismissed as inappropriate, but the point which emerges is that the critical spirit, through its very creativity, can get outside the individual consciousness which Pater so eloquently describes and give it access to the fundamental qualities of man, or, as Wilde puts it, "the race-experience."[35]

[34] Pater makes the statement in the essay on Coleridge (*Appreciations*, p. 68).

[35] Pater's belief in "the accumulative capital of the whole experience of humanity," as he states it in *Plato and Platonism*, p. 159, which appears as early as the review of Morris's poetry as "the composite experience of all the ages is part of each one of us," seems cognate with Wilde's view here, although despite his developing emphasis on moral and even aesthetic responsibility, Pater seems never to have fully seen the relevance of the belief to the function of art.

> For who is the true critic but he who bears within himself the dreams, and ideas, and feelings of myriad generations, and to whom no form of thought is alien, no emotional impulse obscure? And who is the true man of culture, if not he who by fine scholarship and fastidious rejection has made instinct self-conscious and intelligent, and can separate the work that has distinction from the work that has it not, and so by contact and comparison makes himself the master of the secrets of style and school, and understands their meanings, and listens to their voices, and develops that spirit of disinterested curiosity which is the real root, as it is the real flower, of the intellectual life, and thus attains to intellectual clarity, and, having learned "the best that is known and thought in the world," lives—it is not fanciful to say so—with those who are the Immortals.

Thus it is that Wilde returns to Arnold's position on the importance of culture and from this point on the Arnoldian references and echoes become thicker. "What we want are unpractical people who see beyond the moment, and think beyond the day. Those who try to lead the people can only do so by following the mob." "The Critic may, indeed, desire to exercise influence; but, if so, he will concern himself not with the individual, but with the age, which he will seek to awake into consciousness, and to make responsive, creating in it new desires and appetites, and lending it his larger vision and his nobler moods." "It is Criticism, as Arnold points out, that creates the intellectual atmosphere of the age."[36] "How little we have of this [the critical] temper in England, and how much we need it! . . . The intellect of the race is wasted in the sordid and stupid quarrels of second-rate politicians or third-rate theologians."

In divorcing criticism from practical action even more

[36] Wilde's eclecticism is of course what makes it particularly difficult to see his position as a whole. In the passage that immediately follows this Wilde is simultaneously paying homage to Newman and pretending that he is not aware that he has been anticipated by Newman.

completely than Arnold, Wilde makes it clearer that the critic is not merely one who retires from the fray to regain perspective before rejoining it, but one whose creative vision, by making clear the collective consciousness of man, may free the fighters from their futile opposition over lesser things.[37] Arnold's "The Function of Criticism" moves from focus on the literary critic to criticism in its larger meaning, at which point, as John Holloway has made clear,[38] the act of criticism becomes synonymous with the exercise of culture. The critical endeavor set forth in the Preface to *The Renaissance* is one application of the prescription for making the most of life given in the Conclusion. The importance of lying—a way of seeing and presenting the object as it is not—in "The Decay of Lying" is justified in the doctrine set forth in "The Critic as Artist," the argument of the second portion of which expands until it becomes a prolegomena to the social program set forth in "The Soul of Man Under Socialism." The aesthetic doctrines of each, grounded in various conscious degrees of denial of a transcendent world, generate philosophies of life that define the ideal relation of the individual to the world. The total views of Pater and Wilde modify those of Arnold, but the three clarify and in a sense justify each other. Arnold's position, carried far enough, implies Wilde's, and does so in a much more fundamental way than T. S. Eliot has suggested.

Wilde's aesthetic/cultural theory may not finally satisfy us, but I have hoped to make clear that Pater's alterations of Arnold's doctrine and Wilde's alterations of the doctrines

[37] Merritt Y. Hughes pointed out that "the whole practical, political gospel of *Culture and Anarchy* is implied in Gilbert's interpretation of 'self-culture as the true ideal of man.'" But more, the emphasis on the critic as one whose impressions are ultimately reports of the possibilities of the human mind makes clearer *how* one critic can affect the course of society without engaging in the practical. See M. Y. Hughes, "The Immortal Wilde," *University of California Chronicle*, XXX (1928), 317.

[38] Holloway, *The Victorian Sage*, pp. 222–23.

of both grow out of unresolved problems inherent in the metaphysical assumptions all three partially share. If it cannot be shown that the object "in itself" is a possible object of knowledge, we are left with only the effects or impressions of objects; if we have only impressions, we are seeing the object as "in itself" it is not; but in the act of creativity which gives form to the impression, which is the object as in itself it is not, we discover the range of qualities, powers, and desires that make up the race of man as in itself it really is. And that, perhaps, is as far toward transcendence as Arnold's starting point will take us.

X

Fin-de-Siècle

THE WEARINESS, tedium, and melancholy expressed so strongly in the literature of the 1890s have been explained as manifestations of aesthetic irresponsibility, moral collapse, racial degeneration, and mere literary imitation. It is probably closer to the truth to assign them to intellectual exhaustion. The slogan *fin-de-siècle* was at least as much a sigh of relief as a boast or lament, and if certain writers of the late eighties and nineties looked to Pater as a master, it was partly at least because he sanctioned the retreat from the philosophical trenches.

Arthur Symons set the tone for almost all subsequent discussion of the nineties in his article "The Decadent Movement in Literature."[1] Acting more as publicist than objective analyst, Symons announced that decadence was the primary new literary force of the time and went on to define it in what were intended to be shocking terms: "an intuitive self-consciousness, a restless curiosity in research, an over-subtilizing refinement upon refinement, a

[1] *Harper's New Magazine*, LXXXVII (1893), 858–67.

spiritual and moral perversity." Moralistic reviewers, Francophobes staunchly guarding England's shores against Gallic lubricity, and critics disturbed by the possibility that the depressing analysis of the nineteenth century offered by Max Nordau's *Degeneration* might be at least partially true were happy enough to take the word of writers like Symons who flaunted their taste for the perverse and forbidden and sighed forth their ennui. Symons's analysis is echoed in one form or another in almost all the subsequent influential critical assessments of the decadence of the nineties. Holbrook Jackson found the chief characteristics of decadence to be perversity, artificiality, egoism, and curiosity; to Granville Hicks the central thread was the belief in "the superiority of the neurotic personality"; Albert Guérard suggested that decadence results from having excessive faith in "art for art's sake."[2]

All of these formulas turn out to point to the same thing, the valuing of experience (or even the expression of one's experience) for itself. All, that is, can be reduced to Pater's "not the fruit of experience, but experience itself, is the end." Such in fact is the argument of C. E. M. Joad's poorly organized, sometimes extravagant, but nevertheless valuable study of cultural decadence in which a wide variety of attempted definitions are found to point toward "the view that experience is valuable or is at least to be valued for its own sake, irrespective of the quality or kind of experience. . . ."[3] The relationship of "decadence" so defined to the impressionism dear to Pater and the end of the century as a whole is clear enough as a kind of corollary. If experience cannot be known "in itself" and is not to be judged by imposed categories of value, widely varying impressions derived by different individuals from seemingly the same experience are of equal value. Thus Pater's "what

[2]H. Jackson, *The Eighteen Nineties*, p. 76; Hicks, *Figures of Transition*, p. 254; Guérard, *Art for Art's Sake*, pp. xii–xiv.

[3]Joad, *Decadence*, p. 95.

is this song or picture, this engaging personality presented in life or in a book, to *me*?" or Hubert Crackanthorpe's "a work of art can never be more than a corner of Nature, seen through the temperament of a single man," or Henry Harland's "you start with an impression. But an impression is never a simple thing. . . . It is always a complex thing, it is always elusive. It is in its very nature intensely personal, it is an intimate thing."[4]

But the question remains as to the source of the "decadent" attitude and the impressionism so easily allied with it. Those literary historians who emphasize the importance of the battle cry (or perhaps plea) "art-for-art's-sake" most often look toward the obvious links between Rossetti, Swinburne, Pater, Wilde, and the Symons-Dowson-Harland-Beardsley-Johnson group. Clearly a line descends from the *Germ* through Swinburne's defense of art-for-art's-sake, the Preface and Conclusion to Pater's *Renaissance*, Wilde's paradoxically phrased elevation of art to supremacy in human life, and finally to the assumptions behind the coteries around the *Yellow Book* and the *Savoy*. However, the ease with which such an approach leads to studies of the intellectual and emotional peculiarities of individuals who make up portions of this chain should give us warning. For example, Barbara Charlesworth's *Dark Passages: The Decadent Consciousness in Victorian Literature* gives us penetrating brief studies of Rossetti, Swinburne, Pater, Wilde, Johnson, and Symons. Professor Charlesworth puts in relief the way each, seeking heightened consciousness and experience for its own sake, found isolation. But why each of these men set out on such a quest is left unexplored; one gathers that inherent psychological imbalances are the primary cause. Only a very few writers have gone outside of what has been, from the be-

[4] Pater, *The Renaissance*, p. viii; Crackanthorpe, "Reticence in Literature," *Yellow Book*, II (1894), 251; Harland, *Academy*, LI (1897), p. 6 of the June 5 supplement.

ginning, the main line of critical study of the nineties: analysis of the neurotic and bizarre side of the individual figures who seem to fit under the decadent label. Even Bernard Muddiman's carefully unexaggerated *The Men of the Nineties* pauses, for instance, to call attention to the strange mixture of subtlety and intensity in the period which made its key figures seem devoted to the unusual and unnatural. "They took Byron's satanism and inflamed it with the lurid light of Baudelaire. *Buveurs de lune* after the manner of Paul Verlaine, they evoked something of the ethereal glamour of the moonlight itself. A realist like Crackanthorpe tried to tread the whole *via dolorosa* without faltering by the wayside. Poetry caught the mood of bizarre crises and Edgar Wilson wrought a strange delicate world of vision. In Max Beerbohm, irony took on a weird tinge of grace almost Pierrot-like."[5]

A second line of explanation looks to France. Graham Hough goes so far as to say that the nineties "were a state of mind that originated in France."[6] French influence there undoubtedly was, both on the members of what we have come to regard as the aesthetic movement—the influence of Baudelaire on Swinburne for example—and on central figures of the nineties—as in Symons's thievery of the idea of "decadence" from Gautier, Baudelaire, and Bourget or the probably overestimated influence of Maupassant on Crackanthorpe or that of Zola on George Moore. But literary influences that suggest new subjects, forms, themes, or even moods are one thing; the prevailing attitude that makes the nineties, in Osbert Burdett's observation, not a period but a point of view, is a different and larger phenomenon.

Another approach to the nineties has been to view them as the final disintegration of a romantic tradition which was long a-dying. Mario Praz's *Romantic Agony* is

[5] Muddiman, *Men of the Nineties*, p. 136.

[6] Hough, *The Last Romantics*, p. 188.

the chief of such studies; a much more recent and very interesting specialized study is that of Masao Miyoshi which traces the divided self, both as theme and biographical reality, from the romantic period to the end of the century, finding the themes and personal lives of key writers increasingly intertwined in the latter part of the century. Such approaches beneficially call attention to continuities that run through the whole of the century; they do not, for that very reason, adequately explain what was unique in the atmosphere of the eighties and nineties.

Finally, a direct and convincing causal relationship between the culture as a whole and the *fin-de-siècle* point of view which has been increasingly explored is that between "decadent" disillusionment with its search for madder music and stronger wine and the radically disturbing implications of scientific theories. That which made the literature of the nineties a "haunted literature, with disillusion for its spectre or refrain,"[7] as Osbert Burdett phrased it, was the interpretation of life which made its authoritative, and for the great majority of Victorians first, statement in the *Origin of Species* in 1859. That Darwin's work, along with the new criticism of the Bible, whipped up dust clouds which darkened the latter third of the century is a commonplace, but John Lester's *Journey Through Despair, 1880–1914* sharpens the outlines of the relationship between scientific theory and cultural response at the turn of the century. "By the end of the century the main features of the challenge were manifest to every observant mind. There had been a crescendo of scientific observations and theories which seemed to prove finally that man was not a special creation, that he was rather a product of external and predetermined terrestrial forces and forever cut off from a heaven or a haven of absolutes corresponding to human aspirations."[8]

[7] Burdett, *The Beardsley Period*, p. 33.

[8] Lester, *Journey Through Despair, 1880–1914*, p. 22.

The new theories of science undoubtedly had their influence. However, one finds almost nothing that directly implies distress with the products of scientific endeavor in reading the *Yellow Book*, the Rhymers' Club's two volumes, *Dorian Gray*, the Keynotes series, or other examples of presumably quintessentially *fin-de-siècle* literature. The writers of the "decadent" group were not turning away from concern with physical science—all in all, there had been little such concern among poets, essayists, or novelists at any time in the nineteenth century. Among the controversial essayists even, Huxley stands almost alone as a man who based his thought on the discoveries of physical and biological science or devoted his literary gifts to debate over questions of a scientific nature. It was not the dawn of the new science so much as the twilight of the transcendental vision that filled the last quarter of the century with melancholy.

WRITERS hardly need a faith in the transcendental to achieve stature as essayists or novelists, but through the first three fourths of the nineteenth century the great tradition in nonfiction prose had been the transcendental—in the countermovement only Mill and Huxley were able to generate any degree of rhetorical excitement—and if the novelists and poets appear less transcendentally committed, especially to the eyes of modern critics, one has to admit that among them no one but George Eliot spoke with literary power for the empiricists. By the 1880s, the transcendental vision was lost; the remaining choices of allegiance seemed for a time to lie between the uninspiring logic of the empiricists and the creation of one's own private solipsistic universe. That the recognition of the undoubted but aesthetically dismal victory of empiricism, or at least loss of faith in transcendental values, coincided with the end of the century was of considerable rhetorical value. A *fin-de-siècle* attitude could be either a refuge from or defiance of the triumph of a mode of thought that ignored or dismissed certain of men's aspirations. The cry art-for-art's-sake could be an admission that art was an escape from the practical world of the empiricists or an assertion that it was really the only practical point of view.

The thinness of much of even the best-known writing of the 1890s reflects a philosophical shallowness, while the frequent shrillness and exaggeration reflect the recognition of this defect; the arduous pursuit of fine style, painstaking draftsmanship, and striking form reflect attempts to find appropriate substitutes. The egoism, the smallness, the triviality, the sometimes peevish reduction of the significance of all things to their effect on oneself which we associate with the nineties reflect the loss of the transcendent vision coupled with the forlorn defiance of the empiricist interpretation of life—Wilde's aesthetic poses, Beardsley's disillusioned insistence on lust, Le Gallienne's quest for the golden girl, Dowson's reduction of the redemptive ideal to mere dreams of a lost mistress, Symons's equation of life with a dance which has no meaning beyond itself, Machen's preoccupation with evil which is powerful and pervasive but without significance because not opposed to any universal striving for good, all express the hectic or melancholy sense of the loss of intellectual force and direction. Wilde's occasionally brilliant paradox and fantasy, Beardsley's sense of the power of line and mass, the concentrated force of the spare, economical realistic short story emerging at the time, the merely decorative success of artists like Patten Wilson, Charles Condor, and Laurence Housman, Yeats's rediscovery of the power of folktale and mythology, all of these are, in their way, means of avoiding the need for metaphysical building materials.

The writers of the nineties were following the example of Rossetti and his pre-Raphaelizing friends and disciples in turning away from any question that could be answered only on the basis of metaphysical considerations. Professor Lester argues that not only was scientific determinism disillusioning to those without scientific allegiances, but their insistence on the unique validity of "empirical observation and inductive logic" was dessicating to the creative faculties. But the threatening voices he quotes were hardly issuing new, unheard-of challenges: "'. . . physical theories which lie beyond experience are derived by a process of abstraction from experience'; '. . . that dry light of reason . . . is the sole human test of truth'; 'Logic, after all, has always the last word here below.'"[9] These voices, repeating nothing not to be found in Bentham and his followers (and there applicable to much wider questions than that of physical science), could hardly have been perceived as an unprecedented danger.

Philip Appleman has perceptively argued that "Darwin's influence on Pater was more significant than is usually assumed . . . [and] that this influence led Pater's literary criticism toward two antithetical positions, the impressionistic and the historical."[10] Appleman makes a strong point in linking Pater's recognition of the importance of the historical process to his approach to art and literature; Pater, like J. A. Symonds and Vernon Lee, found enormous interest in the origin, growth, and decline of aesthetic techniques and viewpoints. However, one cannot overlook the constant growth of this interest from the beginning of the nineteenth century. The sense of historical change, like the growth of the theory and practice of impressionism, was reinforced and given new directions by the current of evolutionary thought which swelled into an overwhelming torrent after the publication of *Origin of*

[9] *Ibid.*, p. 25.

[10] "Darwin, Pater and a Crisis in Criticism," from *1859: Entering an Age of Crisis*, p. 81. Helen Young persuasively pointed out Darwin's influence on Pater in *The Writings of Walter Pater*.

Species, but both tendencies were already not only visible but effective before Darwin. The "relative spirit," to use Pater's term, was abroad in the land by the midpoint of the century. We remember that Pater used that phrase in describing the forces against which Coleridge had fought, and that the argument of Mill's *Spirit of the Age*, written in 1831 under the influence of Saint-Simon, is as much a relativist manifesto as the analysis of "rights" which makes up the last portion of the post-Darwinian *Utilitarianism* of 1863.

On balance, then, it seems at least plausible that what those literary and artistic figures we think of as typical of the nineties were dramatizing and suffering from was not so much the displacement of traditional modes of thought by science as the repudiation of *all* attempts to understand the world by traditional philosophical analysis grounded in assumed first principles.

I HAVE SUGGESTED that the great importance of Pater for late nineteenth-century literary and intellectual history lies in the wholeheartedness with which he bids farewell to transcendentalism. The hedonism, cyrenaicism, pursuit of experience for its own sake, life-tasting, arranging of one's life according to the canons of art, and other formulas generally assumed to sum up the nineties are traditionally buttressed by reference to the Conclusion to Pater's *Renaissance*. Opinions may differ as to the central assertion of the Conclusion; it offers God's plenty for the interpreter of the nineties. The famous few pages consist of one well-turned statement about the meaning of human experience after another packed together so closely that an unquestionable rhetoric produces the effect of inexorable logic. Pater begins by telling us not that "all things and principles of things" *are* "inconstant modes and

fashions" but that the modern tendency is so to regard them—which tendency, presumably, is itself an inconstant fashion. All of the apparently categorical statements that follow are thus presumably provisional, inasmuch as they are intended as support for and illustration of a mode of thought that is itself inconstant. One of these statements, made halfway through the Conclusion, is the well-known "the service of philosophy, of speculative culture, towards the human spirit, is to rouse, to startle it to a life of constant and eager observation." That is an audacious dismissal of the claims of the mighty metaphysical opposites which contended for men's allegiance through the nineteenth century (and, in one form or another, had contended through all the known history of human thought). Such a mode of thought may be an inconstant fashion, but in its implications it is far more daring and significant than more celebrated passages in the Conclusion. Nor is that statement about philosophy a heedless exaggeration; generalization, especially philosophical generalization, Pater tells us in *Plato and Platonism*, "is a method, not of obliterating the concrete phenomena, but of enriching it, with the joint perspective, the significance, the expressiveness of all other things besides."[11] In addition, philosophy is itself a source of aesthetic delight, not knowledge. The *Republic* is to be read "for its dramatic interest, the spectacle of a powerful, of a sovereign intellect, translating itself, amid a complex group of conditions which can never in the nature of things occur again . . . into a great literary monument."[12]

Pater's transmogrification of the role of philosophy arises out of more than his fondness for Heraclitus or the reagent-like reaction of the scientific thought of his time on assumptions of stability and progress. It arises out of the perceived failure of the orthodox transcendentalism of Coleridge's *Aids to Reflection* and lay sermons, the hereti-

[11] Pater, *Plato and Platonism*, p. 159.

[12] *Ibid.*, p. 11.

cal transcendentalism of Carlyle, the moral-aesthetic transcendentalism of Ruskin, or the qualified transcendentalism of Arnold.[13] For all the power of argument lavished on the undeniable insights these men offered the world, they had lost the battle to their common foe.

Pater was indeed perceptive enough in that essay on Coleridge which, as his first published critical essay, fully anticipates the relativism around which the Conclusion to *The Renaissance* is built. Like Mill in finding Coleridge's most central characteristic to be his "disinterested struggle against the relative spirit," Pater is much more concerned with the emotional than the philosophical consequences of Coleridge's transcendentalism. "From his childhood he hungered for eternity. . . . More than Childe Harold, more than Werther, more than René himself, Coleridge, by what he did, what he was, and what he failed to do, represents that inexhaustible discontent, languor, and home-sickness, that endless regret, the chords of which ring all through our modern literature."[14] Coleridge might have regarded that description of himself as a seeker of the absolute with a certain equanimity, for he himself described his much-admired Plato in very similar terms. ("For Plato was a poet of such excellence as would have stood all other competition but that of his being a philosopher. His poetic genius implanted in him those deep impressions and the love of them which, mocking all comparison with after objects, leaves behind it thirst for something not attained, to which nothing in life is found commensurate and which still impells the soul to pursue.")[15] Pater could understand

[13] That Pater attempted to restate the case for faith in the transcendent, or, as Barbara Charlesworth has it, that in *Marius* he was "generously taking for granted the hypothesis that there is a transcendent reality" (*Dark Passages*, p. 50) is frequently argued. Nevertheless, it is clear by the close of *Marius* that although Pater may have opened the door and gazed longingly in, he did not enter the transcendental shrine.

[14] Pater, "Coleridge," in *Appreciations*, p. 104.

[15] Coleridge, *The Philosophical Lectures*, p. 158.

such hunger, for he shared it, but he was quite sure that nothing but "great passions" could satisfy it.

But Pater's point of view arises equally out of the perceived inadequacies of the empiricism which had won the day. The common philosophy that lay behind Bentham, the Mills, Morley, Harrison, and Huxley was essentially supreme in all areas of thought, not merely science, by the 1880s, but the culture that paid its respect to empiricism seemed no fitter a milieu in which to live, no more logical in its structure, no more in tune with empirically discovered laws. Nor as much as Pater accepted the findings of science, and even the philosophical arguments of the empiricists,[16] could his spirit live in that region. One notes, incidentally, that the difficulties in logically analyzing history that Mill increasingly came to admit lead toward the interpretation of the flow of time as the concurrence of forces beyond analysis which Pater evokes in the Conclusion. Better to savor the moment than search for the eternal or scrutinize dull and profitless fact. The function of philosophy becomes that of providing piquancy to experience.

Nor should we forget that if Pater proposed art as the antidote to man's realization that his brief life is set in the midst of forces not to be weighed by the subtlest philosophy, it was an antidote to essentially the same realization that Stevenson, Henley, and what have come to be known as the anti-decadents proposed the full-blooded embrace of adventure. Against empiricism and the realism it spawned, they opposed romance.

Stevenson's "Aes Triplex" and Pater's Conclusion are

[16] One finds, for instance, that Pater accepted certain of the key empiricist philosophical positions such as the Bentham/Mill explanation of Plato's Ideas. "The 'Ideas' of Plato are, in truth, neither more nor less than those universal definitions, those universal conceptions, as they look, as they could not but look, amid the peculiar lights and shadows, in the singularly constituted atmosphere, under the strange laws of refraction, and in the proper perspective, of Plato's house of thought" (*Plato and Platonism*, p. 163).

as mutually illuminating as the works of Pater and Wilde that we are more accustomed to compare. Philosophy, for Pater, offers not principles but "points of view . . . to help us gather up what might otherwise pass unregarded by us." Stevenson dismisses philosophy with a Wildean jest at the expense of Mill's definition of life as "a Permanent Possibility of Sensation." Pater flees to the delights of art, looks to consciously individual experience: "For what man has sought for is, indeed, neither pain nor pleasure, but simply life. . . . Pleasure is Nature's sign of approval." Stevenson is more robust. "To be deeply interested in the accidents of our existence, to enjoy keenly the mixed texture of human experience" leads man, says Stevenson, "to disregard precautions and risk his neck against a straw." It is not necessarily art which gives "the highest quality to your moments as they pass" but perhaps the actions of "an Alpine climber roping over a peril, or a hunter riding merrily at a stiff fence." Still, the uncertainty of life's term in a world no longer susceptible of axiological, ontological, or epistemological analysis is the starting point for both. Both writers set the same problem—how closely "accidents of our existence" suggest "concurrence . . . of forces parting sooner or later on their ways" and "mixed texture of our existence" suggests "the passage and dissolution of impressions, images, sensations . . . that strange, perpetual weaving and unweaving of ourselves."[17] "We are all under sentence of death but with a sort of indefinite reprieve," writes Pater. "All the world over, and every hour, some one is parting

[17] The sense of man's existence as the result of mighty, imponderable, and eternal forces is of course part of the nineteenth-century consciousness of both history and science and is to be found in writers of differing persuasions. We have seen how strong this sense is in Carlyle, for instance; in the empiricist camp we find John Morley writing, "if a man has intelligently followed the very shortest course of universal history, it will be the fault of his teacher if he has not acquired an impressive conception, which will never be effaced, of the destinies of man upon earth; of the mighty confluence of forces working on from age to age, which have their meeting in every one of us here tonight. . ." (*Critical Miscellanies*, III, 12).

company with all his aches and ecstasies. For us also the trap is laid. . . . It is a honeymoon with us all through, and none of the longest."[18] So Stevenson.

Recognition that the "decadent" art of the nineties is very much a reaction against metaphysical or philosophical endeavors casts light on a number of other characteristics of that art. The realistic fiction and the sentimental fiction and poetry of the nineties are equally results of a conscious restriction of vision, of the negation of the broader views implied by an intellectual system. One limits one's regard to personal emotional responses, to personally significant episodes, refusing to correct for the individual, egoistic, or fantasy-colored viewpoint by reference to general principles, and one produces the sentimental stories and poems of Dowson, Symons, Harland, and Le Gallienne. "The poetry of the period is essentially an expression of moods and sentiments," writes Muddiman;[19] he could have described the majority of the essays and a good third of the short stories of the period in the same way. Alternatively, one concentrates on the sordid, painful, or wholly commonplace details of an episode, refusing to set that episode against an explanatory (and thus potentially reassuring) background, and one produces the realistic fiction of Hubert Crackanthorpe, or Ella D'Arcy, or Vincent O'Sullivan.

But we must recognize that not only did the dismissal of the prophetic function by writers of the time contribute largely to both the realistic and sentimental writing of the

[18] "Aes Triplex," in *The Works of Robert Louis Stevenson*, XXV, 78. See also "Crabbed Age and Youth" (XXV, 43, 45): "We theorise with a pistol to our head; we are confronted with a new set of conditions on which we have not only to pass a judgment, but to take action, before the hour is at an end. And we cannot even regard ourselves as a constant; in this flux of things, our identity itself seems in a perpetual variation. . . ." "We sail in leaky bottoms and on great and perilous waters; and to take a cue from the dolorous old naval ballad, we have heard the mermaidens singing, and know that we shall never see dry land any more."

[19] Muddiman, *The Men of the Nineties*, p. 79.

nineties, but it gave writers a sense of liberation, even while leading them to produce darkly realistic and romantically melancholy stories and poems. It is also important to remember, as Holbrook Jackson reminds us, that many of the writers of the time found joy in their lives and work, and that a feeling of expectancy was in the air.[20] The "newfound freedom" which Jackson finds symbolically expressed in the nonsense chorus "Ta-ra-ra-boom-de-ay" was not unconnected with the sigh of relief as the burden of serious metaphysical speculation ceased to oppress the muse.

The sprightly fantasy and frivolity of Beerbohm's essays and stories, Beardsley's poems, and Wilde's prose, the rage for "fine writing" in the little magazines of the time, and the frankly decorative impulses behind much of the illustration of the time was possible to a generation little concerned for larger meanings. As Professor Lester put it, "The ecstasies of this time were prized more for the subjective rewards they brought than for their confirmation of some higher harmony or for their promise of some higher sphere which may exist behind and beyond the phenomenal world known to man."[21] The very tendency to concentrate on the smaller, sometimes slighter genres is at least partly explained by the more limited intentions of its creators. Vignettes, brief essays, short short stories, brief lyrics, simple black-and-white drawings were appropriate to reproducing fleeting impressions, imposing form on passing moments, or offering quickly absorbed aesthetic bon-bons. Such, it had come to seem, could offer all the understanding or delight man could hope for. The men of the nineties did not feel required to state anew the grounds of the imaginative faculty, pluck away the world's vestments, revise the basis of law and government, rescue the "secret" of Jesus from the *Aberglaube* which concealed it, reveal the re-

[20] H. Jackson, *The Eighteen Nineties*, p. 30.

[21] Lester, *Journey Through Despair*, p. 159.

lationship between architectural forms and eternal principles, or offer a vision of the new world that is to be.

They, like Swinburne in "Wordsworth and Byron," tended to regard phrases like "a criticism of life," when applied to art and considered too curiously, as leading the reverent reader down "the high road to distraction" and the irreverent to "the verge of laughter."[22] It is interesting for instance to compare J. A. Symonds's conception of culture as set forth in a brief essay in his most "*fin-de-siècle*" volume, *In the Key of Blue*,[23] with Arnold's views in *Culture and Anarchy*. Symonds's "culture" is much closer to Wilde's—and Mill's—than to Arnold's: it has its uses, in making men more tolerant for instance, but the Arnoldian view of culture as something which brings men finally to a common sense of values is not to be found here. Symonds has no doubt that the highest possible development of the potential of each person is of mutual benefit to all. "Society would reach something like perfection if each individual succeeded in self-effectuation, fulfilling the law of his own nature, and being distinguished from his neighbors by some marked quality, some special instrument."[24] But the latter portion of that sentence indicates the Mill-like emphasis, as does the following sentence from the essay's penultimate paragraph: "While recognizing our own right and duty to struggle for the truth as we perceive it, we acknowledge the same right and the same duty in our opponents." It is shown equally by the completeness with

[22] Swinburne, *Complete Works*, XIV, 158.

[23] The earnest portrayal of the inconsequential represented by the title essay of *In the Key of Blue* is a part of the satisfaction many of the writers of the nineties were able to find in minor genres and even trivial exercises in the curious: "It struck me that it would be amusing to try the resources of our language in a series of studies of what might be termed 'values and blouses.' For this purpose I resolved to take a single figure—a *facchino* with whom I have been long acquainted—and to pose him in a variety of lights with a variety of hues in combination" (p. 4).

[24] Symonds, *In the Key of Blue*, pp. 213–14.

which he embraced the results of empirical science. "If we attempt to seize the main fact in the intellectual development of the last half-century, we shall find that this may be described as the triumph of the scientific method in relation to all man's thought about the universe. We have gained our present standing-point by a long process of experimental and philosophical labour, which has been carried on through three centuries in Europe, and which culminated recently in the hypothesis of Evolution."[25] On that hypothesis, Symonds builds much of his aesthetic theory.

The ease with which the art-and-beauty-worshipping Symonds accepted the characteristic moral and political premises of the utilitarians shows how thorough the rout of the transcendentalists had been. Unlike Harrison, who felt it necessary to reply to Arnold in his witty "Culture: A Dialogue," Symonds can happily ignore Arnold even when writing on the subject of culture. Symonds's love of the Renaissance—announced again in the essay in question—is part of that wholesale rejection of the values which the transcendentally oriented had found, or tried to find, in the Middle Ages. The preference shared by Symonds, Pater, Wilde, and Vernon Lee for Renaissance vitality, individualism, and even eccentricity over the social unity that earlier anti-empiricists had found in the Middle Ages is one of the more interesting manifestations (or reactions to) the loss of the transcendent vision.

WHAT INDEED the men of the nineties devoted themselves to was the pursuit not merely of experience for its own sake but of *form* for its own sake as well. I earlier cited the way in which Pater substituted the artist's im-

[25] Symonds, *Essays Speculative and Suggestive*, p. 1.

pression of a thing for Arnold's "thing in itself as it really is." Pater's essay on "Style" defines style finally as the translation of that impression which is a product of the interaction of the seer and the thing seen into form. Style for Pater *is* form. Wilde, as usual, takes this one step further. If we grant that the style or form is at least as much the result of the perceiving artist as the thing perceived, and the unique mind and soul (to use Pater's terms in that essay) which the artist brings to the scene really antecedent to the experience that, interacting with them, produces the impression, can we not therefore regard form as anticipating content? Wilde never works out this, or any argument, in so explicit a way, but the preeminence of the unique style or form in which the individual grasps his vision and, through art, offers it to others is the real basis of that individuality which writers on Wilde constantly identify as the center of his thought. Individuality is at least as much the subject of *The Soul of Man Under Socialism* as socialism. The third subject of *The Soul of Man* is, naturally for Wilde, art. This he can introduce into the essay because "art is the most intense mode of individualism that the world has known." Or, in other words, "A work of art is the unique result of a unique temperament. Its beauty comes from the fact that the author is what he is."[26] In such statements Wilde sharpens and clarifies a point of view which lies half hidden in "The Critic as Artist." One way of regarding what at first glance seems like the trivial paradox of the aesthete—"life is terribly deficient in form"[27]—is as the assertion of the necessity of imposing one's individual style or form on all one sees so that one is in control of one's impressions. The point is made on a lower plane when Wilde turns from individual style and form to analysis of conventional forms of art.

[26] Wilde, "The Soul of Man Under Socialism," in *Complete Works of Oscar Wilde*, p. 1090.

[27] Wilde, "The Critic as Artist," in *Complete Works*, p. 1034.

> For the real artist is he who proceeds, not from feeling to form, but from form to thought and passion. He does not first conceive an idea, and then say to himself "I will put my idea into a complex metre of fourteen lines," but realising the beauty of the sonnet-scheme, he conceives certain modes of music and methods of rhyme, and the mere form suggests what is to fill and make it intellectually and emotionally complete.[28]

That is why the artist is no longer the prophet, but rather the bringer of delight and the stirrer of the imagination. The latter part of "The Critic as Artist," strongly echoing Arnold, assigns criticism the task of rejuvenating the culture. "It is Criticism, as Arnold points out, that creates the intellectual atmosphere of the age. . . . It is Criticism, again, that by concentration makes culture possible. . . . It is Criticism that makes us cosmopolitan. . . ."[29] But though here criticism and, elsewhere in his writings, art are made to minister to the evils of the world, Wilde holds back always from assigning either art or criticism the mission of directly teaching, or in Arnold's terms, edifying. Art being simply the expression of one's individuality, it can only be fully enjoyed by those who, having achieved their own individuality, are able to use it as the raw material of the more complex impression which results when they impose their own forms (styles or visions) upon it. If art were prophetic, Wilde would be concerned to maximize the effect of art on mankind rather than to minimize the effect of ignorant mankind on the artist, as he is in *The Soul of Man*. One of the most curious things about that essay is Wilde's concern with protecting the artist's individuality from destruction by the uncomprehending public. The cultivation of one's individuality—whether in order to produce

[28] *Ibid.*, p. 1052.

[29] *Ibid.*, pp. 1055–56.

art or savor experience (including art), whether counseled by a conscious recognition of one's isolation, as in Pater, or a desire for harmony and self-realization as in *The Soul of Man*—offered an obvious alternative to the sense of mission which faded with the transcendental and empiricist visions.

One notices, incidentally, that Wilde was both freed from the constraints of a philosophical commitment and deprived of a foundation on which to build his arguments. Paradox became his way of simultaneously celebrating his freedom and avoiding the necessity of concatenated argument. Wilde's delight in paradox and exaggeration was, of course, partly an important constituent of his attention-getting pose, but it served very well as a means of divorcing his aesthetic "philosophy" from traditional aesthetic currents. For instance, the word "lying" in the title of the essay "The Decay of Lying" is not chosen simply for its shock effect. L. F. Choisy comments that "si on remplace le mot 'mensonge' par le mot 'creation' ou 'imagination,' beaucoup d'objections s'evanouisment."[30] Yes, but both alternatives call up tritely traditional or metaphysically based aesthetic controversy; "imagination" especially has strong transcendental overtones. The word "lying" short circuits outworn responses.

George Moore's "conversations" and autobiographical excursions among books were also one way of demonstrating the importance of the impression or the experience itself over theorizing about it. One might, indeed, regard Moore's egoistic volumes of criticism, beginning with *Confessions of a Young Man* (1888) and *Impressions and Opinions* (1891), as going one step beyond Wilde's "Critic as Artist"; where Wilde talks about the importance of the individual's response and affirms the value of accurate expression of one's own impression over mere comment on

[30] Choisy, *Oscar Wilde*, p. 151.

the original artist's own meaning, Moore simply writes from an apparent total acceptance of such views without bothering to defend them.

Of course, writers of the nineties found many other substitutes for philosophical orientations. Kipling's jungle code, Stevenson's code of honor, Wilde's and Shaw's socialism, Conrad's ordeal-perfected personal integrity, and Yeats's devotion to folklore, patriotism, ceremony, symbolism, and occultism replaced philosophical systems.

The interest in occultism or magic that we find in both Yeats and Symons is of particular interest. Frank Kermode remarked in *Romantic Image* that "to Yeats and Symons it was clear that the magic element must be reintroduced, in order to affirm, or re-affirm, the status of the image as a means of tapping "'inepuisable fonds de l'universelle analogie.'"[31] The point is that both felt that the powers of poetry must have a ground in something more powerful, more significant, than could be accounted for by any logical, rhetorical, or merely aesthetic theory, yet they did not care to begin that long journey back to a transcendental explanation which Coleridge had hoped to achieve or Carlyle had symbolically sketched. Magic provided an explanation that was neither abstract nor logical.

Alternatively, of course, it was possible to regard the world as having no meaning that could be intellectually formulated—art then becomes the *only* means of grasping, of expressing one's sense of life. And if one feels life as an unanalyzable flow, the art which would seem to most directly express this is the dance. Thus Symons:

> As they dance, under the changing lights, so human, so remote, so desirable, so evasive, coming and going to the sound of a thin, heady music which marks the rhythm of their movements like a kind of clinging drapery, they seem to sum up in themselves the appeal of everything in the world that is passing, and coloured, and to be enjoyed; everything that bids us

[31] Kermode, *Romantic Image*, p. 112.

take no thought for the morrow, and dissolve the will into slumber, and give way luxuriously to the delightful present.[32]

Once say that life is simply flux, however, and the melancholy which characterizes the twentieth century more than the 1890s is only a paragraph away.

> Realising all humanity to be but a masque of shadows, and this solid world an impromptu stage as temporary as they, it is with a pathetic desire of some last illusion, which shall deceive even ourselves, that we are consumed with this hunger to create, to make something for ourselves, of at least the same shadowy reality as that about us. The art of the ballet awaits us.[33]

THE TRANSCENDENTALIST assumes the existence of a model which is esoteric, pre-existent, perfect, and peremptory. The empiricist assumes that any model or ideal man might attempt to follow is exoteric, self-constructed, tentative, and heuristic. The two intellectual faiths into which that distinction cleaves Victorian thought never come together; only when the one had lost so much of its power over men's minds that the other came to seem the natural way of regarding the world did the antagonism between the system-builders and the cloud-piercers disappear—to be replaced by that near-sighted concentration on minor objects of thought that characterizes the end of the century and the opening of our own.

[32] Symons, "The World as Ballet," in *Studies in Seven Arts*, p. 389.

[33] *Ibid.*, p. 390.

VOLUMES CITED

Abrams, Meyer. *The Mirror and the Lamp*. New York: Oxford University Press, 1953.

Alexander, Edward. *Matthew Arnold and John Stuart Mill*. New York: Columbia University Press, 1965.

———. *Matthew Arnold, John Ruskin, and the Modern Temper*. Columbus: Ohio State University Press, 1973.

Appleman, Phillip, ed. *1859: Entering an Age of Crisis*. Bloomington: University of Indiana Press, 1959.

Appleyard, J. A. *Coleridge's Philosophy of Literature*. Cambridge, Mass.: Harvard University Press, 1966.

Archer, William, and Robert Lowe, eds. *Dramatic Essays by John Forster and George Henry Lewes*. London: W. Scott, 1896.

Arnold, Matthew. *The Complete Prose Works of Matthew Arnold*. Ed. R. H. Super. 11 vols. Ann Arbor: University of Michigan Press, 1960–1977.

Arnold, Thomas. *Lectures on Modern History*. London: B. Fellowes, 1844.

———. *The Miscellaneous Works of Thomas Arnold*. New York: D. Appleton, 1845.

Bain, Alexander. *John Stuart Mill*. London: Longmans, Green, 1882.

Barfield, Owen. *What Coleridge Thought*. Middletown, Conn.: Wesleyan University Press, 1971.

Beatty, Richmond. *Lord Macaulay*. Norman: University of Oklahoma Press, 1938.

"Beauchamp, Philip" [Jeremy Bentham/George Grote]. *Analysis of the Influence of Natural Religion on the Temporal Happiness of Mankind*. London: R. Carlile, 1822.

Benn, A. W. *The History of English Rationalism in the Nineteenth Century*. London: Longmans, Green, 1906.

Bentham, Jeremy. *The Works of Jeremy Bentham*. Ed. John

Bowring. 11 vols. Edinburgh and London: William Tait, 1843.

Boulger, James D. *Coleridge as Religious Thinker*. New Haven: Yale University Press, 1961.

Brinton, Clarence Crane. *English Political Thought in the Nineteenth Century*. Cambridge, Mass.: Harvard University Press, 1949.

Burdett, Osbert. *The Beardsley Period*. London: John Lane, 1925.

Cairnes, J. E. *The Character and Logical Method of Political Economy*. London: Macmillan and Co., 1875.

Campbell, J. D. *Samuel Taylor Coleridge: A Narrative of the Events of His Life*. London and New York: Macmillan, 1896.

Carlyle, Thomas. *Carlyle's Complete Works*. Sterling Edition. 20 vols. Boston: Estes and Lauriat, 1885.

Cassirer, Heinrich W. *A Commentary on Kant's* Critique of Judgment. London: Methuen, 1938.

Chambers, E. K. *Samuel Taylor Coleridge: A Biographical Study*. Oxford: Clarendon Press, 1938.

Charlesworth, Barbara. *Dark Passages: The Decadent Consciousness in Victorian Literature*. Madison: University of Wisconsin Press, 1965.

Child, Ruth C. *The Aesthetic of Walter Pater*. New York: Macmillan Co., 1940.

Choisy, Louis Frédéric. *Oscar Wilde*. Paris: Perrin, 1926.

Clark, Kenneth. *The Gothic Revival*. 3rd ed. New York: Holt, Rinehart and Winston, 1962.

Coleridge, Samuel Taylor. *Biographia Literaria*. Ed. John Shawcross. 2 vols. Oxford: Clarendon Press, 1907.

———. *Coleridge's Miscellaneous Criticism*. Ed. T. M. Raysor. Cambridge, Mass.: Harvard University Press, 1936.

———. *The Collected Works of Samuel Taylor Coleridge*. Kathleen Coburn, gen. ed. 16 vols. Princeton: Princeton University Press, 1969–. (This edition is cited in the notes as *Collected Works*; the 7-volume Shedd edition of 1853 is cited as *Complete Works*.)

———. *Complete Works of Samuel Taylor Coleridge*. Ed. W. G. T. Shedd. 7 vols. New York: Harper, 1853.

———. *Confessions of an Inquiring Spirit*. Ed. H. S. Hart. Stanford, Calif.: Stanford University Press, 1957.

———. *The Philosophical Lectures*. Ed. Kathleen Coburn. London: Pilot Press, 1949.

———. *S. T. Coleridge's Treatise on Method*. Ed. Alice D. Snyder. London: Constable, 1934.

Collingwood, R. G. *The Idea of History*. Oxford: Clarendon Press, 1946.

Colmer, John. *Coleridge: Critic of Society*. Oxford: Clarendon Press, 1959.

Dale, Peter Allan. *The Victorian Critic and the Idea of History*. Cambridge, Mass.: Harvard University Press, 1977.

Dallas, Eneas Sweetland. *The Gay Science*. 2 vols. London: Chapman and Hall, 1866.

———. *Poetics*. London: Smith, Elder, 1852.

DeLaura, David. *Hebrew and Hellene in Victorian England*. Austin: University of Texas Press, 1969.

Dutton, Geoffrey. *The Hero as Murderer: The Life of Edward John Eyre*. London: Collins, 1967.

Ellmann, Richard. *Wilde and the Nineties*. Princeton: Princeton University Library, 1966. (Ellmann's essay, "The Critic as Artist as Wilde," was reprinted in *Encounter*, XXVIII (1967); also in *The Poet as Critic*, ed. F. P. W. McDowell [Evanston: Northwestern University Press, 1967].)

Ewing, A. C. *A Short Commentary on Kant's* Critique of Pure Reason. London: Methuen, 1938.

Freeman, Kathleen, ed., trans. *Ancilla to the Pre-Socratic Philosophers*. Oxford: Basil Blackwell, 1948.

Froude, J. A. *Thomas Carlyle: A History of His Life in London 1834–1881*. 2 vols. London: Longmans, Green, 1919.

Fruman, Norman. *Coleridge: The Damaged Archangel*. New York: George Braziller, 1971.

Grennan, Margaret. *William Morris, Medievalist and Revolutionary*. New York: King's Crown Press, 1945.

Gross, John. *The Rise and Fall of the Man of Letters*. New York: Macmillan Co., 1969.

Guérard, Albert Léon. *Art for Art's Sake*. New York: Schocken Books, 1936.

Halévy, Eli. *The Growth of Philosophical Radicalism*. Trans. Mary Morris. London: Faber and Faber, 1952.

Hamilton, Sir William. *Lectures on Metaphysics and Logic*. 4 vols. Edinburgh: W. Blackwood and Sons, 1849–1850.

Harrison, Frederic. *The Choice of Books.* London: Macmillan and Co., 1886.

———. *Tennyson, Ruskin, Mill and Other Literary Estimates.* London: Macmillan and Co., 1899.

Harrold, C. F. *Carlyle and German Thought: 1819–1834.* New Haven: Yale University Press, 1934.

Hazlitt, William. *The Complete Works.* Ed. P. P. Howe. 21 vols. London: J. M. Dent and Sons, 1930–1934.

Hewison, Robert. *John Ruskin: The Argument of the Eye.* London: Thames and Hudson, 1976.

Hicks, Granville. *Figures of Transition.* New York: Macmillan Co., 1939.

Höffding, Harald. *A History of Modern Philosophy.* 2 vols. New York: Dover, 1955.

Holloway, John. *The Victorian Sage.* London: Macmillan and Co., 1953.

Hough, Graham. *The Last Romantics.* London: Duckworth, 1949.

Houghton, Walter. *The Victorian Frame of Mind, 1830–1870.* New Haven: Yale University Press, 1957.

Hume, Hamilton. *The Life of Edward John Eyre.* London: R. Bentley, 1867.

Jackson, Holbrook. *The Eighteen Nineties.* New York: Mitchell Kennerly, 1914.

Jackson, J. R. de J. *Method and Imagination in Coleridge's Criticism.* Cambridge, Mass.: Harvard University Press, 1969.

James, D. G. *Matthew Arnold and the Decline of English Romanticism.* Oxford: Clarendon Press, 1961.

James and John Stuart Mill: Papers of the Centenary Conference. Ed. John M. Robson and Michael Laine. Toronto: University of Toronto Press, 1976.

Joad, C. E. M. *Decadence.* New York: Philosophical Library, 1949.

Kaminsky, Alice. *George Henry Lewes as Literary Critic.* Syracuse: Syracuse University Press, 1968.

Kermode, Frank. *Romantic Image.* London: Routledge and Kegan Paul, 1957.

Lee, Vernon. *Althea.* New Edition. London: John Lane, 1910.

———. *Baldwin.* London: T. F. Unwin, 1886.

———. *The Beautiful.* Cambridge: Cambridge University Press, 1913.

———. *Belcaro*. London: W. Satchell, 1883.
———. *Laurus Nobilis*. London: John Lane, 1909.
———. *Proteus, Or, The Future of Intelligence*. London: K. Paul, Trench, Trubner, 1925.
———. *Renaissance Fancies and Studies*. 2nd ed. London: John Lane, 1909.
Lee, Vernon, and C. Anstruther-Thomson. *Beauty and Ugliness*. London: John Lane, 1912.
Leroy, Gaylord. *Perplexed Prophets: Six Nineteenth-Century British Authors*. Philadelphia: University of Pennsylvania Press for Temple University Publications, 1953.
Lester, John. *Journey Through Despair, 1880–1914*. Princeton: Princeton University Press, 1968.
Levine, George Lewis. *The Boundaries of Fiction: Carlyle, Macaulay, Newman*. Princeton: Princeton University Press, 1968.
Lewes, George Henry. *A Biographical History of Philosophy*. London: G. Routledge, 1900. (Fourth edition: London, 1882, 2 vols.)
———. *Life of Goethe*. London: Smith, Elder, 1875.
———. *Literary Criticism of George Henry Lewes*. Ed. Alice Kaminsky. Lincoln: University of Nebraska Press, 1964.
———. *The Principles of Success in Literature*. Ed. F. N. Scott. Boston: Allyn and Bacon, 1891.
———. *Problems of Life and Mind*. 2 vols. 3rd ed. London: Trubner, 1874.
Locke, John. *Essay Concerning the Human Understanding*. Fraser edition. 2 vols. Oxford: Clarendon Press, 1894; rptd., New York: Dover, 1959.
Lovejoy, A. O. *The Great Chain of Being*. Cambridge, Mass.: Harvard University Press, 1936.
Lovejoy, A. O., and George Boas. *Primitivism and Related Ideas in Antiquity*. Baltimore: Johns Hopkins Press, 1935.
Macaulay, Thomas Babington. *The Complete Writings of Thomas Babington Macaulay*. Cambridge edition. 10 vols. Boston: Houghton Mifflin, 1901.
McCarthy, Patrick J. *Matthew Arnold and the Three Classes*. New York: Columbia University Press, 1964.
Madden, William. *Matthew Arnold: A Study of the Aesthetic Temperament in Victorian England*. Bloomington: Indiana University Press, 1967.

Masson, David. *Recent British Philosophy*. London: Macmillan and Co., 1877.

Mill, James. *Analysis of the Phenomena of the Human Mind*. 2 vols. London: Longmans, Green, 1869.

———. *Essays on Government, Jurisprudence, Liberty of the Press and Law of Nations*. Reprints of Economic Classics. New York: A. M. Kelley, 1967.

———. *The History of British India*. 5th ed. 6 vols. London: James Madden, 1830; rptd. 6 vols. in 4. New York: Chelsea House, 1968.

———. *James Mill on Education*. Ed. W. H. Burston. London: Cambridge University Press, 1969.

Mill, John Stuart. *Autobiography*. Library of the Liberal Arts edition. Indianapolis: Bobbs-Merrill, 1957.

———. *Collected Works of John Stuart Mill*. Ed. F. E. L. Priestley and J. M. Robson. 15 vols. Toronto: University of Toronto Press, 1963–.

———. *Dissertations and Discussions*. 3 vols. London: Longmans, Green, 1867.

———. *Essays on Politics and Culture*. Ed. Gertrude Himmelfarb. Garden City: Doubleday, Anchor, 1963.

———. *On Liberty*. Library of the Liberal Arts edition. Indianapolis: Bobbs-Merrill, 1956.

———. *Principles of Political Economy*. Ed. Sir W. J. Ashley. London: Longmans, Green, 1920.

———. *System of Logic*. 8th ed. London: Longmans, Green, 1900; rptd., 1965.

———. *Three Essays on Religion*. Ed. Helen Taylor. London: Longmans, Green, 1923.

Miyoshi, Masao. *The Divided Self*. New York: New York University Press, 1969.

More, Thomas. *Yale Edition of the Complete Works of St. Thomas More*. 14 vols. New Haven: Yale University Press, 1963–.

Morley, John. *Critical Miscellanies*. 3 vols. London and New York: Macmillan, Chapman & Hall, 1871.

———. *Notes on Politics and History*. London: Macmillan and Co., 1913.

Morris, William. *The Collected Works of William Morris*. Introductions by May Morris. 24 vols. London: Longmans, Green, 1910–1915.

———. *William Morris: Artist, Writer, Socialist.* Ed. May Morris. 2 vols. Oxford: Basil Blackwell, 1936.
Muddiman, Bernard. *The Men of the Nineties.* London: H. Danielson, 1920.
Muirhead, J. H. *Coleridge as Philosopher.* New York: Macmillan Co., 1930.
———. *The Platonic Tradition in Anglo-Saxon Philosophy.* London: George Allen and Unwin, 1931.
Neff, Emory. *Carlyle and Mill.* New York: Columbia University Press, 1926.
Orsini, G. N. G. *Coleridge and German Idealism.* Carbondale: Southern Illinois University Press, 1969.
Pater, Walter. *Appreciations.* Library edition. London: Macmillan and Co., 1910.
———. *Plato and Platonism.* London: Macmillan and Co., 1910.
———. *The Renaissance.* London: Macmillan and Co., 1910.
Praz, Mario. *The Romantic Agony.* Trans. Angus Davidson. 2nd ed. London: Oxford University Press, 1951.
Robbins, Lionel C. *The Theory of Economic Policy in English Classical Political Economy.* London: Macmillan and Co., 1952.
Robbins, William. *The Ethical Idealism of Matthew Arnold.* Toronto: University of Toronto Press, 1959.
Rosenberg, John. *The Darkling Glass: A Portrait of Ruskin's Genius.* New York: Columbia University Press, 1961.
Ruskin, John. *The Works of John Ruskin.* Ed. E. T. Cook and A. D. O. Wedderburn. 39 vols. London: George Allen, 1903–1912.
Semmel, Bernard. *The Governor Eyre Controversy.* London: MacGibbon and Kee, 1962.
Seth, James. *English Philosophers and Schools of Philosophy.* London: Dent, 1925.
Shelley, Percy Bysshe. *The Complete Works of Percy Bysshe Shelley.* Ed. R. Ingpen and Walter E. Peck. 10 vols. London and New York: Charles Scribner's Sons, 1926–1930.
Sherwood, Margaret. *Coleridge's Imaginative Concept of the Imagination.* Wellesley, Mass.: Hathaway House Bookshop, 1937.
Smith, John. *Selected Discourses.* Delmar, N. Y.: Scholars' Facsimiles and Reprints, 1979.

Smith, Norman Kemp. *A Commentary on Kant's* Critique of Pure Reason. New York: Macmillan, 1918.

Snyder, Alice D. *Coleridge on Logic and Learning.* New Haven: Yale University Press, 1929.

Somervell, David C. *English Thought in the Nineteenth Century.* London: Methuen, 1929.

Sorley, W. R. *A History of British Philosophy to 1900.* Cambridge: Cambridge University Press, 1920; rptd., 1965.

Southey, Robert. *Sir Thomas More: Or, Colloquies on the Progress and Prospects of Society.* 2 vols. London: J. Murray, 1829.

Spencer, Herbert. *Philosophy of Style.* New York: D. Appleton, 1900. (Rptd. from *Westminster Review*, LVIII [1852].)

Stanley, Arthur Penrhyn. *The Life and Correspondence of Thomas Arnold.* London: B. Fellowes, 1844.

Stanlis, Peter. *Edmund Burke and the Natural Law.* Ann Arbor: University of Michigan Press, 1958.

Stephen, Leslie. *The English Utilitarians.* London: Duckworth, 1900; rptd. 3 vols. in 1. New York: Peter Smith, 1950.

Stevenson, Robert Louis. *The Works of Robert Louis Stevenson.* Tusitala edition. 35 vols. London: Wm. Heinemann, 1924.

Swinburne, Algernon Charles. *The Complete Works of Algernon Charles Swinburne.* Ed. E. Gosse and T. J. Wise. Bonchurch edition. 20 vols. London: Wm. Heinemann, 1925–1927.

Symonds, John Addington. *Essays Speculative and Suggestive.* New York: Charles Scribner's Sons, 1894.

———. *In the Key of Blue.* London: E. Mathews and John Lane, 1893.

Symons, Arthur. *Studies in the Seven Arts.* New York: E. P. Dutton, 1906.

Tennyson, G. B. *Sartor Called Resartus.* Princeton: Princeton University Press, 1966.

Tuveson, Ernest. *The Imagination as a Means of Grace.* Berkeley and Los Angeles: University of California Press, 1960.

———. *Millenium and Utopia.* Berkeley and Los Angeles: University of California Press, 1949.

Wellek, René. *Immanuel Kant in England, 1793–1838.* Princeton: Princeton University Press, 1931.

Wilde, Oscar. *Complete Works of Oscar Wilde.* 1-vol. edition. London: Collins, 1966.

Willey, Basil. *More Nineteenth Century Studies.* London: Chatto and Windus, 1956; rptd., New York: Harper Torchbooks, 1966.

———. *Nineteenth Century Studies.* London: Chatto and Windus, 1949; rptd., New York: Harper Torchbooks, 1966.

———. *The Seventeenth Century Background.* London: Chatto and Windus, 1942; rptd., New York: Columbia University Press, 1967.

Williams, Raymond. *Culture and Society, 1780–1850.* London: Chatto and Windus, 1958; rptd., Harmondsworth, England: Penguin, 1961.

Young, Helen Wadsworth. *The Writings of Walter Pater: A Reflection of British Philosophical Opinion from 1860 to 1890.* Lancaster, Pa: Lancaster Press, 1933; rptd., New York: Haskell House, 1965.

INDEX

Names that appear in the text only to provide continuity or that figure incidentally in quotations are not here cited, nor are the works and authors listed as standard authorities in the Preface. Only those footnotes are cited that include a quotation from or specific opinion of a twentieth-century critic.